LOL AND SORROW

Enjoy Moments of Laughter and Tears

Charles Cawv Thao

Copyright © Charles Cawv Thao 2024

All Rights Reserved

No part of this publication may be reproduced, distributed, or transmitted in any form or by any means, including photocopying, recording, or other electronic or mechanical methods, without the author's prior written permission, except in the case of brief quotations embodied in critical reviews and certain other non-commercial uses permitted by copyright law. For permission requests, please get in touch with the author.

DEDICATION

Dedicated to

My beloved wife, Mai L. Thao,

Cherished son, Theophilus Thao, and

Esteemed father, Pao Thao (Txwj Pov Thoj),

You are the cherished pillars of my life.

ACKNOWLEDGMENTS

I would like to express my deepest gratitude to the many individuals who have played significant roles in my life; without them, this book would not have been possible.

To all my dear friends, relatives, and family, especially my in-laws, for your unwavering love and support during both good and bad times. Without you, I would not have come this far.

Special mention and thanks to my publishing editorial team for their diligent work in reviewing my manuscript. To my special assistant editor, Christopher Baum, for his meticulous review and editing, and to Anthony Harrison for crafting the insightful prologue. I am thankful to Xeng Djoua Xiong, a role model during my formative years in Wheaton, Illinois, and to Mr. and Mrs. Jean Dusek, who welcomed me into their home and helped me adjust to life in America during the late 1970s and early 1980s. I also extend my gratitude to Mr. and Mrs. Jean Burton for their encouragement and support and to Mrs. Reams, my influential fourth-grade teacher at Longfellow School in Wheaton, Illinois, whose lessons have had a lasting impact. I remember Mrs. Hall, my Sunday school teacher at Wheaton College Church, who introduced me to the teachings of God.

My heartfelt thanks to Mr. John Anderson, a teacher and mentor at Franklin Junior High School in Wheaton, Illinois, who imparted valuable life lessons beyond academics. I am grateful to Rev. Kxf. Nyaj Tswb Yaaj for enlightening me about God during my younger years. To my friend, Roberto Corona, for his love and support. I am grateful to Daniel and Elizabeth Diaz for their unwavering love, kindness, and support during my darkest days. To my friend, Danny Rook, for your help and support. To Anthony Phillips, my spiritual brother in Christ. To Michael Collins for helping me a lot. To Mike Clinton, you are resilient. To Bobby Woods, you're a great friend and an inspiring rock mover. To Linda Kauffman in Tennessee, thanks for your love and friendship. To Xf. Ntxoov Lis Hawj for showing agape love and kindness, and to Yawm and Tais David Vaj Neeb Lis for being there for me through both good and bad times; and Mr. & Mrs. Tsaav Xyooj Thoj for your gift of joy and love.

In memory of my good friends, Anthony Keagle of Tennessee and Ray Siegfried, III, of Nordam Corporation, Tulsa, Oklahoma.

To all my church family in Wheaton, Illinois, and Springfield, Missouri.

Last but most importantly, I thank Jesus Christ, the anchor of my soul and life, who saved me from myself and granted me the promise of God's kingdom. There are countless others who have shaped my life but cannot be mentioned here due to space constraints. To all of you, I extend my heartfelt thanks. Your impact on my life is immeasurable. Thank you from the bottom of my heart!

ABOUT THE AUTHOR

Charles Cawv Thao, a Hmong native, was born in Laos and found himself displaced as a refugee in Thailand in 1975 amidst the turbulent sociopolitical landscape of Southeast Asia. His journey to the United States commenced in 1979, marking the onset of a new chapter characterized by both promise and adversity. Initially confronted with the formidable task of mastering English as a second language, Thao grappled with the challenges inherent in acclimating to a foreign educational system. Despite these obstacles, his perseverance ultimately yielded fruit as he became the first in his family to proudly graduate from Olive Nazarene University, Kankakee, Illinois.

A talented and multifaceted individual, Thao harbors a profound passion for storytelling, musical composition, and instrumental performance. This innate creativity manifests in his inaugural work of fiction, "LOL AND SORROW," which stands as a testament to his longstanding dream realized—a literary endeavor long deferred now brought to fruition.

Residing in Springfield, Missouri, Thao finds solace and inspiration in the embrace of family life, his marital bond providing a sturdy foundation upon which to pursue his artistic ambitions.

With his wife, son, and father, Thao lived in Springfield, Missouri.

INTRODUCTION MESSAGE

Charles Cawv Thao sat in his favorite corner of the local café, the aroma of freshly brewed coffee wafting through the air. He stared at the title of the book in front of him, "LOL AND SORROW," embossed in gold letters on the cover. It still felt surreal, like a dream he couldn't quite wake up from. His friend, Daniel, walked in and immediately noticed the faraway look in Charles's eyes.

"Hey, Charles," Daniel greeted, sliding into the seat across from him. "What's on your mind?"

Charles shook his head slowly as if trying to clear the fog of disbelief. "Daniel, have you ever woken up and not been sure if you're still dreaming?"

Daniel chuckled. "Every Monday morning. But seriously, what's up?"

Charles pushed the book across the table towards Daniel. "This. This book. I can't believe I wrote it."

Daniel picked up the book, flipping through the pages. "LOL AND SORROW, huh? Quite the title. What's it about?"

"It's about my journey, our journeys," Charles replied. "The laughter, the tears, the ups and downs. It's everything I experienced, everything we all experience."

Daniel's eyes softened as he looked at his friend. "It's incredible, Charles. But why do you seem so...disconnected from it?"

Charles sighed. "Because it doesn't feel real. I remember the late nights, the endless revisions, but now that it's done, it's like I'm in a dream. Seeing my name on this cover feels like I'm looking at someone else's life."

"Let's talk about it," Daniel said, leaning forward. "Maybe it'll help ground you. What was the hardest part of writing this book?"

Charles leaned back, a distant look in his eyes as he recalled the process. "The hardest part? Reliving the sorrow. The moments of loss, the times I felt completely defeated. But it was also cathartic, you know? Writing about it helped me process those feelings."

Daniel nodded. "And the laughter? The 'LOL' part?"

Charles smiled a genuine, warm smile that reached his eyes. "Those were the moments that kept me going. The small joys, the unexpected bursts of happiness. Like when we used to hang out at the old diner and joke about the most ridiculous things."

"I remember those times," Daniel said with a grin. "We laughed so hard we almost got kicked out a few times."

"Exactly," Charles said, his smile growing. "It's those memories that balance out the sorrow. They made the hard times bearable."

Daniel closed the book gently and placed it back on the table. "Charles, this book is a testament to your resilience. It's a reflection of your journey, and it's real. You've poured your heart and soul into it, and that's something to be proud of."

Charles took a deep breath, feeling the weight of Daniel's words. "You're right. It's just...overwhelming. To see it all laid out like this. To know that others will read it and maybe, just maybe, find some comfort or laughter in their own struggles."

"And they will," Daniel assured him. "Your story is powerful because it's real. It's relatable. People need to know that they're not alone in their sorrow and that laughter can still find its way into their lives."

Charles nodded slowly, a sense of peace settling over him. "Thanks, Daniel. I needed to hear that."

"Anytime, my friend," Daniel said with a warm smile. "Now, how about we celebrate this achievement? My treat."

Charles chuckled. "Sounds like a plan. But let's avoid getting kicked out this time, okay?"

"Deal," Daniel laughed. He then looked at the book again and said, "You know, you should thank your readers in your next public talk or interview. Without them, this dream wouldn't be a reality."

Charles nodded thoughtfully. "You're right. The readers are the ones who make this all possible. Their support, their feedback, their engagement—it's what turns a personal journey into something that can touch so many lives."

"And that's something worth celebrating," Daniel agreed.

As the two friends left the café, the weight of the book now feeling like a badge of honor rather than a dream, Charles felt a deep gratitude for everyone who had supported him along the way.

In the quiet of the night, Charles sat by his window, the book in his lap. He ran his fingers over the embossed title, finally accepting the reality of his accomplishment. "LOL AND SORROW," he whispered to himself. "It's real. I did it. And it's thanks to everyone who believed in me, especially the readers."

And with that, he allowed himself to embrace the dream that had become his reality, feeling a sense of fulfillment he had never known before.

PROLOGUE

In the heart of every story lies a kernel of truth, a seed from which the narrative grows and flourishes. "LOL and Sorrow" is no exception. This collection of short stories, penned by Charles Cawv Thao, invites readers into a world where humor and heartache intertwine, creating a tapestry of human experience that is as rich and diverse as life itself.

Charles Cawv Thao, a Hmong native from Laos, has traversed a journey marked by profound change and resilience. From the verdant landscapes of Southeast Asia to the bustling streets of America, his life story is a testament to the indomitable spirit of a man who, despite numerous challenges, found his voice in the written word. Each story in this book reflects his unique perspective, shaped by the cultural tapestry of his Hmong heritage and the trials of immigrant life.

"LOL and Sorrow" is more than just a collection of anecdotes; it is a mirror reflecting the myriad facets of the human condition. The tales within these pages are inspired by true events, imbued with the authenticity of real emotions and experiences. They capture the essence of life's unpredictability—the moments of joy that catch us by surprise, the sorrow that lingers in the quiet corners of our hearts, and the resilience that propels us forward.

As you delve into these stories, you will encounter a diverse array of characters, each with their own struggles and triumphs. Through their eyes, you will experience the laughter that bubbles up in the most unexpected circumstances and the tears that fall silently in the face of adversity. These narratives celebrate the human spirit, highlighting the strength and vulnerability residing within us all.

Charles Thao never envisioned himself as an author, yet his innate talent for storytelling shines brightly in this debut work. His words paint vivid pictures, transporting readers to different times and places, allowing them to walk alongside the characters and feel their emotions. The cultural insights woven into each story offer a glimpse into the rich heritage of the Hmong people while also addressing universal themes that resonate with readers from all walks of life.

"LOL and Sorrow" is a journey through the full spectrum of human emotion, a testament to the power of storytelling to connect, heal, and inspire. As you turn the pages, may you find yourself laughing out loud at the absurdities of life, shedding a tear for its sorrows, and ultimately feeling a deeper connection to the shared experiences that unite us all.

Welcome to "LOL and Sorrow." May your journey through these stories be as enriching and unforgettable as the life that inspired them.

Anthony Harrison

CHAPTER ONE
NEVER THROW A BRICK STRAIGHT UP; YOU'LL HAVE A VERY BAD DAY.

IN PURSUIT

Tou Lee had been on the road for hours, the monotony of the highway stretching endlessly before him. His eyes grew heavy, and his stomach rumbled in protest of the sparse snacks he'd been surviving on. Spotting a weathered sign indicating a roadhouse cafe just ahead, he decided it was time for a break. He signaled and veered off the main road, the car bumping gently along the gravel path that led to the quaint, inviting establishment nestled amidst towering pines and rolling fields.

The roadhouse cafe exuded a rustic charm, with its wooden beams and flower boxes brimming with bright blooms. Tou pushed open the creaky door, greeted by the warm aroma of freshly brewed coffee and the friendly hum of conversation. The interior was cozy, filled with mismatched furniture that added to its homely appeal. He found a corner table and sank into the cushioned seat, feeling the tension of the drive begin to melt away.

A cheerful waitress approached, her smile wide and welcoming. "What can I get for you today?" she asked, her pen poised over a notepad.

"I'll have a hearty sandwich and a cup of your finest coffee, please," Tou replied, his mouth watering at the thought of a proper meal.

While waiting, he observed the lively atmosphere around him. A group of older men played cards at a nearby table, their laughter echoing through the room. A young couple huddled close, sharing whispered conversations and shy smiles. It was a slice of small-town life, a comforting contrast to the isolation of the open road.

The waitress returned with his order, the sandwich generously stacked with fresh ingredients and the coffee steaming hot. Tou savored each bite, feeling rejuvenated with every sip. As he polished off his meal, he exchanged pleasantries with the staff and a few of the regulars, who welcomed him as if he were an old friend. With its warmth and hospitality, the cafe felt like a temporary home.

After settling the bill, Tou gathered his belongings, thanked the staff for their kindness, and stepped back out into the crisp afternoon air. The sun hung low, casting long shadows as it inched toward the horizon. He took a moment to stretch, breathing deeply the scent of pine and earth, before heading to his car. The gravel crunched underfoot, the only sound breaking the serene silence of the countryside.

He started the engine and pulled back onto the road, the cafe quickly receding into the distance behind him. As he merged onto the highway, he noticed a car rapidly approaching in his rearview mirror. It drew uncomfortably close, its driver swerving erratically. A knot of unease formed in Tou's stomach. He pressed the gas pedal, hoping to put some distance between himself and the erratic vehicle.

The car behind him did not relent. It matched his speed, staying perilously close, its headlights flashing in his mirrors. Tou's pulse quickened, fear gripping his mind. He tried to think of a plan, considering pulling over but dismissing the idea quickly; the road was too deserted, and the driver too unpredictable. Instead, he decided to keep moving, praying that the other car would lose interest or that he would encounter another vehicle to flag down for help.

Minutes stretched into what felt like hours as the nerve-wracking pursuit continued. Tou's hands were slick with sweat, his breath coming in shallow gasps. He reached for his cell phone, desperate to call for help, but in his panic, it slipped from his grasp, tumbling to the floor of the car. He cursed under his breath, unable to retrieve it without stopping.

The car behind him suddenly accelerated, overtaking him with a reckless surge of speed. It swerved sharply, cutting in front of Tou and forcing him to a screeching halt on the desolate road. His heart pounded in his chest as he watched the driver of the other car step out and begin walking toward him.

Tou braced himself for the worst, his mind racing with possibilities. The setting sun cast long shadows, painting the scene in a dramatic twilight. The driver, a middle-aged man with a stern expression, approached his window and knocked gently.

Tou rolled down the window, his hands trembling. "What do you want?" he managed to stammer.

To his astonishment, the man's expression softened. "You left your wallet at the cafe," he said, holding up the familiar leather item. "I was just trying to return it to you. Why didn't you stop? What were you thinking?"

Relief and embarrassment washed over Tou in equal measure. He took a deep breath, the fear dissipating as he realized the misunderstanding. "I'm so sorry," he said, his voice shaking. "I thought you were... I didn't know. Thank you so much."

The man smiled, handing the wallet through the window. "It's alright. Just be careful next time."

Tou nodded, gratitude flooding his heart. As the man returned to his car and drove away, Bee sat for a moment, the twilight deepening around him. He reflected on the ordeal, realizing the importance of not letting fear cloud his judgment. With a renewed sense of calm, he started his car and continued his journey, the day's lesson etched firmly in his mind.

As the road stretched out before him, bathed in the soft glow of the setting sun, Tou felt a deep appreciation for the kindness of strangers and the unexpected turns of life. The country road seemed less lonely now, each mile bringing him closer to his destination and a new perspective on the road ahead.

AN APPOINTMENT WITH DR. DOODLE

Once upon a time, in the bustling town of Springfield, a man named Joe paid a visit to his eccentric doctor, Dr. Doodle. Joe had been feeling under the weather lately and hoped Dr. Doodle could provide some relief.

After an examination that involved a stethoscope, a rubber chicken, and a magnifying glass, Dr. Doodle reached a diagnosis and promptly scribbled out a prescription on a piece of paper that looked suspiciously like a grocery list.

"Aha!" exclaimed Dr. Doodle, waving the prescription in the air dramatically. "This concoction should have you feeling as sprightly as a kangaroo on a pogo stick in no time!"

Joe raised an eyebrow but decided to trust the good doctor and headed to the local pharmacy to fill his prescription.

A month later, Joe returned to Dr. Doodle's office for a follow-up appointment. The doctor, with his bushy eyebrows knitted in concern, asked Joe how he had been feeling and whether the prescribed medication had worked its magic.

Joe scratched his head, a perplexed expression on his face. "Well, Doc," he began hesitantly, "I gotta be honest with ya. I tried taking the medicine just like you said, but I couldn't shake off this funky feeling."

Dr. Doodle's eyes widened in surprise. "Oh dear! That simply won't do! I prescribed the finest elixir this side of Springfield!"

Joe chuckled nervously before sheepishly admitting, "Well, you see, Doc, I did exactly what the label said. It said, 'KEEP IT TIGHLY CLOSED,' so I did just that. I kept the bottle closed tight as a drum!"

Dr. Doodle blinked in disbelief before bursting into laughter, his belly jiggling like a bowl full of jelly. "Oh, Joe, that's not quite what I meant, my friend!"

And so, with a few clarifications on how to properly take medication, Joe left Dr. Doodle's office with a prescription for laughter and a newfound appreciation for the importance of reading instructions carefully.

THE DINNER DATE DILEMMA

Tony, a young businessman with a penchant for adventure, found himself attending a bustling conference in the heart of Chicago. Amidst the sea of faces and the whirlwind of networking, one person stood out to him like a beacon in the fog – Crystal. With her captivating smile and infectious laughter, she effortlessly drew him in, leaving him eager to learn more about her.

After a day filled with insightful seminars and tedious meetings, Tony finally mustered the courage to approach Crystal. He struck up a conversation, and to his delight, she reciprocated with warmth and genuine interest. Sparks flew between them as they exchanged anecdotes and shared laughs, forging a connection that seemed destined to blossom.

With a surge of adrenaline and a flutter of nerves, Tony took a leap of faith and asked Crystal out to dinner. To his delight, she accepted, and they made plans to meet at a cozy Italian restaurant just a few blocks away from the conference venue.

As the appointed hour drew near, Tony found himself anxiously pacing outside the restaurant, his heart racing with anticipation. He arrived a little early, eager to secure the perfect table and impress Crystal with his punctuality. However, as minutes turned into half an hour, there was still no sign of her.

Growing increasingly concerned, Tony checked his watch for what felt like the hundredth time. Where could Crystal be? Had something happened to her? Unable to shake off his worries, he decided to call her at the hotel where she was staying.

Crystal's soft voice greeted him over the phone, but before Tony could utter a word, she spoke, her tone apologetic yet cryptic. "Sorry, Tony, I couldn't make it. I can't leave my room."

Perplexed, Tony furrowed his brow, trying to make sense of her words. "Why is that?" he asked, his concern deepening with each passing moment.

Crystal hesitated for a moment before explaining, her voice tinged with embarrassment. "Well, there's a sign hanging on the doorknob that says, 'PLEASE DO NOT DISTURB.'"

Tony couldn't help but chuckle at the absurdity of the situation. "Crystal, you can just take the sign off the door and come out."

There was a brief silence on the other end of the line before Crystal responded, her laughter ringing out. "Oh my goodness, Tony! I never thought of that. I feel so silly!"

Relieved and amused, Tony reassured her, "It's alright, Crystal. These things happen. Why don't you come down now? The restaurant is still open, and I'd love to have dinner with you."

A few minutes later, Crystal arrived at the restaurant, slightly flustered but smiling. They laughed about the mix-up and enjoyed a wonderful dinner together, sharing stories and dreams late into the night. Their connection grew deeper, and they both felt that this chance meeting at the conference might be the beginning of something special.

As they walked back to their respective hotels, Tony couldn't help but reflect on the evening's events. He had been so nervous and worried, but in the end, everything had turned out better than he could have hoped. Crystal was not just a pretty face but a delightful companion, full of charm and wit.

The next day at the conference, Tony and Crystal were inseparable. They attended seminars together, exchanged ideas, and even started brainstorming a potential business collaboration. Their shared interests and chemistry were undeniable, and by the end of the conference, they had become more than just friends.

In the weeks and months that followed, Tony and Crystal's relationship continued to flourish. They visited each other in their respective cities, explored new adventures together, and supported each other in their professional endeavors. Their bond was strong, and their future promising.

One evening, as they sat together watching the sunset, Tony turned to Crystal with a smile. "You know, meeting you was the best thing that happened to me at that conference."

Crystal squeezed his hand and replied, "And to think, it all started because of a 'DO NOT DISTURB' sign."

They both laughed, knowing that sometimes, the most memorable moments in life come from the most unexpected situations.

Moral: Be careful about hoping for a date with a pretty woman; you might just get it. And when you do, enjoy every moment, no matter how unexpected or amusing it may be.

PAWS FOR THOUGHT

Once upon a time, in the quiet suburb of Oakwood Lane, there were two bumbling burglars named Joe and Bob. They were known throughout the neighborhood for their knack for trouble and their dubious talents in thievery. On one fateful evening, they found themselves on the prowl for their next target.

"Psst, Bob, look over there," whispered Joe, pointing towards a cozy-looking house with a neatly trimmed lawn. "That house looks ripe for the taking. No alarms, no security cameras, just an old lady pottering around. It's a piece of cake!"

Bob nodded eagerly, rubbing his hands together in anticipation. "Let's do it, Joe. This'll be our easiest job yet!"

Under the cover of darkness, the two would-be bandits crept towards the unsuspecting house, their hearts pounding with excitement. With a swift kick, they forced their way inside, ready to fill their pockets with ill-gotten gains. But little did they know, their plans were about to take an unexpected turn.

As they tiptoed through the dimly lit hallway, they were suddenly met with a sight that sent shivers down their spines. Standing before them were not just one but two towering German Shepherds, their deep growls filling the air with menace.

"Uh-oh, Joe, I don't think we're alone," whispered Bob, his voice trembling with fear.

Before they could even think about making a hasty retreat, the ferocious guard dogs sprang into action, their sharp teeth sinking into the seat of Joe and Bob's pants. Yelping in pain, the two hapless burglars stumbled over each other in a frantic attempt to escape the canine onslaught.

Hours later, Joe and Bob found themselves lying in hospital beds, nursing their wounds and nursing a grudge against the very creatures that had foiled their plans. It was during their lengthy recovery that they hatched a plan that was as ludicrous as it was laughable.

"We'll sue her, Bob! We'll sue her for not warning us about those blasted dogs!" exclaimed Joe, his face contorted in pain and anger.

And so, armed with nothing but their misguided sense of entitlement, Joe and Bob embarked on a quest for justice, or rather, revenge. They filed a lawsuit against the old lady, claiming that she had failed to adequately warn them about the presence of her furry guardians.

The news of the absurd lawsuit spread like wildfire through the town, drawing chuckles and guffaws from all who heard it. Even the judge struggled to maintain a straight face as he presided over the courtroom proceedings. In the end, justice prevailed, though perhaps not in the way Joe and Bob had hoped.

LOL AND SORROW

The judge ruled in favor of the old lady, dismissing Joe and Bob's frivolous lawsuit with a hearty dose of common sense. And as they trudged out of the courtroom, defeated but hopefully wiser, Joe and Bob realized that sometimes, the biggest bite comes not from the law but from man's best friend.

9/11: LOVE REUNITED FROM THE RUBBLE

Adam and Eva were only children when they met. Adam was eleven, with an inquisitive mind and a heart full of dreams, and Eva, just a year younger, was a kind-hearted girl with a contagious smile. Their parents, unfortunately, had fallen on hard times, and both families found themselves living in a homeless shelter in Springfield, Missouri. Despite their circumstances, Adam and Eva found joy in each other's company. They played together, studied together, and dreamed of a better future together.

The state of Missouri eventually intervened, rescuing Adam and Eva from their challenging environment. They were placed into the foster care system and soon adopted by separate families. Though they were sad to be apart, their love and memories of each other lingered in their hearts.

Years passed. Adam was adopted by a loving family in Kansas City, where he grew up to be a compassionate and driven man. He excelled in school and later pursued a career in engineering. Eva, adopted by a family in St. Louis, grew into a caring and resilient woman. She became a nurse dedicated to helping those in need.

Twenty-five years later, in the year 2000, the United States faced a devastating attack. On September 11th, the Twin Towers in New York City were plunged into chaos. The nation was in shock, and amidst the rubble and ruin, countless lives were lost or forever changed.

Adam, now thirty-six, felt a calling to help. He volunteered with the American Red Cross, joining a team of brave men and women who traveled to New York City to assist in the rescue and cleanup efforts. It was a daunting task, but Adam was determined to make a difference.

For days, Adam and his team scouted the assigned areas, looking for anyone who might still be trapped beneath the crushed buildings. In 24 hours, they found eleven people alive and four dead. The survivors were rushed to nearby hospitals for treatment. Among the survivors was a woman named Eva.

Two weeks later, Adam visited the survivors at St. Mark's Hospital. He wanted to check on them, to offer support and comfort. He moved from room to room, exchanging kind words and smiles. Then, he arrived at room 2552. The name on the door stopped him in his tracks: Eva.

Adam entered the room, his heart pounding. The woman lying in the bed looked tired but smiled warmly when she saw him. During their conversation, Adam mentioned that he once knew someone very dear to him named Eva. He explained that it was a long time ago and that he had never forgotten her.

The patient, Eva, listened intently, her curiosity piqued. When Adam told her his name—Adam Preston—and mentioned that he used to live in Springfield, Missouri, Eva's eyes widened in recognition. They began to share their pasts, recounting childhood memories and the dreams they once had. It didn't take long for them to realize that they were the same Adam and Eva who had once promised to marry each other when they grew up.

The reunion of the two childhood lovers was nothing short of miraculous. They were shocked and surprised to find each other again, especially under such extraordinary circumstances. Both of them were still single, having never married, as if fate had kept them waiting for this moment.

Adam and Eva reconnected deeply over the following months, their bond stronger than ever. Two years later, in a beautiful ceremony in New York City, they finally fulfilled their childhood promise and were married. Their story became a testament to the enduring power of love and the mysterious ways in which destiny can bring people together.

This heartwarming tale caught the attention of a local newspaper, the New York Life Daily. In a special feature titled "Love Reunited from the Rubble," the paper detailed the incredible journey of Adam and Eva, highlighting their childhood love, separation, and miraculous reunion in the wake of a national tragedy. The article concluded with a reflection on the resilience of the human spirit and the enduring power of love, leaving readers with a sense of hope and inspiration in the midst of difficult times.

CHAPTER TWO
IF YOU THINK YOUR LIFE IS SUCKS, YOU'RE A VACUUM.

THE ROADSIDE RUMBLE

It was a typical day on the bustling city streets when fate decided to throw two strangers into an unexpected encounter that would leave them both reeling with laughter and disbelief.

As the traffic crawled along the crowded road, a stunning woman maneuvered her sleek car through the chaos with effortless grace. But in her haste to reach her destination, she inadvertently cut off a man in a beat-up sedan, sending him into a fit of rage.

Infuriated by the woman's reckless driving, the man honked his horn furiously before finally managing to pull up alongside her car. With a scowl etched on his face, he motioned for her to stop, his anger simmering just below the surface.

"You nearly killed me back there!" he yelled, his voice was laced with outrage.

The woman, caught off guard by his outburst, sheepishly replied, "Sorry."

But apologies were not enough to quell the man's fury. With a stern expression, he reached into his car and retrieved a marker, drawing a bold line on the ground before her car. "Don't you dare cross that line!" he commanded, his voice dripping with authority.

Confused but compliant, the woman nodded, her eyes widening in anticipation of what would come next.

To the woman's shock and disbelief, the man then produced a baseball bat from his car and began furiously pounding on her windshield, each blow resonating through the air with a deafening clang.

As cracks spiderwebbed across the glass, the woman couldn't contain her laughter, her amusement bubbling up from deep within her. "What's so funny? I'm smashing your windshield!" the man barked, his frustration mounting with each passing moment.

But the woman, unable to suppress her joy any longer, chuckled through her tears of laughter. "Well, while you're busy smashing my car," she managed to gasp between giggles, "I stepped over the line!"

TOU AND TENG

Once upon a time, in the wilds of the forest, there were two pals, Tou and Teng. They decided to venture into the woods for a hunting expedition, armed with enthusiasm and a slightly dubious sense of direction.

Tou, the self-proclaimed hunting guru, had a keen eye for any moving target. So, when a plump squirrel scurried by, he couldn't resist the temptation. With a swift motion, he aimed and fired.

Teng, watching in horror, exclaimed, "Tou, what in the world? We're supposed to be hunting deer, not killing innocent squirrels!"

Tou, ever the quick thinker, flashed a grin and replied, "Come on, Teng, I had to shoot them. Are you suggesting I'm just supposed to talk to the squirrels to death?"

Teng shook his head in disbelief. "Tou, that's not how hunting works! Besides, we've got bigger prey in mind."

But Tou was undeterred. "Hey, you never know until you try, right?"

The two continued deeper into the forest, the air thick with the scent of pine and the sound of rustling leaves. As they walked, Teng couldn't help but notice how Tou's trigger-happy approach was scaring away any potential deer they might encounter. Every snap of a twig or flutter of a bird had Tou reaching for his bow, and soon enough, the forest fell eerily silent as if the animals had learned to hide from Tou's reckless enthusiasm.

Hours passed with no sight of deer, and Teng's frustration grew. "Tou, if you keep shooting at everything that moves, we'll never find a deer. Hunting requires patience and strategy, not just a quick trigger finger."

Tou sighed, his initial excitement waning. "I guess I got carried away. But it's hard to resist when there's so much going on around us."

Teng nodded. "I understand, but we need to stay focused. The forest is full of life, but we have to respect it. Every creature has its place, and we have a responsibility to hunt wisely."

Taking Teng's advice to heart, Tou slowed down and began to appreciate the subtle signs of the forest. He noticed the deer tracks in the soft earth, the broken branches indicating recent movement, and the distant sounds of a herd. Together, they moved silently, their senses attuned to their surroundings.

Finally, as dusk approached, they spotted a majestic deer grazing in a clearing. Tou, with newfound patience, carefully aimed and took the shot, making sure it was clean and humane. The deer fell, and the two friends approached, grateful for the success that came from respecting the forest and its inhabitants.

As they prepared to head back home, Teng turned to Tou and said, "You see, Tou, hunting isn't just about the thrill of the chase. It's about understanding the balance of nature and acting with respect and restraint."

Tou smiled, feeling a sense of accomplishment and newfound wisdom. "You're right, Teng. I've learned that sometimes, patience and respect are the greatest skills a hunter can have."

Moral of the story: True success comes from patience, respect, and understanding. In any endeavor, it's important to balance enthusiasm with wisdom and consideration for the world around us.

TITLES DO MATTER

The restaurant manager, Mr. Thompson, was interviewing candidates for a cooking position at his upscale restaurant. He sought someone skilled in creating delicious meals. Reviewing Arriya's application, he called her in for an interview.

"Arriya, we take pride in being one of the top restaurants in town. I'm in need of a talented cook to join my kitchen. Can you cook well?" Mr. Thompson inquired.

Arriya replied, "Actually, no, I'm not a cook. I don't cook."

Confused, Mr. Thompson exclaimed, "What? What do you mean? Your application clearly states that you're applying for a cooking job at my restaurant. Are you a chef?"

Arriya responded softly, "No, I am not a chef."

"Then why did you apply for a job in a restaurant?" Mr. Thompson asked.

Arriya smiled and explained, "But I'm a master chef. I specialize in creating and designing food."

Mr. Thompson's confusion turned into curiosity. "So, you don't cook, but you create dishes? Could you explain what you mean by that?"

Arriya nodded. "Yes, exactly. I'm skilled at inventing new recipes, formulating flavors, and presenting food in elegant ways."

Impressed, Mr. Thompson exclaimed, "That's fascinating! We could use someone with your talents in our kitchen. Can you show me some examples of your work?"

Arriya eagerly shared her portfolio, filled with photos of intricately plated dishes and descriptions of her innovative recipes.

Mr. Thompson was amazed. "Your creations look incredible! We'd love to have you on our team as a chef, Arriya. Welcome aboard!"

Arriya smiled gratefully. "Thank you, Mr. Thompson. I'm excited to bring my creativity to your restaurant's kitchen."

And so, Arriya joined the restaurant as its newest chef, bringing her unique flair and culinary expertise to the esteemed establishment.

HOSPITALITY MATTERS: A LESSON IN ETIQUETTE

In an elegant and refined restaurant nestled in the heart of the city, a scene unfolded that would become the talk of the town. It all began when a particularly ill-mannered customer crossed paths with the restaurant's impeccable service.

The evening started like any other, with the restaurant buzzing with the clinking of glasses and the murmur of contented diners. However, the tranquility was shattered when a disgruntled patron lashed out at one of the servers, his words dripping with disdain.

The manager, a paragon of poise and professionalism, swiftly intervened. With a calm demeanor, he addressed the unruly customer, "Sir, I'm afraid your behavior is not in line with the standards of this establishment. We pride ourselves on providing a welcoming atmosphere for our guests."

Infuriated by the manager's gentle reprimand, the customer erupted in a fit of rage. "You can't do this! I'm a paying customer! I'll sue you!" he bellowed, his voice echoing through the dining room.

Undeterred, the manager maintained his composure. "Here at this restaurant, we don't have customers; we have guests. However, your behavior has extended beyond our hospitality. Please leave."

Fuming with anger, the customer stormed out of the restaurant, vowing vengeance for the perceived slight. But his tirade did not end there. Determined to seek retribution, he dialed the number for law enforcement, eager to enlist their support in his cause.

When the police arrived, they found themselves caught in the midst of a culinary controversy. The customer, with a self-righteous air, proclaimed, "The manager accused me of being rude to the server and kicked me out."

Turning to the manager for clarification, the officers inquired, "Sir, is this true?"

Unfazed by the scrutiny, the manager met their gaze with steely resolve. "Do you see how he's behaving? We don't have servers; we have concierges. Our staff are trained to provide unparalleled service, and when faced with disrespect, we must uphold the dignity of our establishment."

Impressed by the manager's unwavering commitment to hospitality, the officers nodded in understanding. "Thank you for your cooperation, sir. It seems this matter is best resolved outside of the law."

With that, the police bid farewell, leaving the restaurant to return to its usual state of refined elegance. And though the incident left a lingering taste of discord, it served as a poignant reminder that in the world of fine dining, etiquette reigns supreme.

TWENTY YEARS LATER: A REUNION OVER DINNER

It had been two decades since Joe and Bob had last crossed paths, their lives diverging down separate paths after their youthful adventures together. Yet fate had a way of bringing old friends back together. And on this particular evening, they found themselves seated across from each other in the cozy ambiance of a fine restaurant, the clink of silverware and the gentle murmur of conversation providing the backdrop to their reunion.

With a warm smile, Joe broke the ice. "Well, Bob, it's been quite some time! How have you been keeping?"

Bob returned the smile, his eyes alight with nostalgia. "Oh, you know, Joe, navigating the twists and turns of life as best as I can. What about you? What's been keeping you busy all these years?"

Joe leaned in, a spark of pride in his eyes. "I'm an electrical engineer now, working on all sorts of fascinating projects. It's been quite the journey, let me tell you."

Bob nodded appreciatively. "That sounds impressive, Joe! You always did have a knack for tinkering with gadgets. As for me, well, I found my calling in a slightly different realm. I'm an engineer, too."

Joe's eyebrows raised in shocking curiosity. "Oh, really? What kind of engineering do you specialize in?"

A mischievous twinkle danced in Bob's eyes as he delivered his response. "I drive trains."

For a moment, silence hung in the air as Joe processed Bob's unexpected revelation. Then, a burst of laughter erupted between them, echoing through the restaurant and drawing curious glances from nearby diners.

"Of course you do, Bob! Leave it to you to take the scenic route," Joe chuckled, wiping a tear of joy from his eye.

Bob grinned sheepishly, his laughter subsiding into a nostalgic sigh. "Well, you know me, Joe. I've always had a thing for locomotives. Besides, it's been quite the ride, pun intended."

As the evening unfolded, Joe and Bob reminisced about their shared memories, weaving tales of youthful escapades and dreams fulfilled. And though their paths had diverged over the years, their friendship remained as strong as ever, a testament to the enduring bonds forged in the fires of camaraderie.

And so, amidst the clatter of dishes and the hum of conversation, Joe and Bob savored not only the delectable cuisine before them but also the timeless joy of reconnecting with an old friend after twenty years apart.

CHAPTER THREE

THE FAMOUS SAYING GOES,
"A PRETTY FACE MEANS NOTHING IF YOU HAVE AN UGLY HEART."

WELL, THAT'S NOT ALL TRUE IF YOU ASK MARY KAY, CHARLOTTE TILBURY, OR REVLON.

A HISTORY CLASS LESSON

In the bustling corridors of the Franklin Junior High School, Mr. Anderson, a seasoned history teacher renowned for his dedication to his students' education, faced the familiar task of assigning homework to his class of sixty eager young minds. With a confident sweep of his chalk, he set forth their weekend assignment—reading chapter 32, pages 231 to 239, in their history textbooks—before bidding them farewell for the weekend.

As Monday dawned and the students filtered back into Mr. Anderson's classroom, anticipation hung thick in the air, palpable excitement mingling with the lingering echoes of weekend adventures. With a twinkle in his eye and a warm smile on his lips, Mr. Anderson wasted no time in posing the inevitable question to his expectant pupils, "How many of you read the chapter?"

To his surprise, fifty-nine hands shot up in unison, each student eager to showcase their diligence and dedication. But amidst the sea of raised hands, there was one notable exception: Karl, a young lad with a sheepish expression and a confession on his lips.

With a sense of honesty that belied his years, Karl spoke up, his voice tinged with remorse, "I'm sorry, Mr. Anderson, but I didn't read the chapter."

Mr. Anderson's brow furrowed in contemplation as he regarded the earnest young man before him. Then, with a nod of understanding and a hint of admiration, he addressed the class, "My dear students, it seems we have a lesson to learn today—one that transcends the confines of our history textbooks."

With a dramatic flourish, Mr. Anderson revealed the truth that lay hidden within the pages of their assigned reading. "As far as I'm concerned, Karl is the only one who read the chapter," he declared, his voice ringing with conviction. "And for his honesty and integrity, I'm going to award him sixty extra credits: fifty-nine from each of you, plus one for himself."

Gasps of astonishment filled the room as the gravity of Mr. Anderson's words sank in. The students exchanged bewildered glances, grappling with the implications of their teacher's unexpected decree.

But Mr. Anderson was not finished yet. With a solemn expression and a gentle tone, he explained the reason behind his unorthodox decision—there was no chapter 32, pages 231 to 239, in their history books. In the face of this revelation, the truth dawned upon the class, casting a shadow of realization over their previous assumptions.

And so, with heads bowed and hearts heavy, the students accepted their teacher's judgment, each one silently reflecting on the importance of honesty and integrity in both their academic pursuits and their lives beyond the classroom.

As the echoes of the day's lesson lingered in the air, Mr. Anderson couldn't help but smile. History, it seemed, had repeated itself once again—but this time, the students had learned a lesson that transcended the boundaries of time and textbooks, a lesson that would stay with them long after the bell had tolled and the school day had ended.

As the sun dipped below the horizon, casting long shadows across the empty classroom, Mr. Anderson couldn't help but feel a glimmer of hope for the future—a future shaped not only by the events of the past but by the choices and character of those who dared to learn from them.

ECHOES OF REFLECTION

Cindy had always known she was a bit eccentric, but today was an entirely new level of oddity. She found herself engaged in a conversation with her reflection in the mirror. It all started innocently enough. Cindy was brushing her teeth when her reflection, looking more animated than usual, suddenly cleared its throat and spoke up.

"Hey, Cindy, can I ask you something?" the reflection said, making Cindy nearly choke on her toothpaste.

Cindy stared, toothbrush hanging out of her mouth. "Uh, sure?" she mumbled around the foam.

"Why did you stop seeing your shrink?" her reflection's voice echoed, sounding surprisingly calm for a mirror image.

Cindy finished brushing and spat into the sink, pondering the question. "I stopped seeing him because he made me mad. He thinks I'm crazy."

The friend in the mirror, who Cindy decided to name Reflecto (because every imaginary friend needs a good name), tilted her head, contemplating Cindy's words with an exaggerated seriousness that made Cindy chuckle. "So, you're not crazy? Then I'm real?"

Cindy scratched her head. "I think so," she replied, trying to make sense of the bizarre situation.

Reflecto leaned in closer, her face filling up the entire mirror. "Cindy, you're crazy."

Cindy burst out laughing. "You know what, Reflecto? Maybe you're right. Maybe I am a little bit crazy."

Reflecto grinned mischievously. "A little bit? Cindy, you are talking to your reflection. That's not just a sprinkle of crazy; that's the whole darn cupcake!"

Cindy couldn't help but laugh harder. "Okay, okay! But seriously, everyone has their quirks. Look at the world! We've got people who believe in conspiracy theories about lizard people and others who collect toenail clippings. Compared to that, talking to my reflection is nothing."

Reflecto nodded sagely. "True, true. And you know what? Being a little crazy makes life interesting. Imagine how boring it would be if everyone was 'normal.'"

"Exactly!" Cindy agreed, feeling a strange kinship with her reflection. "Besides, I think sanity is overrated. All the best people are a little bonkers. Like Einstein or that guy who invented the pool noodle."

Reflecto's eyes twinkled with amusement. "So what you're saying is, we're in good company?"

"Absolutely," Cindy said, feeling more confident. "We're all crazy in some ways. The world is crazy. We have to be, too, in order to survive. If you can't laugh at yourself and your quirks, you're missing out on half the fun."

Reflecto beamed at her. "Well said, Cindy. Now, what shall we do next? Talk to the toaster? Have a chat with the cat?"

Cindy grinned. "Let's start with the cat. Mr. Whiskers always has the best advice."

And so, Cindy spent the rest of the day having whimsical conversations with her reflection, her cat, and even the toaster. She realized that maybe, just maybe, being a little crazy wasn't so bad after all. It made life more colorful, more unpredictable, and definitely more fun.

Moral: Embrace your quirks and remember, in a world that's gone mad, a little bit of crazy might just be your secret weapon.

THE CHURCH LOCK

Early one Sunday morning, Pastor Gregory Vang found himself in a predicament: he had mistakenly left his keys inside the church, locking himself out. Feeling a bit flustered, he called a local 24/7 emergency locksmith.

Within a short time, Jonas White, the locksmith, arrived and skillfully managed to pry open the door, allowing the pastor to regain access to the church. Grateful for Jonas's help, the pastor invited him inside for a brief conversation.

"Thank you for your assistance, young man," the pastor began warmly. "May I ask you something?"

"Of course," Jonas replied, eager to assist further.

"A few weeks ago, we had a break-in here at the church," the pastor explained with a hint of concern in his voice.

"I'm sorry to hear that," Jonas sympathized, understanding the gravity of the situation.

The pastor continued, "I wonder if there's a way we can install a lock that's more secure, one that's not easy for intruders to bypass or break."

Jonas nodded thoughtfully. "I could certainly look into that. But to be honest, no lock is completely foolproof. If someone is determined enough, they'll find a way to get in."

Frowning, the pastor asked, "Then what's the point of having a lock if it can't keep the intruders out?"

Jonas paused, considering his response carefully. "Well, Pastor, the lock isn't invented to keep bad people out. It's to keep the good ones from coming in without permission. It's a symbol of respect, reminding the good ones to knock before entering. The bad ones won't bother with it."

The pastor's expression softened as he pondered Jonas's words. "I see," he murmured, realizing the deeper significance of the lock.

Jonas continued, "Locks serve as a reminder to those with good intentions to respect boundaries and ask for permission. It's a sign of mutual respect and trust. While we can always improve security to deter intruders, the essence of a lock is more about honoring these principles."

The pastor nodded in agreement, feeling enlightened. "You know, Jonas, you've given me a new perspective. Sometimes, we focus so much on keeping bad things out that we forget the importance of fostering respect and trust among those with good intentions."

As they continued their conversation, Jonas offered to assess the church's security and suggest improvements that could provide better peace of mind without undermining the essence of mutual respect.

Later that day, Pastor Vang reflected on the encounter. He realized that in many aspects of life, it's essential to balance security with trust. By emphasizing respect and mutual understanding, communities can foster stronger bonds and create environments where trust is valued above all.

Moral of the Story: Locks and barriers are actually made to keep the good ones out.

RUNNING FASTER

Jake always wished he could finish the district marathon race in his hometown. Year after year, for 21 years, he had attempted to cross that elusive finish line, but each time, something held him back. Whether it was fatigue, cramps, or sheer bad luck, the dream seemed to slip further away. But Jake was nothing if not determined. He decided to give it one final try before hanging up his running shoes for good.

His best friend, Wesley, believed in him wholeheartedly. "Jake, you've got to stick with it until you succeed," Wesley urged. "Why not consult a professional trainer? Someone who can give you the edge you need."

Jake was skeptical but decided to follow Wesley's advice. He sought out Tony Yang, a renowned marathon trainer with a reputation for pushing his trainees to their limits. Jake met Tony at the local gym, feeling a mixture of hope and apprehension.

"Hi, Jake. How're you doing? I understand you want to talk about how to improve your marathon run?" Tony greeted him with a confident smile.

"Of course," Jake replied, trying to match Tony's enthusiasm.

"Alright, let's do some workouts and talk about it," Tony suggested, leading Jake to the weight area.

"Yes, let's do that," Jake responded, feeling a surge of determination.

As they worked out, Tony shared various strategies. He talked about pacing, nutrition, mental stamina, and the importance of strength training. Jake listened intently, absorbing every piece of advice.

"So, Jake, do I understand you correctly? You just want to run faster and longer," Tony asked, wiping sweat from his brow.

Jake nodded emphatically. "Yes, exactly."

"Alright, then, we need to start intense training. Meet me at the vacant field tomorrow morning at dawn," Tony instructed.

The next morning, Jake arrived at the abandoned field, the rising sun casting long shadows on the dew-kissed grass. Tony was already there, his sports van parked nearby.

"Jake, today you'll learn how to run faster. And trust me, you will run faster," Tony said with a mysterious grin. He walked over to his van and opened the back doors. Out bounded two large, muscular German Shepherds, their eyes sharp and their bodies taut with energy.

Jake's eyes widened in shock. "What's going on?"

"Jake, you better run fast, or they'll bite your ass!" Tony shouted as he unleashed the dogs.

Without a second thought, Jake took off, his heart pounding not just from exertion but from sheer adrenaline. The sound of the dogs' paws thudding against the ground behind him pushed him to move faster than he ever had before. Each stride was a desperate bid to stay ahead, each breath a fierce commitment to not give up.

The thrill of the chase activated a primal part of Jake's brain, driving him to tap into reserves of speed and endurance he didn't know he possessed. He ran like his life depended on it, zigzagging through the field, his muscles burning but his spirit soaring.

After what felt like an eternity, Tony called off the dogs. Panting and exhilarated, Jake collapsed onto the grass, a triumphant smile spreading across his face.

"You see, Jake," Tony said, walking over and helping him to his feet. "Motivation comes in many forms. Sometimes, a little fear can push you beyond your limits."

Jake laughed breathlessly, realizing the truth in Tony's words. He had just run faster and farther than ever before. The experience was transformative, showing him that with the right motivation, he could achieve anything.

Over the next few months, Tony put Jake through a grueling but effective training regimen. The initial shock of the dogs was replaced with disciplined workouts, meticulous planning, and constant encouragement. Jake's times improved, his stamina increased, and his confidence soared.

Finally, the day of the district marathon arrived. As Jake stood at the starting line, he felt a calm wash over him. The gun fired, and he surged forward, each stride filled with purpose and strength. Throughout the race, he recalled Tony's training, Wesley's unwavering belief, and the exhilarating chase with the dogs.

As he approached the finish line, the crowd's cheers grew louder. With a final burst of energy, Jake crossed the line, arms raised in victory. He had done it. After 21 years, he had finally finished the marathon.

The lesson was clear: with the right motivation, determination, and support, people can achieve anything. Jake's journey was a testament to the power of perseverance and the incredible things one can accomplish when people are motivated properly.

THE CONTRAST

Bob, a Vietnam veteran and member of the Pure America, had always harbored a deep-seated disdain for foreigners. Yet, amidst his fervor for patriotism, there was a gentle passion for painting that he could never quite shake off. Despite his efforts, his artistry never seemed to blossom enough to support him financially.

One fateful day, on a Greyhound bus journey, Bob encountered Vincent, a Hmong renowned for his artistic prowess. Intrigued by Bob's struggle with painting, Vincent offered to mentor him, promising to help him refine his skills.

Eight months later, Bob found himself in Idaho, ready to absorb Vincent's teachings. Vincent began with a simple lesson, starting a painting with just one color: white. As he gradually added more colors - yellow, red, blue, black - the painting transformed, each hue adding depth and dimension.

"I reckon I could do that too," Bob mused, eager to try his hand at Vincent's technique.

Vincent smiled knowingly. "It's not just about adding colors, Bob. It's about understanding contrast."

"Contrast?" Bob queried, unfamiliar with the term.

Vincent patiently explained, "Contrast is the difference between colors. It's what makes them stand out, what gives a painting its beauty."

Enlightened, Bob began to grasp the concept, realizing its significance not only in art but also in life. With newfound understanding, he dedicated himself to perfecting his craft, eventually gaining recognition and popularity as an artist.

Through his journey, Bob underwent a spiritual transformation. He realized that the diversity of races, cultures, and nationalities enriches the world, much like the contrast in a painting. He distanced himself from his former xenophobic beliefs and the Pure America.

One day, a man named Charles wandered into Bob's art gallery. He was intrigued by the painting and couldn't help but stare at it in awe. As he stood there, lost in thought, Bob approached him.

"Beautiful, isn't it?" he said with a smile.

Charles nodded, but there was a hint of confusion in his eyes. "I'm not sure I understand. It's just a bunch of people...different colors, different clothes."

Bob chuckled softly. "Ah, but that's where the beauty lies, my friend. You see, this painting isn't just about colors and clothing. It's about the richness of diversity and the beauty of contrast."

Bob went on to explain how each person in the painting represented a different race, culture, and nationality. And while they were all unique in their own way, it was their differences that made the painting so captivating.

"Imagine if everyone in this painting looked the same," Bob mused. "It wouldn't be nearly as interesting, would it? It's the contrast—the difference between the colors—that makes it beautiful."

As Charles listened to his words, a realization dawned on him. He had always been taught that differences were something to be wary of, something to fear. But looking at the painting before him, he saw things in a new light.

"Without contrast, people wouldn't see the beauty in diversity," he murmured to himself.

Bob smiled, knowing that his message had resonated with him. "Exactly. Racism, discrimination, and hate are ugly, but race, culture, and nationality—they're what make the world such a vibrant and beautiful place."

CHAPTER FOUR

THE FAMOUS SAYING GOES,
"STAND UP AND CHANGE THE WORLD."

WELL, YOU CAN ALSO DO IT WHILE
SITTING DOWN TOO.

A FOLDED PIECE OF PAPER

Once upon a time, in a serene Hmong village nestled among rolling hills, Master Xi Chao, at the age of 102, lay on his deathbed, surrounded by his devoted disciples. They gathered around him, their hearts heavy with sorrow, yet eager to hear his final words of wisdom.

Master Xi Chao began to speak, his voice soft but steady, "Listen closely, my dear disciples, for I wish to share with you a story—a story that carries a lesson of great importance."

Many years ago, in a village much like this one, there lived a wise teacher named Master Dao. Renowned far and wide for his profound wisdom, Master Dao's teachings on love and happiness drew many eager disciples who sought to learn from him.

One bright morning, Master Dao gathered his disciples in the tranquil courtyard of the village temple. In his hands, he held a crisp, white piece of paper for each of his students. With a gentle smile, he instructed them, "My dear disciples, please write your name on this paper and fold it neatly."

The disciples obeyed, and soon the courtyard was filled with neatly folded pieces of paper, each bearing a name written in elegant script. Master Dao then collected all the papers, mixed them thoroughly, and scattered them across the courtyard. The disciples exchanged puzzled glances; their curiosity piqued.

"Now, my dear students," Master Dao announced, "you have five minutes to find your own piece of paper among the scattered notes." The disciples sprang into action, their eyes scanning the ground as they darted back and forth, searching for their names.

Frustration soon set in. "I can't find my paper anywhere!" one disciple exclaimed; his voice tinged with anxiety. "How are we supposed to do this in such a short time?"

"This is impossible!" another disciple echoed, worry evident in his tone. "I've checked every corner, but I still can't find mine. What if we fail?"

As the minutes ticked by, the frantic search continued, the disciples' voices blending into a chorus of worry and doubt. Despite their best efforts, they could not locate their respective pieces of paper amid the chaotic jumble.

Sensing the rising tension, Master Dao stepped forward, his presence calming the anxious group. "Do not despair, my dear ones," he said, his voice soothing. "There is a deeper lesson within this exercise. I want each of you to pick up the first piece of paper you find and deliver it to the person whose name is inscribed upon it."

Though still confused, the disciples followed his instructions. To their surprise, within just five minutes, every disciple held their own paper with their name on it. The courtyard, once filled with frantic energy, was now filled with smiles and relieved laughter.

Master Dao gathered his disciples around him, his eyes filled with warmth and wisdom. "These pieces of paper," he said, "represent love and happiness. Remember this: true happiness is not found by solely seeking our own desires and needs. It is discovered when we selflessly love and care for others. When we take the time to bring joy to someone else's life, we find our own hearts filled with love and happiness."

The disciples nodded in understanding, their hearts touched by the simplicity and depth of the lesson.

Master Xi Chao paused, allowing the story to sink in, then revealed with a gentle smile, "I was one of Master Dao's students."

The disciples gasped softly, realization dawning upon them. The story they had just heard was not merely a tale, but a reflection of the life their beloved Master Xi Chao had lived—a life of selfless love, compassion, and wisdom.

From that day forward, the disciples strived to embody Master Xi Chao's teachings, spreading love and happiness wherever they went. They understood that true fulfillment comes not from seeking one's own happiness but from selfless acts of kindness and love.

And so, the legacy of Master Dao, passed down through Master Xi Chao, lived on in the hearts of his disciples, a beacon of love and wisdom guiding them through the journey of life.

BEYOND THE GOLD MEDAL

In the heart of Beijing, China, amidst the flurry of excitement surrounding the Beijing World Olympic Marathon, Pam stood at the starting line, her determination shining brighter than the morning sun. With every fiber of her being, she was ready to take on the challenge that lay ahead. The cheers of the crowd fueled her spirit as she embarked on the grueling 26.2-mile journey.

Pam had trained tirelessly for this moment, pouring her sweat, tears, and dreams into each stride. But as fate would have it, early into the race, a misstep sent her tumbling down, costing her precious time. Despite the setback, Pam refused to let disappointment overshadow her resolve. She dusted herself off and continued onward, her eyes fixed on the finish line.

Hours passed, and Pam found herself falling further and further behind the pack. Yet, she pressed on, her perseverance unwavering. As the sun began its descent and the shadows grew long, Pam remained undeterred. For her, the race was not about winning a gold medal but about honoring the commitment she had made to herself – to finish what she started.

As Pam crossed the finish line, long after the other runners had already claimed their accolades, a wave of admiration swept through the crowd. Reporters clamored to hear her story, eager to capture the essence of her unwavering determination.

"Why did you keep going, even when you knew the race was over?" one reporter asked, microphone poised expectantly.

Pam smiled, her eyes reflecting the fire that burned within her. "Winning isn't always about receiving a medal," she replied. "It's about pushing through the pain, overcoming obstacles, and never giving up on yourself."

Her words echoed across news stations, capturing the hearts of people around the world. In a larger scheme, Mia became a symbol of resilience, a testament to the power of the human spirit.

In living rooms and coffee shops, her story was shared in hushed tones, inspiring countless individuals to chase their dreams with unwavering determination. Pam may not have received a gold medal that day, but she emerged as the true champion – a beacon of hope, courage, and unwavering perseverance.

FRED'S DYING

Fred lived a life that many would envy. He possessed wealth, a loving family, and all the trappings of success. Despite the facade of contentment he displayed, an enduring ache nestled within him, an emptiness that no material abundance could dispel.

For years, Fred had suppressed this sense of dissatisfaction beneath the busyness of daily life. He immersed himself in work, pursuing success and recognition in hopes of silencing the restless void within him. Yet, no matter his efforts, the emptiness persisted, a silent specter haunting him even in moments of triumph.

Then, on an ordinary day turned extraordinary, his car spluttered to a stop on a lonely, desolate road. Frustration and helplessness washed over Fred as he realized he was stranded, miles from civilization. Just when he felt at his lowest, a stranger emerged like a beacon of hope.

Benjamin, a man with a warm smile and gentle eyes, pulled over and extended a helping hand. As Benjamin tinkered with the engine, a profound conversation unfolded between the two men, delving into depths Fred hadn't anticipated.

Amidst their exchange, Fred found himself blurting out the words he'd long kept locked away. He confessed his inner turmoil, acknowledging to Benjamin the emptiness gnawing at his soul, even amidst his seemingly perfect life.

To Fred's astonishment, Benjamin didn't offer hollow platitudes or quick fixes. Instead, he reached into his pocket and withdrew a weathered Bible, flipping to a passage that resonated deeply with Fred's heart.

"'Whoever drinks the water I give them will never thirst. Indeed, the water I give them will become a spring of water welling up to eternal life,'" Benjamin read, his voice steady and sure.

"How do you know this is going to work?" asked Fred, skeptical.

"I can't guarantee it will work for you. It's up to you. I was once in your shoes. I understand your feelings and struggles," replied Benjamin.

Fred's skepticism faded as Benjamin explained that genuine fulfillment couldn't be found in material possessions or external achievements. It lay in nurturing the spirit, in forging a connection with something greater than oneself.

"I'm not religious," Fred protested, grappling with the unfamiliar terrain of spirituality.

"You don't need religion," reassured Benjamin. "You just need a willingness to open your heart to the possibility of something beyond what you can see and touch."

As their conversation unfolded, Fred felt a glimmer of hope ignite within him. Could it be that the answers he sought lay not in external validation but in the quiet whispers of his soul?

With Benjamin's guidance, Fred embarked on a journey of exploration, delving into the teachings of spirituality with an open mind and a hungry heart. He devoured books and attended gatherings, eager to drink deeply from the wells of wisdom revealed to him.

As he delved deeper into the realms of the spirit, Fred sensed a transformation within him. The emptiness that had long tormented him began to dissipate, replaced by a sense of peace and purpose previously unknown.

In the end, Fred realized that true fulfillment wasn't a destination but a journey to be embraced. It wasn't about acquiring more or achieving greater success but about listening to the quiet whispers of the soul and following where they led.

Armed with this newfound wisdom, Fred embarked on a quest for genuine fulfillment, guided by the belief that happiness lies not in possessions but in authenticity and how one chooses to live. Though the road ahead may be long and uncertain, Fred knew that as long as he remained true to the whispers of his own soul, he would never be alone.

UNEXPECTED REUNION

Separated by the passage of time and the twists of fate, John and Pete found themselves unexpectedly reunited after over three decades in a chance encounter at a local bar in a town far from their childhood stomping grounds. As they exchanged surprised greetings, the weight of years melted away, leaving only the warmth of their long-forgotten camaraderie.

"Hey, Pete, it's been thirty years! How have you been?" John's voice carried a mixture of nostalgia and genuine curiosity.

Pete, visibly taken aback by the unexpected reunion, managed a sheepish grin. "Definitely, I'm doing fine."

John's eyes sparkled with intrigue. "It's a surprise to see you here, Pete. What have you been up to all these years?"

With a nonchalant shrug, Pete replied, "Nothing much. What 'bout you?"

"I'm a lawyer now," John responded, a hint of pride coloring his voice.

However, as the evening wore on and the drinks flowed freely, Pete's inhibitions began to wane, and the bitterness that had simmered beneath the surface for years came bubbling to the forefront.

Inebriated and lacking coordination, Pete's words turned sharp as he raised his voice above the din of the bar. "I hate lawyers! You hear me? All you f---ing lawyers, except you…" His tirade was cut short as he tumbled off his bar stool, the impact echoing through the crowded room.

Feeling a mix of concern and empathy, John sprang into action, helping Pete to his feet and deftly relieving him of his car keys. With a solemn determination, he guided his old friend out of the bar and into the cool night air.

Arriving at Pete's doorstep, John rang the doorbell, his heart pounding with a mixture of apprehension and resolve. When a young lady answered the door, confusion flickered across her face at the sight of her father in such a state.

"Is this your dad?" John asked, his voice gentle yet firm.

The young lady nodded, her eyes widening with concern. "Yes, he is. Thank you for bringing him home. Can I help you?"

With a weary smile, John explained, "I'm bringing him home to you. Can I come in?"

As they entered the house, the young lady's gratitude poured over. "Thank you for bringing my dad home. I'm glad he can walk now. But where is his wheelchair?"

LAST DAY

In the heart of Springfield, Missouri, Ma Her had been counting down the days to her retirement. After toiling away for 24 long years at the local CINTAS factory, she had finally paid off her beloved Toyota car just a few months before her anticipated freedom. July 2, 2022, was supposed to be the dawn of a new era for her, one filled with relaxation and the simple joys of life.

As Ma made her way to her second shift at CINTAS on that fateful afternoon, there was an undeniable buzz of excitement in the air. Her coworkers and friends had been eagerly awaiting her retirement, and that night, they threw her a small celebration filled with heartfelt gifts, laughter, and well-wishes. Ma couldn't help but be touched by their kindness, and she left work that day with a heart brimming with gratitude and joy.

But fate had cruel intentions for Ma Her. Late that night, as she drove home from work, she realized she had left something important behind at the factory. Turning her car around to retrieve her forgotten belongings, she found herself traversing the bridge atop I-65, a seemingly ordinary structure in the Springfield night.

Then, in a blink of an eye, tragedy struck. Ma's car veered suddenly, crashing into a utility pole at the center of the bridge. The impact was catastrophic, leaving her vehicle mangled and herself gravely injured. Emergency services rushed to the scene, but the damage was already done. Ma was whisked away to Mercy Hospital, her life hanging in the balance.

Despite the efforts of skilled surgeons and the prayers of her loved ones, Ma's injuries proved insurmountable. After a month-long battle for survival, she tragically passed away, leaving behind a shattered community and devastated family and friends.

The news of Ma's untimely demise reverberated through the streets of Springfield, leaving a somber pall in its wake. No one had anticipated such a cruel twist of fate, especially on the eve of Ma's long-awaited retirement.

Her death served as a stark reminder of life's fragility, a harsh lesson learned by those who had known and loved her. In their grief-stricken state, they clung to the memories of Ma's infectious laughter and boundless kindness, finding solace in the warmth of her spirit.

As they mourned her loss, they made a solemn vow to honor Ma's memory by cherishing each fleeting moment, for they knew all too well that tomorrow was never promised. In the quiet streets of Springfield, amidst tears and sorrow, they whispered their farewells to Ma Her, a beloved soul taken too soon.

CHAPTER FIVE

A CLEVER AD SAYS,
"HERE'S YOUR 14-DAY TRIAL. SERIOUSLY."

THEN THEY HOPE YOU FORGET TO CANCEL IT.

RELIGIOUSLY

"Wait, you're going to church, you're religious?" Ted inquired, raising an eyebrow.

"No," Susie exclaimed, her tone puzzled. "But what's going to church got to do with religion?"

"I thought religious people go to church?" Ted questioned, trying to make sense of Susie's response.

"Indeed, religious people typically attend church. However, I'm just going to get some fried chicken at Church for our dinner date," clarified Susie, with a hint of amusement in her voice.

"Oh, I thought…" Fred mumbled, his disappointment evident.

Susie rolled her eyes. "Fred, I thought you knew me better than that. I'm not religious; I'm just food-curious!"

Fred's face lit up with understanding. "Oh! So, you're not into praying; you're into poultry!"

Susie chuckled. "Exactly! Besides, I've heard their chicken is divine."

Ted couldn't help but laugh at the pun. "Well, I guess that makes sense. But seriously, you had me worried there for a moment. I thought I was going to have to start confessing my sins or something."

The trio shared a laugh as they made their way to Church the restaurant, where they were bound to have a clucking good time.

As they entered the restaurant, they were greeted by the heavenly aroma of crispy fried chicken. Susie's eyes sparkled with excitement as she scanned the menu, already envisioning the delicious meal ahead.

But just as they were about to place their order, they noticed something peculiar. The waiter, dressed in a chef's hat and apron, had a strange glint in his eye.

"Welcome to Church, where our chicken is so good, it's almost religious," the waiter proclaimed with a dramatic flair.

Fred exchanged a puzzled glance with Susie and Ted. "Um, did he just... make a pun about chicken and religion?"

Susie shrugged. "I guess so. But hey, if the chicken is as good as they say, I'm willing to convert!"

They burst into laughter once again, their worries about religion and disappointment about the misunderstanding now nothing more than a humorous memory.

And as they dug into their crispy, golden pieces of fried chicken, they couldn't help but agree that sometimes, the best things in life are worth worshiping, even if it's just for a delicious dinner date at a Church.

ADAPTATION

The Hmong people made a valiant effort to adapt to life in the United States. Coming from a predominantly primitive culture, isolated from urban areas and lowlands, approximately 95% of the Hmong population lacked formal education and were unable to read or write. Consequently, their transition to American life posed significant challenges.

In 1980, three sisters embarked on their journey to assimilate by enrolling in an ESL (English as a Second Language) class in Chicago, Illinois. Armed with only a smattering of English acquired during their time in a refugee camp in Thailand, the sisters faced a daunting task. When the ESL teacher prompted them to introduce themselves to the class, the sisters encountered a linguistic hurdle. One sister bravely pointed to herself and declared, "My name is Her Neng," and pointed to her other sister, "Her name is My Neng." Perplexed, the teacher turned to the third sister and inquired about her name. In response, the third sister confidently stated, "My name is You."

In another instance, one of the sisters went to a job interview. The interviewer asked, "What is your name?" The sister replied properly, "My name is…" The interviewer responded, "Hi, My Neng. It's nice to meet you."

LOL AND SORROW

This amusing anecdote encapsulates the humor and the immense challenge faced by both the teacher and the Hmong sisters in navigating language barriers. It highlights the resilience of the Hmong community in embracing the complexities of a new culture while humorously showcasing the difficulties encountered in mastering a new language. Despite the initial confusion, such moments fostered understanding and camaraderie between the Hmong immigrants and their educators as they embarked on their shared journey of adaptation and learning.

THE ALIEN

Once upon a time, nestled within the heart of the Hmong mountains, there lived the Thao family. Their days were woven with the threads of tradition, their nights whispered with the stories of their ancestors. But when the winds of war swept through their homeland, they were forced to flee, seeking refuge far across the oceans in a land unknown to them – America.

Arriving in the United States, the Thao family found themselves surrounded by towering buildings and bustling streets, a world unlike any they had ever known. Their new home brimmed with strange contraptions: microwaves that hummed, refrigerators that chilled, and toilets that flushed with a mysterious whoosh.

As they settled into their first rental house, the Thao family gathered around at the dinner table, their hearts heavy with the weight of uncertainty. Amidst their chatter, the daughter-in-law, her eyes wide with curiosity, turned to her grandmother-in-law and asked, "Grandma, where do you get water to cook our rice?"

With a gentle smile, Grandma pointed to a gleaming fixture in the corner of the room. "Why, from the well in the bathroom, of course. It never runs dry," she replied.

Gasps of disbelief echoed around the table as the family realized the truth. "Grandma, that's the toilet!" a relative exclaimed, aghast. "That's where we relieve ourselves!"

Shock rippled through the Thao family, followed by nervous laughter. They had stumbled upon one of the many mysteries of their new American home. But this moment was just the beginning of their journey.

In the days that followed, the Thao family navigated the labyrinth of modern conveniences with a mixture of awe and confusion. They learned to coax heat from the stove, chill from the fridge, and even music from the radio. Each discovery was met with laughter, each mistake with understanding.

But beyond the realm of appliances lay a deeper challenge – the unfamiliar landscape of American culture. With each misunderstanding came a lesson, a bridge between the old ways and the new. Through perseverance and laughter, the Thao family forged ahead, their bonds strengthened by shared experiences, and their spirits buoyed by the promise of a brighter tomorrow.

And so, amidst the whirlwind of change, the Thao family embarked on a journey of discovery, laughter, and growth. Through the trials and tribulations of adapting to their new homeland, they found not only a place to call home but a community to call family. And in the tapestry of their lives, woven with threads of tradition and resilience, they discovered the true essence of the American dream.

DARK SHADOW

Once upon a time, in a cozy little cottage nestled among the rolling hills, there lived a mother named Sarah. She was a kind-hearted woman with a warm smile and gentle eyes, and her family meant everything to her. Her husband, John, was a hardworking man who loved his children fiercely, and together they raised three wonderful sons and two beautiful daughters.

But despite the love that filled their home, there was a shadow that hung over their family—a shadow named Jason. He was the eldest of the siblings, a bright and charming young man with a quick wit and a mischievous grin. But behind his laughter, Sarah could sense a sadness, a loneliness that seemed to weigh heavily on his shoulders.

As the days passed, Sarah watched her son carefully, her heart heavy with worry. She longed to reach out to him, to wrap him in her arms and chase away the darkness that clouded his mind. But Jason was always so guarded, so reluctant to share his burdens with anyone.

One morning, as Sarah sat at the kitchen table, a letter arrived in the mail. Her hands trembled as she opened it, her heart nearly pounding out of her chest. Tears welled in her eyes as she read the words written by her beloved son.

"Dad, Mom, I need to talk to you," Jason's voice echoed in her mind as she read his words aloud to her family. "I've been struggling with something for a long time now, something I can't seem to shake. I know you love me, but I haven't been able to bring myself to share this with you..."

Her voice faltered as she reached the end of the letter, her tears flowing freely and sorrowfully now. Beside her, John wrapped an arm around her shoulders, his own eyes glistening with unshed tears.

"Oh, Jason..." Sarah whispered, her voice choked with emotion. "Why didn't you tell us? Why did you have to go through this alone?"

Her daughters exchanged worried glances, their eyes red-rimmed with tears. "We should have noticed," Emily said softly, her voice trembling. "We should have seen that he was hurting."

"We couldn't have known," Sarah murmured, her heart aching with regret. "But we have to honor his memory. We have to be there for each other. Now more than ever."

And so, as the sun set behind the hills and the stars twinkled overhead, Sarah and her family gathered together in their grief. They shared memories of Jason, laughter mixed with tears as they remembered the boy who had brought so much joy into their lives.

In the days that followed, they reached out to others who were struggling, offering a kind word or a listening ear to those who needed it most. And as they comforted each other, Sarah felt a glimmer of hope beginning to stir in her heart—a hope that even in the darkest of times, love would always shine through.

YOU CHICKEN!

In 1975, as the Americans withdrew from Southeast Asia, Laos succumbed to the Pathet Lao, a communist regime. Due to the Hmong people's involvement in the United States' covert operations in Laos, approximately 50,000 Hmong fled to Thailand as refugees. In 1976, the United States began resettling these refugees, including my aunts and uncles, Su Thao and Mai Thao. They found a new home in Wheaton, Illinois, arriving in February 1979 during a harsh winter.

The Hmong people cherished fresh, farm-grown chicken. One day, my uncle and aunt asked me to take them to a farm to purchase some chickens. Upon arrival, before I had the chance to speak, my aunt Mai blurted out, "You chicken!" The farmer, a burly man with a handlebar mustache and a confused look, responded angrily, "What the heck did you say?" My aunt exclaimed again, "You chicken!" with a fervor that made the whole situation even more bewildering.

Sensing the confusion, I quickly intervened. "No, no," I said, stifling a laugh. "She means, do you have any chickens for sale?"

The farmer's face transformed from anger to a hearty laugh. "Oh, sorry. I thought... Never mind. Of course, we do have some chickens."

Mai, still smiling, seemed completely unfazed by the confusion she had caused. The farmer led us to the back where the chickens were kept, and as soon as my uncle saw the birds, his eyes lit up like a child on Christmas morning. He immediately began to inspect each one, lifting their wings and examining their feet, much to the amusement of the farmer.

Adjusting to life in America proved challenging. We had to do whatever we could to survive and adapt. One particularly memorable incident was when my uncle tried to use a lawnmower for the first time. Determined to master the strange contraption, he ended up chasing it around the yard as it sputtered and roared, zigzagging wildly. The neighbors gathered to watch the spectacle, some offering tips and others simply enjoying the show.

Despite these humorous challenges, my aunt and uncle worked tirelessly to build a new life. They learned English through trial and error, often mixing up words in ways that brought laughter to everyone around. My uncle once proudly announced he had "fished" the lightbulb instead of "fixed" it, and my aunt's attempts at baking American pies often resulted in what we lovingly called "pie soup."

Today, my aunt and uncle have passed away, but I still fondly remember those humorous and nostalgic moments. They are a testament to our journey and the resilience it took to navigate a new language and culture. Those early days in Wheaton were filled with laughter, learning, and an unbreakable spirit that carried us through the toughest times.

CHAPTER SIX

THE SAYING GOES,
"MIRACLE WILL HAPPEN IN YOUR LIFE;
IT WILL CHANGE EVERYTHING."

NO, THANKS. I AM COMFORTABLE. I
DON'T WANT THINGS TO CHANGE.

MEET GRACE

Charlie was one of those kids who aced every math test without breaking a sweat. But one day, he found himself facing a math exam he hadn't prepared for. Instead of hitting the books like he usually would, he chose to spend the weekend having a blast with his buddies. Come test day, he was in a panic. So, he took the easy way out and cheated.

Now, Mr. Anderson wasn't just any teacher. He was sharp, and he noticed Charlie's shenanigans right away. But instead of calling him out then and there, he waited. After class, he asked Charlie to stick around.

"Charlie," Mr. Anderson began, "I know you cheated on that test. I saw it. But I wanted to see how you'd handle it."

Charlie felt a mix of relief and guilt flood over him. At first, he tried to defend himself, but Mr. Anderson wasn't having any of it.

"Look," Mr. Anderson said gently, "I could punish you. But I'm not going to. Instead, I'll let you keep the A you cheated for."

Charlie was stunned. He hadn't expected this. But deep down, he knew he didn't deserve that A.

"I... I can't do that," Charlie stammered, his guilt overwhelming him. "I cheated. I should get an F."

Mr. Anderson nodded, understanding written all over his face, but had compassion on him. Mr. Anderson didn't want an F to be a record on him. So, he said, "Alright, Charlie. That's what you want. But I am not going to do that. I'm not going to punish you or let you have an F. Instead, I'm going to let you keep that A, and I hope that you learn something from this." Tears welled up in Charlie's eyes as he apologized profusely to Mr. Anderson. It was a moment of realization for him.

Charlie was a PK, a pastor's kid. For years, he'd brushed off his father's sermons as boring and irrelevant. But now, as he reflected on what Mr. Anderson had done for him, he finally understood the concept of grace and mercy. Grace, he realized, was getting something you didn't deserve. And mercy? Well, that was not getting what you did deserve. From that day on, Charlie listened to his father's sermons with newfound respect. He even mustered up the courage to confess his wrongdoing to his dad, apologizing for his behavior. And as Charlie learned his lesson, he knew that sometimes, the most profound teachings come not from a pulpit but from unexpected acts of kindness and forgiveness.

HMONG-AMERICAN

After the conclusion of the Vietnam War in 1975, approximately 25,000 Hmong refugees found resettlement in the United States. These Hmong individuals played crucial roles in clandestine operations for the United States in Laos under the leadership of General Vang Pao. Fast forward 40 years since the Hmong community's arrival in the United States, and some of the native-born Hmong Americans begin to undergo a mysterious transformation into zombies-like.

While many Hmong Americans born in the U.S. have excelled in education, business, and various careers, a subset finds themselves succumbing to language-zombification. They exhibit a marked deficiency in common sense, requiring written instructions for even the most rudimentary tasks. What's more, they have forsaken proficiency in the Hmong language, appearing inept or unversed during familial gatherings or social events where Hmong and English fluency reigns supreme. Astonishingly, some even necessitate interpreters for casual exchanges with their own parents or elder siblings. Such was the case for a particular Hmong family meeting their son stationed at a military training facility in Oklahoma (the exact location remains undisclosed), prompting them to seek assistance from a translation agency.

Parents: "Koj sim has rua wb tug tub hastas wb ncu nwg. Wb txhale tuaj saib nwg."

The Hmong-born American interpreter: "Your parents convey their yearning to see you."

The son responded, "Kindly relay that I miss them too."

The interpreter: "Nwg hastas, nwg ncu meb hab."

The father inquired, "Koj sim nug hastas, nwg puas muaj noj haus txaus hab pw txaus?"

The Interpreter: "Your father asked about your well-being, specifically regarding your eating and sleeping habits."

The son affirmed, "Please tell my father that I maintain proper nourishment and rest."

The interpreter, "Meb tug tub hastas nwg kheev kev noj haus hab pw zoo nua."

The father continued, "Koj has rua wb tug tub hastas, wb laug lawm. Wb nyob tsi tau tom teb dleb ntawm cov kwvtij lawm. Yog muaj ib sab ob qeg ntshai yuav tsi muaj leejtwg paab tau wb. Ntshai wb yuav tau tsiv moog nyob ze cov kwvtij lwm xyoo lawm."

The interpreter relayed, "Your father says that they are getting old now. They find it increasingly difficult to reside far from their relatives. Should they experience one high two low, they lack support. Consequently, they contemplate about relocating closer to relatives in the coming year."

Perplexed, the son inquired, "Uh, what's 'one high two low'?"

The Hmong-born American interpreter missed the subtlety of the expression.

CALL JESUS

Once upon a time, nestled in Springfield, lived an elderly man, Mr. Thompson. He had spent many years nurturing his little abode, filled with cherished memories and a serene garden. However, as time passed, Mr. Thompson's physical capabilities waned, leaving him unable to tend to the maintenance tasks that once came effortlessly.

One sunny morning, a crumpled note caught his eye, wedged between the weathered wood of his front door. Scribbled hastily on a scrap of paper was a message from his neighbor, Mr. Johnson, a notorious stickler for neighborhood aesthetics. It read, "Look, buster, cut your grass. You're ruining our hood!"

Mr. Thompson sighed, feeling a pang of frustration mixed with a touch of resentment. He wasn't neglecting his lawn intentionally; age had simply caught up with him. Yet, rather than stewing in resentment, he resolved to find a solution.

With a determined spirit, Mr. Thompson set out to seek assistance. His aging bones couldn't manage the task, but surely there were capable hands within reach. One day, as he trundled along in his battered sedan, he found himself trailing behind a weathered pickup truck. Bold lettering on its tailgate caught his attention: "NEED HELP? Call Jesus 1-800-234-5555."

Intrigued by the promise of aid, Mr. Thompson's lips curved into a tentative smile. Perhaps, he mused, this was the answer to his silent prayers. With trembling fingers, he dialed the number, his heart fluttering with hope.

A courteous voice answered on the other end, and Mr. Thompson hesitantly explained his predicament. "I need someone to come and cut my grass," he confessed, his voice tinged with vulnerability.

A few days later, a knock resounded at his door, accompanied by the low hum of a lawnmower. Mr. Thompson opened the door to find a kindly-faced man standing on his doorstep, a lawnmower at his side.

"Hi there," the man greeted warmly. "My name is Jesus. I'm here to cut your grass."

Relief flooded Mr. Thompson's weary heart as he shook Jesus's hand gratefully. It seemed that sometimes, help arrived in unexpected forms, and perhaps, just perhaps, there was a glimmer of hope for his cherished home and his place within the community once more.

COME BACK

Life presents itself with myriad challenges. For some, it unfolds as a realization of their dreams, while for others, it is a constant struggle. Jane found herself amidst the latter. As a single mother of two, she grappled with financial burdens that seemed insurmountable. Falling behind on utility bills, delinquent on credit card payments, and teetering on the brink of inability to pay rent, Jane felt the weight of her responsibilities bearing down upon her. With young children to care for, hiring babysitters to pursue better job opportunities remained a distant luxury. Despite resorting to part-time work, the meager earnings barely made a dent in her mounting debts, which loomed ominously over her.

One fateful day, a customer entered the restaurant where Jane worked as a waitress, accompanied by a young girl. As she served them water, Jane couldn't shake the feeling that something was wrong. The child seemed visibly uneasy in the presence of the man, leading Jane to suspect that she wasn't his daughter. Alerting the restaurant manager, she was instructed to contact the authorities. Promptly, the police arrived to investigate, uncovering the startling truth that the little girl had been abducted a month prior.

In a modest ceremony facilitated by the local sheriff, the girl's grateful parents expressed their heartfelt gratitude towards Jane, presenting her with a small Bible as a token of appreciation. Though touched by their gesture, Jane harbored a sense of frustration and indifference towards religious sentiments. Reluctantly accepting the gift, she stowed away the Bible in the trunk of her modest sedan, relegating it to the recesses of her mind.

After the ceremony, the restaurant manager commended Jane for her courage and initiative. "Congratulations on the recognition and reward," he offered warmly. "You've brought positive attention to our establishment. We're immensely proud of you."

Jane, however, remained modest in her response. "Oh, it's nothing," she shrugged.

"Nonsense," the manager persisted. "What you did was remarkable. Tell me, did the family offer any reward for reuniting them with their daughter?"

"Nothing big or significant," Jane dismissed nonchalantly. "Just a small, stupid Bible," she added with a hint of disdain.

A year later, Jane found herself facing eviction from her apartment, compelled to seek refuge with her children at the local shelter. Amidst the upheaval, she contemplated selling her car to alleviate their financial strain. While cleaning up the vehicle, she stumbled upon the forgotten Bible. Retrieving it, she brought it to her meager shelter accommodations. One evening, her eldest daughter, Jennifer, aged ten, excitedly informed her of a discovery—a Bible with an envelope nestled within its pages. Curiously, Jane retrieved the envelope, opening its contents: a cashier's check amounting to $100,000 and, the key to a new home from a billionaire-parents and a $10,000 cashier's check from the FBI for information leading to rescuing the little girl.

KEEP OUT

Once upon a time, in the lively and bustling town of Springfield, there lived a loving and dedicated mother named Lily. Lily had a vibrant 5-year-old son named Timmy, whose boundless energy and cheerful laughter filled their cozy home with joy. One crisp autumn morning, Timmy awoke with a persistent cough and a fever that left him listless and unusually quiet. Concerned for her precious boy, Lily wasted no time and decided to take him to the local doctor for a thorough check-up.

Springfield's doctor, Dr. Harold, was known for his gentle demeanor and vast knowledge. He listened attentively to Lily as she described Timmy's symptoms, and after a careful examination, he prescribed a special medicine. Handing Lily a small amber bottle with a bright yellow label, Dr. Harold gave her specific instructions on how to administer the medicine. The label prominently read, "KEEP OUT OF REACH OF CHILDREN," which made Lily's heart race with anxiety. She was determined to do everything right to help her son recover swiftly.

Back home, Lily, being the epitome of a cautious and caring mother, carefully read the label once more. She pondered over the warning, her mind racing with the potential dangers of mishandling the medicine. Determined to protect Timmy from any possible harm, she placed the bottle on the highest shelf in the kitchen, far beyond Timmy's inquisitive reach.

Days passed, and despite Lily's diligent efforts, Timmy's condition showed no signs of improvement. His cough grew harsher, and his fever stubbornly persisted. Lily's worry deepened with each passing day. She meticulously followed the doctor's instructions, ensuring Timmy stayed hydrated and comfortable, but the nagging question of why the medicine wasn't working haunted her thoughts.

One rainy afternoon, as the wind howled outside and raindrops tapped persistently against the windows, Lily sat by Timmy's bedside, her heart heavy with frustration and fear. She watched over him, gently stroking his forehead, wondering if she had missed something crucial. Desperation gnawed at her, and she knew she had to seek Dr. Harold's advice once more.

With renewed determination, Lily bundled Timmy in a warm blanket and set off for the doctor's office. The journey felt longer this time, the weight of worry pressing heavily on her shoulders. When they arrived, Dr. Harold greeted them with a warm smile, though it quickly turned to concern as he noticed Lily's troubled expression.

"Dr. Harold, I did everything the label said," Lily began, her voice trembling with emotion. "But Timmy is still so sick. I don't understand why the medicine isn't working!"

Dr. Harold took the small bottle from Lily's hand and examined it closely. After a moment, a chuckle escaped his lips, which quickly turned into hearty laughter. Lily looked at him, bewildered, as he tried to compose himself.

"Oh, dear Lily," Dr. Harold said, wiping a tear of laughter from his eye. "I think there's been a bit of a misunderstanding. The warning on the label is just a standard precaution to ensure the medicine isn't accidentally ingested by children who don't need it. It's not meant to keep the medicine away from the child who actually requires it!"

Lily's eyes widened in realization, and a blush of embarrassment crept up her cheeks. She had been so focused on protecting Timmy that she hadn't given him the medicine at all. Dr. Harold's gentle explanation brought a sense of relief and a wave of light-heartedness to the room.

"Let's start the treatment properly now," Dr. Harold said kindly, handing the bottle back to Lily. "Give Timmy the medicine as prescribed, and you'll see him bounce back in no time."

With heartfelt gratitude and a touch of lingering embarrassment, Lily thanked Dr. Harold and hurried home. She carefully administered the medicine to Timmy, watching over him with renewed hope. Within a few days, Timmy's cough subsided, his fever broke, and his laughter once again filled their home with joy.

From that day on, Lily always made sure to double-check instructions and never hesitated to ask for clarification when in doubt. And as for Timmy, he grew up to be a healthy, happy boy, his mother's love and dedication forever etched in his heart. And thus, in the bustling town of Springfield, the tale of Lily and Timmy became a gentle reminder to all parents about the importance of understanding and careful caregiving.

CHAPTER SEVEN

THE SAYING GOES, "YOUR BIGGEST FAILURE IN LIFE IS TO NEVER TRY."

WELL, THAT'S THE PROBLEM- I HAVE BEEN TRYING, NOW I'M DROWNING IN DEBT.

FLATLINE

Tom sat on the park bench, his head hanging low as he stared at the ground, his thoughts swirling in a whirlpool of frustration and despair. The park around him was vibrant with life; children laughed and played, couples strolled hand-in-hand, and the elderly walked their dogs, basking in the warmth of the afternoon sun. Yet, for Tom, all this seemed distant and unattainable, a stark contrast to the turmoil inside him.

His friend David, having noticed Tom's slumped shoulders and the weight of an invisible burden pressing down on him, quietly approached and sat down beside him. The bench creaked softly under David's weight, but Tom didn't seem to notice. David observed Tom for a moment, his brow furrowed with concern.

"What's on your mind, Tom?" David asked, his voice gentle but filled with genuine concern.

Tom sighed deeply, his shoulders rising and falling with the weight of his breath. He hesitated before replying, his voice tinted with bitterness and resignation. "I just can't shake this feeling that life isn't fair. No matter how hard I try, it seems like everything is stacked against me."

David listened intently, his expression one of empathy and understanding. He knew that Tom had been facing a series of setbacks recently—lost job opportunities, a broken relationship, and the mounting pressures of everyday life. After a few moments of contemplation, David spoke, choosing his words carefully.

"Tom, I understand where you're coming from," David began, his tone thoughtful. "But have you ever thought that maybe struggling in life is a sign that you're truly alive?"

Tom looked up, puzzled by David's words, his brows knitting together in confusion. "What do you mean by that?"

David leaned back against the bench, gazing up at the canopy of leaves above them, their green hues shimmering in the sunlight. He took a deep breath before explaining, "Think about it like this—when there's a flatline on a heart monitor, it means you're dead. But when there are ups and downs, peaks and valleys, it means you're alive. Struggling with life is like those peaks and valleys; it's a sign that you're still in the game, still fighting, still living."

Tom pondered David's words, letting them sink in slowly like the sun's rays penetrating through the leaves. A new perspective began to form in his mind, reshaping his understanding of his own struggles. Perhaps life wasn't about avoiding difficulties but about confronting them head-on and emerging stronger on the other side.

After a moment of silence, where only the distant laughter of children and the rustling of leaves could be heard, Tom turned to David with a newfound appreciation in his eyes. There was a glimmer of hope where there had been only despair moments before. "You know what, David? You're right. Struggling with life doesn't mean I'm defeated. It means I'm alive, I'm fighting, and I'm growing. Thank you for helping me see things differently."

David smiled warmly at his friend, a sense of relief washing over him. He was glad to see the change in Tom's demeanor, to see the spark of resilience reigniting within him. Together, they sat in companionable silence, watching the world go by, each lost in their own thoughts but sharing a silent understanding.

As the afternoon light began to soften, casting long shadows across the park, Tom and David continued to sit on the bench, side by side. The struggles of life were still there, looming on the horizon like distant storm clouds. But now, Tom felt better equipped to face them, armed with a renewed sense of hope and a deeper understanding of what it meant to be alive. Life's struggles may be tough, but with the right perspective, they could be the very things that make us feel truly alive.

911

One chaotic morning at precisely 2:45 AM, the 911 emergency station received a call that would soon become the talk of the town. The usually serene night was abruptly interrupted by the shrill ring of the phone. Miss Twee, a seasoned 911 operator known for her perpetual caffeine buzz and upbeat demeanor, picked up the call. With a voice that was both perky and slightly bewildered, she answered, "911, how may I help you?"

On the other end of the line, the caller's voice was a whirlwind of panic and desperation. "Hello, my little girl is dying, and I need help!" she blurted out, her words tumbling over each other in a frantic rush. Miss Twee's eyes widened as she grasped the severity of the situation. She took a deep breath, trying to maintain her composure amidst the chaos.

"Alright, ma'am, I need you to stay calm. What's your name?" Miss Twee asked, her fingers poised over the keyboard, ready to dispatch help as soon as she had the necessary information.

"Tiffany," the woman gasped, her voice trembling with fear and urgency.

"Okay, Tiffany," Miss Twee continued, her voice steady and reassuring. "What is your little girl's name?"

There was a brief, agonizing pause before Tiffany responded, her voice barely more than a whisper. "Julie. Her name is Julie."

Miss Twee's heart sank at the thought of a child in distress, but she knew she had to stay focused. "Tiffany, can you tell me your address or location? Where are you right now?"

The next words out of Tiffany's mouth sent a wave of confusion and disbelief through Miss Twee. "We're here in the ER lobby," she replied, her voice quivering with a mix of fear and helplessness.

Miss Twee blinked, momentarily stunned by the surreal turn of events. "You're in the emergency room lobby?" she repeated, trying to make sense of the situation. It seemed almost impossible, yet here was a mother calling 911 from within the very place designed to handle medical emergencies.

Suppressing a mix of exasperation and amusement, Miss Twee quickly dispatched help to Tiffany and Julie in the ER lobby. As she did so, she couldn't help but ponder the cosmic irony of the situation. How had a mother ended up calling emergency services from inside an emergency room?

The paramedics responded swiftly, rushing to the scene with a sense of urgency that belied the absurdity of the call. As they arrived at the ER lobby, the hospital staff exchanged bewildered glances, shaking their heads at the bizarre twist of fate that had unfolded right under their noses.

In the midst of the chaos, confusion, and dark humor, Tiffany and Julie were swiftly attended to by the medical team. The little girl's condition, while serious, was stabilized, and the immediate crisis was averted.

In the days that followed, the story of Tiffany and Julie's misadventure in the hospital ER lobby became the stuff of legend. It was retold with a mix of cautionary lessons and odd hilarity in the hallowed halls of the emergency room. The tale served as a reminder of the unpredictable nature of emergencies and the sometimes inexplicable behavior of those caught in their throes.

And so, in the annals of the town's emergency services, the story of the frantic 911 call from the ER lobby became a cherished anecdote. It was a testament to the resilience of both the responders and the community, a quirky yet poignant chapter in the ongoing saga of life, where even in the most chaotic moments, a touch of humor could be found.

SHOPPING

One sunny afternoon in the bustling town of Springfield, Missouri, Leng decided to take his wife, Mee, to the local grocery store. They had been living in Springfield for years, enjoying the warmth of the community and the charm of the town. Mee loved the local market, with its wide selection of fresh produce, homemade goods, and friendly vendors.

As they pulled into the parking lot of the Springfield Supermart, Leng turned to Mee and said, "I'll wait in the car while you go shopping. Take your time, enjoy looking around." Mee smiled, grateful for the opportunity to leisurely browse through the aisles.

Leng leaned back in his seat, scrolling through his phone and occasionally watching the people coming and going from the store. He passed the time by catching up on the latest news and social media updates. An hour slipped by, then another. Leng began to grow restless and a bit worried. Two hours had passed, and there was still no sign of Mee.

Concerned, Leng decided to go into the store to look for her. He walked through the sliding glass doors and was immediately enveloped in the buzz of the crowded supermarket. The familiar hum of chatter, the clinking of shopping carts, and the scent of freshly baked bread filled the air.

Leng started his search in the produce section, thinking Mee might be picking out the best apples or checking for ripe avocados. He moved through each aisle, scanning for her familiar figure, but she was nowhere to be seen. Leng's worry grew as he checked every corner of the store, including the restrooms, but still, no Mee.

Growing more anxious by the minute, Leng approached the store manager, Mr. Johnson, a tall, kind man who had been working at Springfield Supermart for over two decades. "Excuse me, sir," Leng began, "I can't find my wife. She's been in here for over two hours, and I've looked everywhere."

Mr. Johnson immediately understood the gravity of the situation. "Don't worry, sir, we'll find her," he assured Leng. The manager quickly made an announcement over the store's PA system, asking all employees and customers to be on the lookout for Mee. He also organized a systematic search, closing down the store temporarily to aid in the effort.

Despite their combined efforts, they couldn't locate Mee. Mr. Johnson suggested that Leng call the police, and soon enough, officers from the Springfield Police Department arrived on the scene. They took down Leng's information and details about Mee but advised him that they had to wait 24 hours before filing an official missing person report.

Distraught and exhausted, Leng returned home, his mind racing with worry and fear. He could hardly believe the day's events. As he opened the door to their cozy home, he was hit with an unexpected sight. There was Mee, standing in the kitchen, humming softly to herself as she prepared dinner.

Leng stood frozen in the doorway, a mix of confusion and relief washing over him. "Honey! Where were you? I've been searching the store for hours. The police were involved in the search, too!" he exclaimed, his voice shaky with emotion.

Mee turned to him, her brow furrowed in confusion. "What do you mean you were looking for me at the store? You left to go to the store without me!" she replied, her voice filled with bewilderment.

Realization dawned on Leng as he processed her words. In his absent-mindedness, he had indeed left for the grocery store without Mee that day. He had driven off, assuming she was with him, but she had stayed home all along.

Leng let out a sigh of relief, followed by a chuckle at the absurdity of the situation. He walked over to Mee and pulled her into a tight embrace. "I'm so sorry, honey. I must have been out of my mind. I'm just glad you're safe."

They both laughed at the misunderstanding, their worry melting away into a shared moment of gratitude. They sat down to enjoy the dinner Mee had prepared, recounting the day's events with a mix of amusement and relief.

LOL AND SORROW

The couple learned an important lesson that day about communication and attentiveness. From that moment on, they made sure to double-check their plans and always ensure they were on the same page. Life in Springfield continued, with its familiar rhythms and routines, but Leng and Mee never forgot the day their grocery store trip turned into an unexpected adventure.

LABOR PAIN

Steve's heart raced as he frantically paced the living room, the reality of the situation dawning on him: his wife's water had broken, and she was gripped by intense labor pains. This was the moment they had both been anxiously anticipating for months. The arrival of their first child was imminent, and every second felt like an eternity.

"Steve, we need to go now!" his wife, Emily, gasped, clutching her swollen belly as another contraction wracked her body.

Steve's mind was a whirlwind of fear and excitement. He helped Emily to her feet, his hands trembling as he supported her to their brand-new car, a sleek sedan they had bought just a month ago in preparation for their growing family. His breath came in short, sharp bursts as he revved the engine and sped out of their driveway, tires screeching on the asphalt.

"Hang in there, honey. We're going to make it," Steve reassured her, his voice a mix of determination and anxiety. "Just keep breathing. We're almost there."

The car sped through the quiet suburban streets, a blur of lights and shadows whipping past as Steve pushed the speed limit, knowing every minute counted. As they approached a busy intersection, the light turned red. Steve's heart pounded as he made a split-second decision, swerving around the stopped cars and racing through the red light, the sound of angry honks fading into the background.

But their dramatic dash didn't go unnoticed. A police patrol car, hidden in the shadows of a side street, sprang to life, its sirens wailing and lights flashing. Steve's heart sank as he saw the blue and red lights in his rearview mirror. Panic surged through him, but he couldn't afford to stop. Not now.

"Steve, the police!" Emily gasped; her voice strained with pain.

"I know, I know," Steve replied, glancing nervously at the flashing lights. "Just hold on a little longer, Em. I can't stop now."

The police car closed in, and the officer inside motioned for Steve to pull over, even showing him a pair of handcuffs as a warning. Steve rolled down his window and shouted, "My wife is due! She's in labor! I need to get to the hospital!"

The officer's expression softened, but his sense of duty remained. He signaled again for Steve to pull over. Desperation clawed at Steve's chest. He had no choice. With a final, desperate push, he floored the accelerator, the car rocketing forward toward the hospital.

Minutes felt like hours as they sped through the streets, finally skidding to a halt at the emergency room entrance. Steve jumped out, adrenaline coursing through his veins, and ran to the triage station inside.

"Help! I need help! My wife is in labor in the car!" he shouted, his voice echoing through the sterile, fluorescent-lit room.

Hospital staff sprang into action, grabbing a gurney and following Steve outside. But as they reached the car, confusion spread across their faces.

"Where is she?" a nurse asked, looking around.

Steve's heart plummeted into his stomach. He stared at the empty passenger seat, his mind reeling. "No... no, no, no!" he muttered, realization dawning on him with crushing weight. In his panic, he had forgotten to bring Emily with him. She was still at home, alone and in labor.

Without wasting another second, Steve raced back to the car, shouting apologies and explanations to the bewildered hospital staff. He tore out of the parking lot, tires screeching once more, and sped back home, his mind a flurry of self-recrimination and worry.

As he approached their house, he noticed their good neighbor, Mrs. Thompson, standing outside, waving him down. He jumped out of the car, barely stopping before he ran toward her.

"Steve! Thank goodness you're back. Emily's fine; she's already delivered the baby," Mrs. Thompson called out, her voice filled with relief.

Steve skidded to a halt, his eyes wide with shock and confusion. "What? How?"

Mrs. Thompson smiled warmly. "Emily called me right after you left. I rushed over and helped her through it. The baby is healthy, and both of them are doing well."

Steve's knees went weak with relief. "Thank you, thank you so much," he managed to say, his voice choked with emotion.

Mrs. Thompson patted his shoulder. "You should go inside. They're waiting for you."

With a newfound sense of urgency, Steve bolted into the house. There, in the living room, Emily lay on the couch, cradling their newborn daughter, her face glowing with the joy of motherhood.

"Steve," she said softly, tears of happiness in her eyes. "Meet our little girl."

Steve's heart swelled as he knelt beside them, tears streaming down his face. "I'm so sorry, Emily. I was so scared and panicked... I didn't think."

Emily smiled through her tears. "It's okay. We're all safe and together now. That's what matters."

Steve gently took his daughter's tiny hand, his heart overflowing with love and gratitude. Despite the chaos and his momentary lapse, everything had turned out all right, thanks to the kindness and quick thinking of their wonderful neighbor. And in that moment, surrounded by his family, Steve knew that they could face anything together.

PARKING

Xeng, a workaholic software engineer, and his wife, Molly, a dedicated schoolteacher, decided to make a rare trip to PriceRight Grocery Store for some much-needed household supplies. Their lives had become a whirlwind of work, chores, and responsibilities, leaving little time for leisurely activities or mundane tasks like grocery shopping. This particular Saturday afternoon, however, they managed to carve out a small window of time to tackle the growing list of essentials.

As they arrived at the bustling store parking lot, Xeng and Molly were already deep in conversation about the various errands they needed to complete after their grocery trip. Molly reminded Xeng about the dry cleaning that needed to be picked up while Xeng mentally noted the oil change due for their car. The couple parked their silver Toyota Highlander and made their way into the store, both holding the detailed shopping list Molly had meticulously prepared.

Inside PriceRight, the atmosphere was a blend of families doing their weekly shopping, couples like Xeng and Molly catching up on household needs, and employees stocking shelves with fresh produce and goods. Grabbing a shopping cart, Xeng and Molly began navigating the aisles with a sense of purpose. They moved swiftly from the produce section, where they picked up crisp apples and leafy greens, to the dairy aisle for milk and cheese and then to the pantry section for dry goods and cereal.

Their focused shopping spree, characterized by efficient teamwork and quick decision-making, was suddenly interrupted by a sudden announcement on the store's PA system, which echoed through the aisles and caught their attention.

"Attention, valued customers! If the owner of a silver Toyota Highlander with license plate XY 456 is present, please come to the parking lot immediately. Your vehicle has ended up in a ditch," the voice blared through the speakers, causing Xeng and Molly to exchange worried glances.

"That's our car!" Molly exclaimed, her eyes wide with shock.

Without hesitation, they abandoned their half-filled cart and rushed out of the store to investigate the unexpected situation. As they hurried through the parking lot, thoughts raced through Xeng's mind. How could this have happened? Had someone tampered with their car? He replayed the parking sequence in his head but couldn't recall any missteps.

To their dismay, they found their own silver Toyota Highlander precariously perched in a ditch at the edge of the parking lot, its rear end lifted slightly and the front bumper scraping the ground. A small crowd of curious onlookers had gathered, adding to Xeng and Molly's embarrassment.

Moments later, a police officer arrived on the scene to assess the situation. With a raised eyebrow, the officer inquired, "Did you forget to put your car in park, sir? Your vehicle seems to have rolled away and landed in this ditch."

It dawned on Xeng that amidst the hustle and bustle of their daily lives, coupled with the distractions of their shopping trip and the weight of his workaholic tendencies, he had indeed overlooked the crucial step of securing their car properly. He had been so preoccupied with discussing their to-do list that he had left the car in neutral without engaging the parking brake.

Feeling a mix of embarrassment and regret, Xeng sheepishly nodded. "I guess I did, officer. I'm really sorry about this."

The police officer, understanding but firm, issued Xeng a ticket for obstructing traffic due to the unexpected parking mishap. As they waited for assistance to tow their car from the ditch, Xeng and Molly stood silently, reflecting on the absurdity of the situation. Molly gently squeezed Xeng's hand, offering him a small smile of reassurance.

"It's okay," she said softly. "Things like this happen. Maybe it's a sign we need to slow down a bit."

Xeng sighed, nodding in agreement. As they watched the tow truck carefully extricate their vehicle, Xeng made a silent vow to himself to be more present and mindful, even amidst the demands of their hectic lives. This incident, though embarrassing, served as a valuable lesson in the importance of attention to detail and the necessity of occasionally stepping back to breathe and appreciate the moment.

As they finally drove home, their car safely back on the road, Xeng and Molly couldn't help but laugh at the absurdity of the day. It was a story they would recount many times, a humorous reminder of the day their car ended up in a ditch and taught them a lesson about life's unexpected turns.

CHAPTER EIGHT

"DON'T WORRY ABOUT YOUR CRIMINAL RECORD, ROBERT," I SAID.

"MCDONALD'S MIGHT NOT HIRE YOU, BUT YOU COULD STILL BECOME THE PRESIDENT OF THE UNITED STATES. JUST LOOK AT TRUMP—IN AMERICA, EVEN A FELON CAN BE PRESIDENT."

"ALRIGHT, I'LL RUN FOR PRESIDENT THEN," ROBERT REPLIED.

TAILLIGHT'S OUT

Dang Yang had been tirelessly dedicated to his work for several years, neglecting to take a well-deserved vacation. His days were consumed by endless meetings and project deadlines, often leaving him little time to spend with his growing children or to savor quiet moments with his wife, Eva. The weekends, once a haven for family bonding, had become an extension of his workweek. Eva, patient and understanding, longed for the days when they could reconnect as a family, sharing laughter and creating new memories.

One evening, after missing yet another family dinner, Dang found himself looking at a recent photo of his children, Anya and Kai. They had grown so much, their faces radiating the innocent joy of youth. The realization hit him hard: time was slipping away, and he was missing out on the most important moments of their lives. Determined to make a change, Dang decided it was time to prioritize his family.

After much deliberation, he announced to Eva and the kids that they would be taking a grand adventure—a family road trip. Dang rented a spacious camping trailer to attach to his trusty F150 truck, envisioning a journey filled with adventure, bonding, and the creation of lasting memories. The excitement was palpable as they planned their route, filled with national parks, scenic byways, and quaint little towns. Anya and Kai eagerly marked spots on the map, dreaming of campfires and starry nights.

The year was 1988, and with no cell phones to keep them connected or distracted, the family relied on paper maps and the simple joys of each other's company. The day of departure arrived, and the Yang family set off, the trailer in tow. As they embarked on their journey, the freedom of the open road invigorated them. They sang along to their favorite songs, shared stories, and marveled at the beauty of nature unfolding around them. Every stop was an adventure: they hiked through lush forests, swam in crystal-clear lakes, and explored charming small towns. Each night, they would gather around the campfire, roasting marshmallows and sharing laughter under the vast, starlit sky.

However, as they cruised toward their next destination, the flashing lights of a highway patrol car interrupted their joyful expedition. Pulling over to the side of the road, Dang's heart raced as the officer approached their vehicle.

"I stopped you because one of your taillights is out," the officer informed Dang with a stern expression.

Concerned but eager to address the issue, Dang quickly stepped out of the truck to inspect the taillight. He walked to the back of the vehicle, but as he turned the corner, his focus shifted from the minor mechanical problem to a more pressing concern. The trailer was gone.

"No, no, no," Dang exclaimed in a panic, "forget about the taillight! Where is my family?"

Perplexed by Dang's response, the officer replied, "What family?"

Realization dawned on Dang as he scanned the surroundings in disbelief. "My camping trailer," he exclaimed frantically, his heart sinking at the realization.

"You mean you forgot your trailer back there?" the officer questioned a hint of disbelief in his tone.

Dang's mind raced. He remembered their last stop—a scenic overlook where they had taken a short break to stretch their legs. In his haste to get back on the road, he must have forgotten to reattach the trailer securely.

"I'm dead," Dang muttered, his thoughts swirling with images of Eva and the kids waiting anxiously by the roadside. The precious memories they had packed into that trailer, the camping gear, the family photos, the little mementos collected along the way—all left behind.

The officer, seeing the genuine panic in Dang's eyes, softened his tone. "Let's get you turned around and back to that overlook," he said. "I'll follow you and make sure you get there safely."

Grateful for the officer's understanding, Dang hurried back into the truck and turned it around, driving as quickly yet safely as he could. His heart pounded with each passing mile, praying that Eva and the kids were safe.

As they approached the overlook, Dang spotted the trailer, still parked where they had left it. Eva stood by the roadside, her face a mixture of relief and amusement. Anya and Kai were playing nearby, seemingly unfazed by the temporary separation.

Dang leaped out of the truck and ran to Eva, enveloping her in a tight embrace. "I'm so sorry," he whispered, his voice choked with emotion. "I can't believe I left you behind."

Eva smiled, her eyes twinkling with affection. "It's alright, Dang. We knew you'd come back for us. And look, we made some new friends while we waited," she said, gesturing to a family parked nearby who had kept them company.

Relieved and thankful, Dang made sure to attach the trailer this time, double-checking every latch securely. As they resumed their journey, the incident became a story they would laugh about for years to come—a reminder of the importance of family and the adventures that come with the unexpected twists and turns of life, especially in an era without cell phones to call for help.

IT'S MARY

Aunt Martha was busy cooking in the kitchen, the aroma of her famous apple pie filling the air. She hummed softly to herself, enjoying the rhythmic chopping of vegetables and the sizzle of the stovetop. The kitchen was her sanctuary, a place where she felt in control and at peace.

Her daughter, Mary, approached her with a bright smile and a lightness in her step. "Mom, I'm heading to the mall to do some shopping. Is there anything you need?" she asked, her voice cheerful.

Aunt Martha turned, wiping her hands on a checkered apron, and smiled warmly at Mary. "No, dear. Enjoy your shopping!" she replied, feeling a swell of pride at how independent and thoughtful her daughter had become.

As Mary left, the sound of the front door closing echoed through the house, leaving Aunt Martha to the quiet solace of her kitchen once more. She continued her cooking, stirring the pot of soup and checking on the pie in the oven. She was lost in her thoughts, planning the family dinner for the evening and reminiscing about Mary's childhood.

Suddenly, a loud knock on the door shattered her tranquility. Startled, Aunt Martha wiped her hands again and hurried to the door, a sense of unease prickling at her skin. When she opened it, she was met with the solemn faces of two police officers standing on her doorstep.

"Ma'am, we apologize for the interruption. Is Mary your daughter?" one of the officers inquired, his tone grave and respectful.

Aunt Martha's heart began to race. She felt a cold wave of dread wash over her. "Yes, she is. What is this about?" she asked, her voice trembling slightly.

The officer took a deep breath, his eyes filled with sorrow. "It's regarding your daughter, Mary. She has been in an accident, and unfortunately, she passed away at the scene."

Aunt Martha's world seemed to stop. Her heart sank, and her legs felt like they might give out beneath her. Disbelief and shock overwhelmed her as she stammered, "But that can't be possible. I just spoke to her a few minutes ago."

The officers expressed their sincere condolences, their voices soft and empathetic. "We are very sorry for your loss, ma'am. If there is anything we can do to help, please let us know."

Aunt Martha nodded numbly, her mind unable to fully grasp the reality of the situation. The officers handed her a card with contact information and left her standing in the doorway, the weight of their words crushing her.

She closed the door slowly, leaning against it for support as tears began to flow freely down her cheeks. Her kitchen, which had been a place of joy and comfort just moments ago, now felt empty and cold. The scent of apple pie, once so inviting, now seemed to mock her with its normalcy.

Aunt Martha sank to the floor, clutching her apron, her sobs echoing through the empty house. The reality of losing Mary was too much to bear. The minutes ticked by, each one a painful reminder that her daughter was gone.

As the hours passed, family and friends began to arrive, having heard the devastating news. They offered their support and love, but nothing could fill the void left by Mary's absence. Aunt Martha sat in the living room, surrounded by loved ones, yet feeling utterly alone.

In the days that followed, the community rallied around Aunt Martha, helping with arrangements and providing comfort. But the pain of losing a child is a unique and profound agony, one that time can only partially heal.

Aunt Martha found solace in the memories of Mary, cherishing the moments they had shared. She vowed to keep her daughter's spirit alive in her heart, holding on to the love and joy that Mary had brought into her life.

Life would never be the same, but Aunt Martha knew that Mary's memory would live on in the hearts of those who loved her.

And in the quiet moments, when she was alone in her kitchen, Aunt Martha could still feel Mary's presence, a comforting reminder of the bond they would always share.

A TWISTED LEGACY

Fred, the seemingly upstanding family man with a dark secret, had shocked his community to its core with his gruesome confession. The revelation of his heinous crimes had left everyone reeling in disbelief, struggling to reconcile the image of the beloved church elder and volunteer firefighter with the cold-blooded serial killer he had been all along.

As Fred sat in his prison cell, staring blankly at the gray walls that enclosed him, a young journalist named Sarah was assigned to cover his story. Intrigued by the enigma of a man who had lived a double life for so long, she requested an interview with Fred, hoping to uncover the truth behind his twisted actions.

During their first meeting, Sarah couldn't help but feel a shiver run down her spine as she looked into Fred's calm, unassuming eyes. "Why did you do it, Fred?" she asked, her voice barely above a whisper.

Fred's lips curled into a chilling smile as he leaned in closer, his gaze unwavering. "I did it because I enjoyed it," he replied, his voice devoid of remorse. "Those women were nothing but playthings to me, pawns in my twisted game."

Sarah recoiled in horror at his callous words, but she pressed on, determined to unravel the mystery of his motives. "But why confess now, after all these years of hiding in plain sight? What made you finally come clean?"

Fred's smile widened, a glint of amusement dancing in his eyes. "Ah, that's the twist, isn't it?" he said cryptically. "You see, Sarah, there's a reason I chose to reveal the truth now. A reason that goes far beyond mere guilt or remorse."

Intrigued by his cryptic words, Sarah leaned in closer, her heart pounding in her chest. "What do you mean, Fred? What reason could possibly justify the horrors you've committed?"

Fred's smile faded, replaced by a steely resolve as he fixed her with a piercing gaze. "Because," he said slowly, each word dripping with malice, "I wanted to ensure that my legacy of fear and death would live on long after I'm gone. I wanted to leave behind a mystery that would keep people guessing for years to come."

Sarah's blood ran cold as she realized the full extent of Fred's twisted plan. He had confessed not out of guilt or remorse but out of a desire to manipulate and control even from behind bars. His legacy of terror would haunt the community long after his conviction, a chilling reminder of the darkness that lurked beneath the facade of a seemingly good man.

As Sarah left the prison that day, her mind reeling with the implications of her conversation with Fred, she knew that the story of the enigmatic serial killer would continue to unfold long after the final chapter had been written. And she vowed to uncover the truth behind the man who had shattered the illusion of safety and trust in their once-peaceful community.

DAD'S CELL PHONE

In the year 1997, back in the good ol' days when cell phones were more like bricks with antennas, I found myself in the vibrant city of Tulsa, Oklahoma. It was a time when dial-up internet was the height of technology, and the phrase "surfing the web" made people think you were catching waves on a computer screen.

I decided to get my dad, Txwj Pao Thao, his very first cell phone.

With great excitement, I presented him with the shiny new cell phone. It was one of those models that weighed a ton and looked like it could double as a weapon if needed. My dad examined it with the curiosity of someone inspecting an alien artifact.

"Look, Dad," I said, my voice brimming with enthusiasm. "This is your new cell phone. Let me show you how it works."

For the next hour, I explained every little detail, from how to turn it on to how to dial a number. I even went through the painstaking process of explaining what a ringtone was. My dad nodded along, absorbing every word as if I were unveiling the secrets of the universe.

Finally, he said with a confident smile, "Okay, I got it. I know how to use it now."

Feeling quite proud of myself, I decided to put his new skills to the test. "Great. Now, let's pretend I'm calling you. Let's see if you know how to answer the phone."

He gave me a serious nod, the kind of nod that generals give before going into battle. I asked him to step back a few feet, creating a dramatic distance between us. Then, with all the suspense of a Hollywood thriller, I dialed his number.

The phone rang. And rang. And rang.

But there stood my dad, staring at the phone as if it were a ticking time bomb. His face was a mix of confusion and intense concentration. I couldn't hold back any longer.

"Dad, why aren't you answering the phone?" I asked, trying to stifle my laughter. "We're supposed to be pretending!"

He looked at me, completely serious, and said, "But why do I need to answer it when you're just right there?"

That did it. I burst out laughing, nearly doubling over. For my dad, everything was literal. The concept of pretending was as foreign to him as a sushi restaurant in a cowboy town. His world was one where reality reigned supreme, where a phone call meant someone was far away, not standing a few feet in front of you.

Despite his confusion, I couldn't help but smile at his genuine response. It was moments like these that reminded me how wonderfully unique my dad was. His sincerity, his straightforwardness, and his unintentional humor made every day an adventure.

As I wiped away tears of laughter, I realized that this was just another chapter in the ongoing comedy that was life with my dad. And honestly, I wouldn't have it any other way.

TRANQUILITY ISLAND

In the quaint town of Wildberry resided Michael and Michelle, both individuals of homosexual orientation. Michael, originally born female, and Michelle, similarly born biologically female, shared a profound bond, their love transcending societal norms.

One evening, Michael turned to Michelle with a determined look. "Michelle, I can't hide our love any longer. We deserve to be happy, no matter what anyone says."

Michelle nodded, her eyes shining with resolve. "You're right, Michael. Let's pledge our commitment to each other, no matter the risks."

They pledged their commitment in a discreet ceremony held in the clandestine alcoves of Las Vegas. Despite the clandestine nature of their union, the citizens of their small township harbored a vehement disdain towards them. Their families, regrettably, chose to sever ties.

Michelle sighed heavily one night, staring into the distance. "Do you think they'll ever understand?"

Michael shook his head. "I don't know. But we have each other, and that's what matters."

A decade elapsed, and fate smiled upon them with a lottery windfall. Michael couldn't contain his excitement. "Michelle, can you believe it? We've won! We can finally escape this place."

Michelle laughed, tears of joy streaming down her face. "Let's buy that island we've always dreamed of, where we can be free."

Armed with newfound prosperity, they invested in an idyllic refuge—a private island acquired for a sum of four million dollars. As they set foot on their new home, Michelle took Michael's hand. "This is it. Our sanctuary."

In a symbolic gesture, they consigned their solitary means of transportation, a boat, to flames, severing their last link to the world they left behind. Michael watched the boat burn, then turned to Michelle. "No more running. We're truly free now."

Their sanctuary promised tranquility and the freedom to revel in their love without fear of persecution. However, destiny dealt a cruel blow when tragedy befell Michael on the island's serene shores. One fateful day, Michelle found Michael struggling after an accident.

"Hang on, Michael. I'll get help," Michelle cried, but there was no one else on the island. Despite valiant efforts to overcome his injuries, after a protracted struggle lasting seven months, Michael succumbed at the age of 47.

Lying in her arms, Michael whispered his last words. "Live for us, Michelle. Make this place our paradise."

Michelle, now bereft and solitary amidst the vast expanse of their sanctuary, grappled with her grief for nearly two decades, her only companion being the relentless passage of time. She often spoke to the ocean, her voice tinged with sorrow and love. "Michael, I'm keeping my promise. This is still our paradise."

As if fate sought to compound her suffering, Michelle was afflicted with cancer. As she lay weak and frail, she whispered to the wind, "I'll be with you soon, Michael. Our love will never die."

The insidious adversary ultimately claimed her life at the age of 59. With her passing, the island lapsed once more into desolation, a haunting testament to the love that once flourished there.

Thirty-six years later, as nature began to reclaim its dominion over the forgotten isle, fate intervened once more in a twist of fortune. Treasure hunters, drawn by whispers of untold riches hidden amidst the island's overgrown foliage, stumbled upon a cache of wealth beyond their wildest dreams.

One treasure hunter, Jake, marveled at the trove. "Can you believe this? We're rich!"

His partner, Sarah, nodded, but she was thoughtful. "This place feels... sacred. I wonder who lived here."

Buried beneath layers of soil and memories, a trove of $256 million lay dormant, awaiting discovery. The revelation sparked a frenzy of activity as news of the discovery spread like wildfire.

Yet, amid the clamor of excavations and the gleeful anticipation of newfound wealth, the specters of Michael and Michelle lingered. Their legacy intertwined with the very soil upon which the treasure rested. Sarah felt a chill as she explored the island. "Do you ever feel like we're not alone here?"

Jake chuckled. "Maybe it's the spirits of the past guarding their treasure."

For those who dared to venture into the heart of the island, the discovery served as a poignant reminder of the love that once thrived in that desolate expanse. As Sarah stood by the shore, she whispered, "Whoever you were, I hope you found peace."

The treasure hunters reveled in their newfound riches, yet they could not help but ponder the fateful journey that brought them to this moment—a journey marked by love, loss, and the relentless march of time.

And amidst the glittering spoils of their discovery, the spirits of Michael and Michelle whispered softly, their love immortalized in the annals of history, forever entwined with the island they called home.

CHAPTER NINE

THE FAMOUS SAYING GOES,
"PEOPLE START HATING YOU BECAUSE
THEY CANNOT CONTROL YOU."

YES, THEY DO.
THEY CONTROL ME.
I HATE THEM.

THE SHADOWS OF THE PAST

Mimi met Tong at a New Year celebration in a remote village in Xiengkhuang, where the remnants of war still whispered through the trees. Tong, with his gentle smile and soft-spoken nature, reminded Mimi of the father she never knew but had always imagined—a protector, a man who would shield her from the world's harshness. Tong was everything she had longed for, and she quickly fell in love with him. They married, and soon after, they welcomed their daughter, Lah, into the world.

For years, they lived a peaceful life in Xiengkhuang, far from the bustle of Vientiane. While the memories of war still lingered in the shadows, they found solace in each other. Tong became a devoted husband and father, and Mimi cherished the life they had built together. Lah grew up surrounded by love, blossoming into a bright and ambitious young woman who dreamed of becoming a nurse. She eventually left for Vientiane to pursue her studies, leaving her parents behind in the quiet village.

But the peace they had known was shattered when Mimi fell ill. It started with fatigue and unexplained bruising. When she finally sought medical help, the diagnosis was anemia. However, further genetic testing revealed a far more disturbing truth.

The day Lah learned of the test results, the world seemed to tilt off its axis. Dr. Somsak, the family physician, had called her into his office. The grave look on his face told her that whatever he was about to say would change everything.

"Lah," Dr. Somsak began, his voice heavy with the burden of his words, "there's something in your mother's genetic test that we didn't expect. The results suggest that your mother and father might be closely related—far closer than a married couple should be."

Lah felt as though the ground had opened beneath her. "What do you mean? How close are we talking?"

Dr. Somsak hesitated, searching for the right words. "Lah, the markers indicate a relationship that could be that of a parent and child."

Lah's breath caught in her throat. "That can't be. My mother never knew her father—he died in the war."

"I understand how difficult this must be," Dr. Somsak said gently. "But sometimes, the past holds secrets we never imagined. You need to talk to your mother and ask her about her past."

Shocked and terrified of what she might uncover, Lah returned to Xiengkhuang. The journey home was a blur of memories and fears, each one more unbearable than the last. She arrived to find her father, Tong, waiting for her, his brow furrowed with concern.

"Lah, what's wrong?" he asked, his voice filled with the love that had always been her anchor.

But now, that love felt tainted, as though a dark cloud had settled over their lives. "I need to talk to Mom," Lah said, her voice trembling. "Alone."

She found Mimi resting in her bedroom, her face pale and weary. Lah sat beside her, struggling to find the right words.

"Mom," she began, her voice barely a whisper, "the doctors found something in your tests. They think... they think you and Dad might be closely related."

Mimi's eyes widened in shock, her hand flying to her mouth. "What? No, that's impossible. My father died in the war. I never knew him."

Lah took a deep breath, her heart aching for the woman who had always been her rock. "What if... what if he didn't die, Mom? What if he came back after the war, and you didn't recognize him?"

Mimi's mind spun as she struggled to grasp the enormity of what Lah was suggesting. Memories long buried began to resurface— memories of her father, who had left to join the Royal Lao Army, a secret guerilla unit of the U.S. Central Intelligence Agency operating in Laos. She had been conceived before he left, and after she was born, her mother had died within a year. Raised by her grandparents, she had grown up with the belief that her father was killed, captured, or missing in action.

As the horrifying possibility began to take shape in her mind, Mimi felt her world crumbling around her. "Oh my God, Lah. Could it be true? Could Tong be my father?"

The next few days were a nightmare. Tong, Mimi, and Lah were consumed by the revelation, unable to escape the thoughts that now plagued them. The once peaceful home was now filled with an unbearable tension, and the silence between them spoke volumes.

Lah decided she needed to confront Tong directly. One evening, as the sun dipped low in the sky, casting long shadows over the river near their home, she sat with him on the bank, her heart heavy with the weight of what she was about to say.

"Dad," she began, her voice steady despite the tears brimming in her eyes, "we need to talk. The genetic tests... they suggest that you and Mom might be closely related. It's possible... it's possible you could be her father."

Tong's face drained of color. He looked at Lah, his eyes wide with shock and disbelief. "Lah, I... I never knew. After the war, I was taken prisoner. I lost my memory for years. When I finally returned, I found the village changed. I met your mother, and I thought it was fate that brought us together. I never imagined... I never imagined she could be my daughter."

The horror of what he was saying hit Lah like a physical blow. This man, the man who had raised her, the man she had loved and admired her entire life, could be her grandfather.

In the village, whispers began to spread like wildfire. Neighbors who once smiled warmly at Tong and Mimi now averted their eyes, their hushed conversations carrying a tone of judgment and disdain. The once-respected family became the subject of cruel gossip, with people speculating on the truth behind the shocking revelation. "Did you hear about Mimi and Tong?" they'd say, voices laced with a mixture of pity and scorn. "It's unnatural... disgraceful. How could they not have known?"

The family's once-proud reputation was tarnished, and they found themselves shunned by the very community that had embraced them. Lah, torn between her loyalty to her parents and the horror of their situation, became a shell of the vibrant young woman she once was. She continued her work in Vientiane but felt a deep, unrelenting sorrow each time she returned to Xiengkhuang.

Mimi, once so full of life, became a shadow of her former self. She couldn't bear to leave the house, knowing the villagers were talking about her behind her back, pointing fingers, and shaking their heads in disgust. Tong, too, was consumed by guilt and shame, unable to look anyone in the eye, least of all his wife and daughter.

But amidst the heartache and despair, there were moments of quiet resilience. One day, as the family sat together by the river,

Mimi spoke, her voice frail but determined. "We can't change what happened, but we can decide how to move forward. We have to find a way to heal."

Lah nodded, her heart breaking for her mother, who had been dealt a cruel hand by fate. "I don't blame you, Dad," she said softly, looking at Tong. "You didn't know. None of us did."

Tong, his face lined with sorrow, looked at his daughter with tear-filled eyes. "I wish things were different. I wish I could go back and change the past."

But the past was immutable, and all they could do was try to pick up the pieces of their shattered lives. They would never be the same, but they were determined to face the future together, no matter how uncertain or painful it might be.

As the sun set over the village, casting a golden glow over the river, the three of them sat in silence, mourning the life they had lost and contemplating the uncertain future ahead. The road to healing would be long and fraught with challenges, but they knew that as long as they had each other, they could find a way to endure.

AN INCIDENT

Charlie's car sat damaged and abandoned on the shoulder of the road, its hood crumpled and steam hissing from the engine. Inside the car, Charlie sat gripping the steering wheel, his knuckles white and his heart pounding from the recent ordeal. The sky was beginning to darken, and he could hear the distant rumble of thunder.

Just as Charlie was contemplating his next move, the flashing red and blue lights of a police car appeared in his rearview mirror. The cruiser pulled up and parked behind his vehicle. The officer, a tall man with a serious expression, stepped out and approached Charlie's window, his footsteps crunching on the gravel.

The officer knocked on the window. "What's going on here, sir? What is your name?" he asked, his tone professional but firm.

Charlie rolled down his window, trying to steady his voice. "My name is Charlie," he responded.

"Charlie, may I see your driver's license, please?" the officer requested, his eyes scanning the damaged car.

With a shaky hand, Charlie reached into his pocket, pulled out his wallet, and handed over his license. "Here you go, officer."

The officer took the license and nodded. "Wait here. Stay in your car. I'll be back," he instructed before walking back to his cruiser.

Charlie watched the officer through his side mirror, feeling a mix of anxiety and relief. The minutes ticked by slowly, the silence only broken by the occasional rumble of distant thunder. Finally, the officer returned and handed the license back to Charlie.

"Tell me, what's going on here?" the officer asked, leaning slightly to get a better look at Charlie's face.

"My car is damaged," Charlie explained, gesturing to the crumpled hood and shattered windshield.

"I can see that. Did you hit something?" the officer inquired, raising an eyebrow.

"No, I did not," Charlie replied, shaking his head vigorously.

The officer frowned, his confusion evident. "No? Then what happened to your car? Why is it damaged?"

Charlie took a deep breath, trying to find the right words. "No, I did not, officer," he repeated, his voice trembling slightly.

Frustrated and confused, the officer's voice grew firmer. "If you did not hit anything, then why is your car damaged?"

Charlie closed his eyes for a moment, the memory of the incident flashing before him. "A deer hit me," he replied finally, opening his eyes to meet the officer's.

The officer's expression softened slightly as he looked over the car again. "A deer, you say? That explains a lot. Are you hurt?"

"No, I'm fine. Just a bit shaken," Charlie said, rubbing the back of his neck.

The officer nodded, his tone now more sympathetic. "Alright, Charlie. Let's get you sorted out. I'll call for a tow truck and make sure you get home safely. Just sit tight for a bit longer."

Charlie managed a small smile of gratitude. "Thank you, officer. I appreciate it."

The officer gave a reassuring nod before returning to his cruiser to make the necessary calls. Charlie leaned back in his seat, the tension slowly easing from his body. The ordeal wasn't over, but at least now, he wasn't facing it alone.

REMEMBERING YOU METHOD

In the heart of Wheaton, Illinois, lived a man named Cheng Kong. For a long time, Cheng felt insignificant and overlooked, often experiencing pangs of loneliness when people forgot his name. This feeling of being invisible weighed heavily on him. One sunny afternoon, at a grand birthday party held in the town's central park, he encountered someone new.

"Hi, I'm Kou," said Kou Xiong, extending his hand warmly.

"I'm Cheng," Cheng replied, shaking his hand. "I must apologize in advance; I have trouble remembering people's names."

"That's alright," Kou responded with a reassuring smile. "I used to have the same problem until I discovered a method that helped me."

Intrigued, Cheng asked eagerly, "Oh? What method is that?"

Kou paused for a moment before replying, "My method is rather unconventional. You might not appreciate it."

"Why not?" Cheng asked, his curiosity piqued.

Without warning, Kou slapped Cheng across the face. "Well, does this help you remember my name?"

Stunned, Cheng stared at Kou, the shock of the slap searing his memory. Though unconventional and abrasive, Kou's method left an indelible mark, ensuring Cheng would never forget his name. The story of that slap became a local legend, a bizarre yet effective reminder of the day Cheng learned Kou's name in Wheaton, Illinois.

THE ACCIDENT

In the heart of Tulsa, Oklahoma, where the Arkansas River snakes through the city and the historic Art Deco buildings loom tall, an ordinary day turned extraordinary for Joe Xiong. It was a sunny afternoon, the kind that made the streets bustle with life and activity. Joe, a young man in his mid-twenties, was hurriedly crossing Main Street when fate took an unexpected turn.

Without warning, a car came barreling down the road, hitting Joe squarely and sending him sprawling across the pavement. Bystanders screamed and rushed to his aid, dialing 911 in a frenzy. Within minutes, the wail of sirens filled the air as paramedics arrived and rushed Joe to Saint Francis Hospital, one of Tulsa's renowned medical centers.

In the hospital's emergency room, the doctors and nurses sprang into action, working tirelessly to stabilize Joe's condition. Time was of the essence, and every second counted. After what seemed like an eternity of frantic efforts, Joe was finally out of immediate danger. He was placed in the intensive care unit, where he remained unconscious for several days.

When Joe finally awoke, he found himself in a sterile hospital room, the steady beep of the heart monitor providing a reassuring rhythm. Dr. Stevens, a seasoned physician with a gentle demeanor, stood by his bedside.

"Joe," Dr. Stevens began, his voice soft but firm, "we almost lost you. But now you're alive, and with time, you'll recover. A police detective is here to talk to you."

Still groggy, Joe nodded. Moments later, two figures entered the room. Detective Samuel Armstrong, a tall man with a no-nonsense air about him, and his partner, Detective Jane O'Connor, a sharp-eyed woman with a kind smile, introduced themselves.

"Joe, I'm Detective Armstrong, and this is my partner, Jane. We'd like to ask you a few questions. Can we do that?" Armstrong asked, his tone professional but not unkind.

Joe, still disoriented but understanding the gravity of the situation, replied politely, "Yes, you may."

Armstrong pulled up a chair and leaned in slightly. "Please tell us what happened. Why were you hit by a car in the middle of a busy street?"

Joe took a deep breath, trying to piece together his fragmented memories. "I don't know," he said slowly. "All I remember is I was texting my girlfriend."

Detective Armstrong and Jane exchanged glances, a brief moment of silent communication passing between them. Then, unexpectedly, they burst into laughter. It was a rare moment of levity in their line of work, and Joe couldn't help but crack a smile despite his confusion.

"Texting while crossing the street," Jane said, shaking her head. "That's a new one."

A week later, the case took another surprising turn. The driver who had hit Joe, a middle-aged man named Mark Reynolds, was released from the Tulsa County Jail while awaiting trial. The news spread quickly, causing further astonishment and confusion among those following the case.

As Joe slowly recovered, the city of Tulsa buzzed with the lessons from his accident. The local news stations ran stories on the dangers of distracted walking and driving, hoping to prevent future incidents. And Joe, forever changed by his brush with death, became a vocal advocate for safer streets, determined to make something positive out of his near-tragic experience.

FLIGHT 79 TO AMERICA

In the early morning of February 1979, Flight 79 departed from Bangkok, Thailand, destined for the United States, with a layover in Manila, the Philippines. Among the diverse passengers was Pao, a Hmong man embarking on a new life in America.

Pao sat quietly, clutching his modest bag of belongings, his heart filled with a mixture of hope and anxiety. The hum of the airplane engines was a constant reminder of the distance he was putting between himself and the war-torn mountains of Laos, his homeland.

As the plane soared above the clouds, a flight attendant began distributing warm, scented washcloths for passengers to freshen up. Unfamiliar with this airline custom, Pao hesitated, then gingerly took the washcloth, his hands trembling slightly. He examined the warm cloth, its soft texture, and pleasant scent, unlike anything he had encountered before.

Confused and hungry from the long journey, Pao brought the washcloth to his mouth, believing it to be a meal provided by the airline. He began chewing on it, hoping to stave off his hunger.

A nearby flight attendant noticed Pao's unusual behavior and rushed over, her face etched with concern. "Sir, are you okay? Why are you chewing that cloth?" she asked, but Pao, not understanding English, continued to chew, his eyes wide with uncertainty.

Realizing the language barrier, the flight attendant sought help from the passengers. A few rows back, a young man raised his hand. "Excuse me, miss. I can help," he said in broken English. He stood up and approached the flight attendant, his demeanor calm and reassuring.

"Who are you?" she asked, relief evident in her voice.

"I'm Lee, also Hmong. I'm traveling to America, too," he replied. "Let me talk to him."

Lee approached Pao with a gentle smile. He spoke in their native Hmong language, his words a comforting bridge to Pao's troubled thoughts. "Brother, why are you chewing the washcloth?" Lee asked kindly.

Pao looked up, visibly relieved to hear his mother tongue. "I thought it was food," he admitted, his voice tinged with embarrassment.

Lee chuckled softly, explaining the situation to Pao. "This is for cleaning your face, not for eating." He then turned to the flight attendant and translated Pao's words.

The flight attendant smiled, her concern easing. She fetched a meal tray and handed it to Pao, who accepted it gratefully. As Pao ate, he exchanged stories with Lee, the shared language and culture forging an immediate bond between them.

Throughout the rest of the journey, Lee continued to assist Pao, explaining the customs and easing his transition. By the time Flight 79 touched down in the United States, Pao felt a renewed sense of hope, buoyed by the kindness of a stranger who became a friend.

This moment on Flight 79 was a small yet profound part of Pao's journey to America—a land of new beginnings where, despite the challenges, the spirit of community and understanding would help him forge a new life.

CHAPTER TEN

THE FAMOUS SAYING GOES, "SURROUND YOURSELF WITH POSITIVE PEOPLE WHO WILL SUPPORT YOU WHEN IT RAINS, NOT JUST WHEN IT SHINES."

WELL, ACTUALLY, YOU MIGHT JUST ALSO NEED AN UMBRELLA.

MINTY FRESH PHONE CALL REUNION

Bob sat in his living room, the familiar number trembling on the screen of his phone. With a deep breath, he pressed "call" and waited as it rang on the other end. After what felt like an eternity, a voice he hadn't heard in years finally answered.

"Bob? Is that really you?" John's voice was filled with a mix of surprise and joy.

"Hey John, long time no speak! How have you been?" Bob replied, a smile evident in his tone.

They began to catch up, sharing memories and laughter as if no time had passed between them. As they talked, Bob suddenly noticed a peculiar sensation, almost as if he could smell something through the phone. Summoning his trademark directness, he hesitated for a moment before blurting out, "John, sorry to say this, but you should really brush your teeth. You kind of... smell."

There was a moment of silence on the other end of the line, followed by John's sarcastic chuckle. "Oh, really? Me? I think you might want to take your own advice, Bob. I can smell your morning coffee breath from here!"

Bob was taken aback for a moment before bursting into laughter. "Touché, John! I'll admit, I might need to freshen up too. How about this? Let's make a deal - we both go brush our teeth and meet back here in two minutes!"

John laughed, the sound warm and familiar. "Deal! Two minutes, Bob."

They both hung up, and Bob couldn't help but feel a sense of happiness and nostalgia. He rushed to the bathroom, quickly brushing his teeth, the sound of John's laughter echoing in his mind. Two minutes later, they were back on the phone, the connection between them stronger than ever.

"Much better," John said with a grin in his voice.

COVID 19

During the COVID-19 quarantine in 2020, Lonna, a charming girl with a heart of gold but not always the brightest ideas, found herself in a humorous predicament that left her boyfriend, Alex, scratching his head in disbelief.

Lonna was engrossed in a phone conversation with her friend from college, discussing the latest updates and sharing their worries about the pandemic. As she chatted away, she wore a mask, firmly believing that it would shield her from catching the dreaded virus.

When Alex stumbled upon Lonna on the phone, his eyes widened at the sight of her masked face. "Lonna, why are you wearing a mask indoors? Are you feeling okay?" he inquired, concern evident in his voice.

With all the earnestness she could muster, Lonna replied, "Oh, Alex, don't worry! My friend told me that wearing a mask can protect me from getting COVID-19, even over the phone. Better safe than sorry, right?"

Alex's confusion deepened as he struggled to comprehend her logic. "Lonna, sweetheart, I think you might have misunderstood something. Masks are for when you're around people in person, not over the phone. The virus can't travel through phone lines!"

Lonna's eyes widened in realization, and then she burst into laughter, realizing her mistake. "Oh, oops! Well, better to be safe than sorry, right?" she quipped, trying to save face.

Alex couldn't help but chuckle at her innocent blunder. "You never fail to surprise me, Lonna. Your dedication to staying safe is truly admirable, even if it means wearing a mask during a phone call."

And so, Lonna's misguided belief in the protective powers of a mask over the phone became a hilarious anecdote that they would fondly reminisce about for years to come. In the end, Lonna learned that while her intentions were sweet, a little bit of accurate information can go a long way in navigating the challenges of a global pandemic.

THE BRICK

A young man named Jake found himself waking up in a hospital bed, a dull throbbing pain pulsating through his head. He blinked groggily at the stark white ceiling above him, trying to piece together how he had ended up there. As he shifted slightly, a friendly but concerned doctor walked in, clipboard in hand.

"Good morning," the doctor said, glancing at Jake's chart. "Can you tell me what happened? Do you remember?"

Jake winced, rubbing the bandage wrapped around his head. "Well, Doc," he began, looking a bit embarrassed, "someone told me that if I wanted to change my life, I should throw a brick straight up in the air. So, I did."

The doctor raised an eyebrow, struggling to suppress a chuckle. "And then?"

"And then," Jake continued, "I woke up here."

The doctor sighed, shaking his head but unable to hide a smile. "You know, Jake, most people would find a less painful way to change their lives. It seems you took some very bad advice."

Jake shrugged sheepishly. "Yeah, I guess common sense isn't my strong suit."

Still chuckling softly, the doctor pulled up a stool and sat down next to Jake's bed. "Well, let's make a pact, shall we? No more taking life advice from random people who tell you to throw bricks in the air."

Jake nodded fervently. "Deal. My head can't take another life-changing experience like that."

The doctor patted Jake's shoulder reassuringly. "That's the spirit. Just remember, change often comes from within, not from bricks. And definitely not from throwing them straight up."

As the doctor left the room, Jake lay back on his pillow, pondering the unexpected wisdom he had just received. He made a mental note to be a bit more discerning about whose advice he would follow in the future.

The next day, Jake was discharged with a clean bill of health and a new perspective on life. He vowed to make changes in smarter, less painful ways. He even started a blog titled "Life Lessons Without the Brick," sharing his humorous tale and newfound insights with others.

Years later, Jake often found himself retelling the story at parties, always to great laughter. It became a signature tale, a reminder to everyone that while changing your life is important, how you go about it is just as crucial.

And every time Jake threw his head back in laughter, he was reminded of the lesson he had learned the hard way, with a brick, a bump, and a wise doctor who showed him to use common sense.

THE CROSSROADS OF ADVICE

Fred sat on the edge of his bed, staring blankly at the wall. The weight of his thoughts pressed down on him, making it hard to breathe. He felt like a nobody, trapped in a monotonous routine that led nowhere. Desperate for a change, he muttered to himself for the thousandth time, "I need to change my life."

Over the past few months, Fred had tried everything. He listened to positive thinking tapes, read countless inspirational books, and attended numerous seminars on self-improvement. Yet, nothing seemed to work. The darkness still loomed over him.

One rainy afternoon, as Fred walked home from yet another job he hated, he encountered a man standing under a streetlamp. The man had a warm smile and a certain spark in his eyes. He introduced himself as Bob.

"Hey there, you look like you could use a friend," Bob said cheerfully.

Fred sighed. "I could use more than that. My life feels like it's going nowhere. I hate my job and my life."

Bob nodded sympathetically. "I understand how you feel. I've been there too. But, you know, sometimes the solution is simpler than we think."

Fred raised an eyebrow. "What do you mean?"

Bob leaned in closer, lowering his voice as if sharing a secret. "There's an easy way to change your life. All you have to do is drive your car across a school bus stop sign."

Fred looked puzzled. "Drive a car across a school bus stop sign? What do you mean?"

Bob smiled mysteriously. "Trust me, it's going to be a life-changer. Just do it, and you'll see. It's that easy."

Despite his skepticism, Fred felt a flicker of hope. He had tried everything else, so why not give this odd advice a shot? The next morning, he drove to a nearby school bus stop. His heart pounded as he waited for the school bus to arrive. When it did, the stop sign extended, signaling the children to board safely. With a deep breath, Fred drove across the street, ignoring the sign.

Almost immediately, a sense of exhilaration washed over him. For the first time in ages, he felt a rush of adrenaline—a break from the monotony of his life. He laughed out loud, feeling an unexpected surge of energy.

However, his elation was short-lived. A police car, parked nearby, had witnessed Fred's reckless act. The officer stepped out, shaking his head.

"Sir, do you realize you just crossed a school bus stop sign? That's illegal and dangerous," the officer said sternly.

Fred's face paled. "I... I didn't think. Someone told me that if I wanted to change my life, I should drive a car across a school bus stop sign. I'm sorry."

The officer sighed. "That's terrible advice. Bad advice can lead to bad choices. You're lucky no one got hurt, but you'll have to face the consequences."

As Fred sat in the police station, waiting for his fine to be processed, he thought about Bob's words. Yes, his life had changed, but not in the way he had hoped. He realized now the importance of discerning good advice from bad.

Weeks later, Fred returned to his usual routine but with newfound wisdom. He still sought change, but this time, he was more cautious about whose advice he followed. He continued to listen to tapes, read books, and attend seminars, but with a critical mind.

One day, he saw Bob again. This time, Fred approached him with a firm stance.

"Bob, your advice got me into trouble. I should have been more careful," Fred said.

Bob shrugged. "Sometimes, a little trouble is what we need to see things clearly."

Fred nodded slowly. "Maybe. But I've learned to be careful who I listen to. Bad advice can indeed change your life."

From that day on, Fred focused on genuine, constructive ways to improve his life. He built a support system of trustworthy friends and mentors. Gradually, the dark clouds lifted, and Fred found the sense of purpose and direction he had been longing for.

And so, Fred's life was never the same. But now, it was a life shaped by careful choices and wise counsel.

*

Moral: Be careful who you listen to and use common sense. Bad advice can change your life.

EMAIL BLUNDER

Mike Yang was known around Thao Corporation for his dedication and hard work. He was the kind of employee who could be relied upon to get the job done, and he always went the extra mile. However, he also had a habit of working late into the night, leading to a few unfortunate incidents of sleep-deprived decision-making.

One fateful evening, as the clock struck midnight, Mike was typing up a storm on his computer. He decided to take a quick break and compose a heartfelt email to his girlfriend, Lisa. In his haze of exhaustion, he poured his heart out, describing his love in the cheesiest, most romantic words he could muster.

"Hey there, my lovely pumpkin pie,

I just can't stop thinking about you. Your smile brightens my darkest days, and your laugh is the sweetest music to my ears. I can't wait to wrap you in my arms and never let go.

With all my love and a million kisses,

Your Mike."

Satisfied with his poetic effort, he hit "send." But as soon as he clicked the button, he realized, with horror, that the email had been addressed not to Lisa but to Cindy, his boss.

The next morning, Mike entered the office with a sense of impending doom. He walked to his cubicle, trying to avoid eye contact with anyone. However, Cindy, a stern but fair woman known for her no-nonsense attitude, was waiting for him.

"Mike," Cindy called out as she approached his desk.

Mike froze. "Good morning, Cindy," he replied, trying to sound as normal as possible.

Cindy held up her phone, the incriminating email glaringly visible on the screen. "Care to explain this?"

Mike turned red. "Oh, um, that was meant for someone else. I'm so sorry. I... I was tired and must have clicked your name by accident."

Cindy raised an eyebrow. "So, I'm not your 'lovely pumpkin pie' then?"

Mike shook his head vigorously. "No, absolutely not! I mean, no offense, but..."

Cindy let out a rare chuckle. "Relax, Mike. It was an honest mistake. Just make sure to double-check your recipients next time."

Mike nodded, relieved that Cindy wasn't angry. "I will. Definitely."

As the day progressed, the story of Mike's mishap spread like wildfire through the office. By lunchtime, his coworkers had gathered around him, eager to hear the details.

"So, Mike," his friend Dave said, trying to suppress his laughter, "how's your new relationship with Cindy going?"

Mike groaned. "Don't start, Dave. It was just a mistake."

"Hey, at least you didn't call her something worse," said Sarah from accounting. "Pumpkin pie is pretty tame."

"Yeah, but now I have to live with everyone calling me 'pumpkin pie' behind my back," Mike replied.

"Who says it's behind your back?" Dave teased. "Hey, Pumpkin Pie, wanna grab lunch?"

Mike rolled his eyes but couldn't help but laugh. "Sure, why not? At least it'll give you guys something to talk about."

As they headed to the cafeteria, Mike's phone buzzed with a new email notification. He opened it, and his face turned pale.

It was from Cindy.

"Dear Mike, or should I say 'Sweetie Muffin,'

Just a quick reminder to check your email recipients next time. Keep up the good work!

Best,

Cindy."

Mike showed the email to Dave, who burst out laughing. "Sweetie Muffin! Oh man, this just keeps getting better."

For the next few weeks, the office buzzed with new nicknames for Mike, each more ridiculous than the last. And although he was the butt of many jokes, Mike took it all in stride. After all, if he could survive accidentally sending a love email to his boss, he could handle anything.

And so, Mike continued to work diligently at Thao Corporation, earning the respect of his colleagues not just for his work ethic, but for his ability to laugh at himself and for turning an embarrassing situation into a source of endless office entertainment.

The moral of this story is that be careful. Computers don't have a heart, and unlike humans, technology obeys orders without question.

CHAPTER ELEVEN

THE FAMOUS SAYING GOES, "YOU WILL NEVER REGRET WORKING HARD BECAUSE HARD WORK ALWAYS PAYS OFF."

WELL, IT'S EASY FOR YOU TO SAY NOW THAT YOU DON'T HAVE TO WORK HARD ANYMORE.

THE ORDERS

The Yang family found themselves in a peculiar situation that seemed to defy any and all logic. Unwanted pizzas would arrive at their doorstep, and mysterious Amazon packages would show up on their porch, all without a single order being placed by anyone in the household. Steve Yang, the head of the family, was determined to unravel the mystery behind these bizarre occurrences.

"Dad, there's another pizza at the door!" Emma Yang shouted, her eyes wide with surprise.

"Not again!" Steve exclaimed, marching towards the door. "That's the third time this week. Who keeps sending us these?"

Helen Yang, Steve's wife, looked up from her book with a mixture of amusement and concern. "Maybe it's a prank, Steve. But who would go to such lengths?"

"I'm going to find out," Steve replied with determination. He took the pizza box from Emma and set it on the kitchen counter. "Whoever is behind this, they're going to get an earful from me."

Later that evening, Steve decided to call the pizza place.

"Hello, this is Antonio's Pizzeria. How can I help you?"

"Yeah, hi. This is Steve Yang. We've been receiving pizzas we never ordered. Can you tell me who's been placing these orders?"

"Let me check," the clerk replied. A few moments later, he came back on the line. "Sir, all the orders were placed online under your name, address, and even your own voice."

"That's impossible," Steve said, perplexed. "None of us ordered them."

The clerk shrugged. "I don't know what to tell you, sir. The orders are legit."

"Thanks for your help," Steve sighed, ending the call.

The next morning, another surprise awaited the Yangs.

"Mom, there's a package on the porch!" shouted little Ethan Yang.

Helen walked to the porch and retrieved the package. "This is getting ridiculous," she muttered, opening it. Inside was a bizarre assortment of items: a rubber chicken, a garden gnome, and a pack of neon shoelaces.

Steve looked at the box in disbelief. "I've had enough. I'm going to track down whoever is behind this."

He spent hours scrutinizing his online accounts, checking order histories, and searching for clues. Then, he noticed something odd. Several of the purchases were made using his credit card, but the orders were placed during times when he was sure he hadn't used it.

Steve's eyes narrowed. "This can't be right."

That evening, as the family gathered for dinner, Steve shared his findings.

"Everyone, I think someone in this house has been using my credit card," he said, looking around the table.

Helen frowned. "But who, Steve? We don't even know your card number."

Steve looked puzzled. "That's the strange part. It's almost like they heard me reading it out or something."

Just then, a squawk echoed from the living room. Polly, their beloved parrot, flapped her wings and mimicked Steve's voice perfectly. "Credit card number, 4532-9081-…"

The family stared in astonishment.

"No way," Emma whispered in amazement.

Steve's face turned a shade of red as realization dawned on him. "It's Polly. She's been listening to my phone conversations and memorizing my card number."

The next day, Steve set up a small camera in the living room to confirm his theory. He couldn't believe he was about to spy on a parrot, but nothing else made sense.

Hours later, they reviewed the footage. To their shock and amusement, they watched Polly expertly mimic Steve's voice, ordering pizzas and random items online.

Helen burst into laughter. "Well, that explains the exotic toppings on those pizzas."

Emma giggled. "And the rubber chicken. Polly has good taste."

Even Steve couldn't help but chuckle. "I have to hand it to her; she's one clever bird."

From that day on, Steve made sure to keep a closer eye on his credit card details, always taking phone calls out of Polly's earshot. The misadventures caused by the parrot's unexpected shopping sprees had brought a new level of excitement and laughter into their lives.

At dinner one night, Ethan asked, "So, no more pizzas?"

Steve smiled. "No more unexpected pizzas. But we can still order one from time to time, just not by Polly's doing."

The family laughed, and Polly, perched on her stand, let out a contented squawk.

And so, the mystery of the mischievous parrot was solved, leaving the Yang family with a tale to tell for years to come.

FATHER AND SON FISHING TRIP

Once upon a time, in a quaint village nestled by a serene lake, there lived a father named Joua Wang Thao and his son, Asthee Thao. They shared a deep bond and a common love for fishing. The father and son had been eagerly anticipating a fishing trip together, and finally, the day arrived when they could embark on their long-awaited adventure.

"Asthee, it's finally the day!" Joua Wang exclaimed as he packed their fishing gear purchased from BassPro into their SUV, which was hitched to a fishing boat.

"I can't wait, Dad! This is going to be awesome," Asthee replied, his eyes sparkling with excitement.

Setting off on a scenic three-hour drive, they journeyed to their favorite secluded spot by the tranquil lake, a place where they had shared many cherished memories in the past.

As they cast their lines into the shimmering waters and basked in the beauty of nature, their spirits soared.

"Remember the first time we came here?" Joua Wang reminisced. "You caught that tiny fish and were so proud."

Asthee laughed. "Yeah, and you made such a big deal out of it. Best day ever!"

Their peaceful reverie was soon interrupted by a commotion on the other side of the lake. A boisterous father and son duo were fishing nearby without a boat, their loud voices echoing across the water and disrupting the tranquility of the surroundings.

"Dad, do you hear that?" Asthee asked, frowning.

"Unfortunately, yes," Joua Wang responded, equally irritated. "Some people have no consideration."

They exchanged disapproving glances and whispered criticisms about the unruly father and son, allowing their irritation to overshadow the joy of their fishing trip.

"Why do they have to be so loud?" Asthee muttered, casting his line again. "They're scaring all the fish away."

Joua Wang nodded. "It's frustrating, but let's try to focus."

Despite their efforts, the fish seemed elusive that day, and as the sun began to dip below the horizon, their hopes of a successful catch dwindled.

"We might have to call it a day, Asthee," Joua Wang said, sighing.

"Yeah, I guess so," Asthee replied, disappointed. "But I was really looking forward to catching something."

Disheartened but unwilling to give up, Joua Wang and Asthee reluctantly started packing up their equipment, preparing to head home empty-handed.

Just as they were about to leave, the noisy father and son approached them with a surprising gesture of kindness.

"Hey there!" the boisterous father called out, holding up a string of fish. "We noticed you didn't catch much. Want some of ours?"

Joua Wang and Asthee were taken aback.

"You... you want to give us your fish?" Joua Wang stammered.

"Yeah, we've got more than we need," the man said with a friendly grin. "It's a shame to see anyone go home empty-handed."

Asthee blinked in surprise. "Wow, thank you! We really appreciate it."

"No problem at all," the other boy said, smiling. "It's all part of the fun, right?"

Caught off guard by their unexpected act of generosity, Joua Wang and Asthee were deeply touched.

"Thank you," Joua Wang said sincerely. "We misjudged you. This means a lot to us."

"At that moment, embarrassed, they realized the error of their judgment and the importance of not jumping to conclusions about others.

Grateful for the unexpected gift and the valuable lesson learned, Joua Wang and Asthee bid farewell to their newfound friends.

"Safe travels!" the boisterous father said, waving as they walked away.

"Thanks again! Hope to see you around," Asthee called back, smiling.

As they drove back home under the canopy of a starlit sky, Joua Wang and Asthee reflected on the events of the day.

"Dad, today was amazing," Asthee said. "We learned something important."

"Yes, we did," Joua Wang agreed. "Sometimes, people surprise you in the best ways. I'm glad we met them."

Cherishing the memories made and the wisdom gained, Joua Wang and Asthee embraced the kindness that lies within every soul, their bond stronger than ever before.

STANDING IN LINE

Neng Chang, a respected pastor at a prominent church, stood in line at the grocery store one afternoon, growing increasingly impatient. The customer ahead of him, an elderly woman, engaged in a prolonged conversation with the cashier, delaying the transaction and stretching Neng's patience thin. He had an important meeting to attend and was already running late, a situation that grated on his nerves, given his steadfast commitment to punctuality.

Neng shifted his weight from one foot to the other, glancing at his watch for the third time in as many minutes. His wife, Maiv, stood beside him, sensing his growing agitation.

"Neng, calm down," she whispered, placing a gentle hand on his arm.

"I know, I know," he replied quietly, clenching his jaw. "But this is ridiculous. I can't be late for this meeting."

Maiv squeezed his arm reassuringly. "Remember, patience is a virtue you often preach about."

Neng sighed, taking a deep breath to steady himself. "You're right, Maiv. It's just… frustrating."

As the minutes dragged on, Neng's irritation morphed into a simmering anger. He contemplated urging the woman to expedite her payment, but Maiv's gentle touch and calm demeanor restrained him, mindful of his role as a spiritual leader and the virtues he preached.

Finally, it was his turn. He placed his groceries on the conveyor belt, ready to pay and rush to his meeting. To his astonishment, the cashier, a young man with a warm smile, informed him, "Sir, the lady before you already paid for your groceries. She gave us a $200 bill, and this is the remaining change." The cashier handed Neng the leftover money.

Dumbfounded and slightly embarrassed, Neng inquired, "Who was that kind woman?"

The cashier smiled wider. "She's my mother, and she's a member of your church."

Neng's eyes widened in surprise. "Your mother? What's her name?"

"Mrs. Lee," the cashier replied. "She often speaks highly of your sermons, Pastor."

Neng's face flushed with a mix of embarrassment and gratitude. He turned to Maiv, who looked at him with a knowing smile. "I guess I needed that reminder more than I realized," he admitted.

As they left the store, Neng couldn't shake the encounter from his mind. "I feel so foolish for being so impatient," he confessed to Maiv. "Here I am, preaching about patience and kindness, yet I was ready to lose my temper over a minor inconvenience."

Maiv nodded. "We're all human, Neng. It's a lesson we all need to learn repeatedly."

That evening, Neng stood before his congregation, the day's events still fresh in his mind. He shared the story with them, his voice tinged with humility. "Today, I was reminded that patience and kindness can have significant, unforeseen impacts. I nearly lost my temper over a small delay, only to discover that the woman causing the delay was showing me a great kindness."

The congregation listened intently, many nodding in understanding. "This experience has shown me that true faith and understanding are demonstrated not merely through words but through consistent practice, especially in the most trying and mundane moments. We are all works in progress, constantly learning and growing."

As Neng walked home with Maiv, he felt a renewed sense of purpose. He realized that maintaining virtues like patience and kindness was a daily challenge, one that required constant mindfulness and effort. But he also understood that it was these very challenges that made him grow, not just as a pastor, but as a person.

The moral of this story is clear: Patience and kindness are powerful forces that can transform even the most frustrating situations into moments of grace and reflection. They serve as poignant reminders that maintaining these virtues is a challenge everyone faces, irrespective of their status or experience. True faith and understanding are demonstrated not merely through words but through consistent practice, especially in the most trying and mundane moments.

THE OSCILLATOR

Electronicorp, a giant in the world of electronic manufacturing and assembly, found itself staring at a daunting seven-million-dollar problem. An error in one of their oscillators had jeopardized a crucial contract. If the news of this blunder leaked, it could trigger massive layoffs or even shutter the company entirely.

Despite hiring additional expert engineers, no solution seemed forthcoming. Frustrated and desperate, the owner decided to delay the project, hoping for a miracle.

One bright morning, as sunlight filtered through the office windows, John, the manager, stumbled upon the problematic oscillator lying on a dry-cleaned table near the engineers' office. Puzzled, he picked it up and took it to the lead engineer, hoping against hope.

"Tom, take a look at this," John said, handing over the oscillator.

Tom inspected the piece meticulously, eyes widening in disbelief. "John, this is... perfect. It's fixed!"

"Fixed? Are you sure?" John's heart raced. This could be the breakthrough they needed.

"Absolutely. But who did this?"

John called for a brief meeting in the conference room, summoning everyone. The room buzzed with curiosity and a bit of tension.

"Alright, everyone," John began, his voice steady but curious, "We found the oscillator fixed perfectly on the table near the engineers' office. Who did this?"

A murmur ran through the room. Then, a petite Hmong woman named See timidly raised her hand. She had been with the company for years, her English halting and simple.

"I did it," See confessed, eyes downcast. "I found the piece on the table near my station, and I decided to reassemble it. I am sorry," she said, her voice trembling. "Am I in trouble now?"

John asked everyone else to leave the room. The door closed behind them, leaving only John, Tom, and See. John's stern expression softened.

"You're not in trouble, See," John said gently. "You just saved the company."

Tears welled up in See's eyes, a mixture of relief and joy.

After much discussion, John and the owner, Mr. Bennett, were still curious about how See had managed to fix the oscillator when seasoned engineers couldn't. But for now, they decided to focus on gratitude.

A week later, the company shut down operations for a day to honor See's incredible contribution. The entire staff gathered in the large assembly hall, which was decorated with banners and balloons. A large sign read, "Thank You, See!"

Mr. Bennett took the stage, microphone in hand. "Today, we celebrate one of our own. See, your skill and dedication have saved us all. On behalf of Electronicorp, we thank you."

See was called up to the stage, where Mr. Bennett handed her a $1,000 check and a beautiful plaque that read, "To See: In Gratitude for Your Extraordinary Contribution."

See, clearly overwhelmed, shook her head modestly. "I was just doing my job," she said softly. "I didn't expect anything."

The crowd applauded, cheering for the humble woman who had saved their jobs and the company. See, with tears streaming down her face, smiled broadly. It was a day of joy, relief, and a testament to the hidden talents within each person.

THE ROSANA

In the heart of the picturesque River Spring nestled an exquisite and upscale restaurant known as Rosana. As the sun began to set on a bustling Friday evening, the restaurant hummed with the chatter of well-dressed patrons. The ambiance was one of sophistication and elegance, with only those in suit and tie attire being welcomed to dine in its opulent halls. Crystal chandeliers cast a warm, golden glow, reflecting off the polished mahogany tables and the fine china that adorned them.

Among the sea of finely dressed guests, there sat a solitary figure at a table reserved for one. An elderly man, dressed casually, awaited his meal with a quiet patience that seemed to contrast the lively atmosphere around him. However, as the moments passed, it became apparent that the man was not in the best of health. He coughed intermittently, drooled, and occasionally gasped for air, much to the discomfort of the other diners seated nearby.

Whispers and glances were exchanged among the guests, their annoyance palpable as they felt that the old man was encroaching upon the perfection of their evening. Some began to voice their complaints to the servers, requesting that the man be moved to a more secluded area or, better yet, away from their vicinity.

"Excuse me," said a well-dressed woman at a nearby table, her voice dripping with irritation. "Can something be done about that man? It's rather unappetizing."

A gentleman at another table nodded in agreement, adding, "This is supposed to be an exclusive establishment. We didn't come here for this sort of disturbance."

The young server, unfamiliar with the nuances of the restaurant and eager to please the patrons, complied with their demands. With a sense of duty, he approached the elderly man and gently guided him to a seat at the farthest corner of the restaurant, away from the prying eyes and disapproving glances of the other guests.

"I'm sorry, sir, but would you mind sitting over here?" the server asked politely, though his voice slightly trembled. "Some of the guests have expressed concerns."

The elderly man nodded slowly, not wanting to cause any trouble. "Of course, young man," he replied hoarsely, allowing himself to be led away.

A sudden hush fell over the restaurant as the commotion subsided, only to be shattered by the commanding voice of the master chef, Mr. Angelo. Having been informed of the incident by a concerned staff member, he emerged from the kitchen in a flurry of anger and disbelief.

"Who moved Mr. Rosana?" Mr. Angelo demanded, his tone sharp and authoritative. The young server, feeling the weight of his mistake, stepped forward and admitted his error in relocating the elderly man.

With a steely gaze, Mr. Angelo revealed the identity of the man. "That is the owner of this establishment," he declared, his words cutting through the silence like a knife. "He sits wherever he pleases. Do you understand?"

The realization dawned on the patrons as they absorbed the gravity of their misjudgment. A sense of shock and embarrassment washed over them, mingled with a tinge of remorse for their lack of empathy and understanding. Some approached Mr. Rosana, offering their apologies and expressing their regret for their behavior.

"Mr. Rosana, I had no idea," stammered the well-dressed woman from earlier, her face flushed with shame. "Please, forgive us."

A couple, who had also complained, echoed her sentiment. "We are deeply sorry, sir," they said in unison. "We didn't mean to offend you."

Mr. Rosana, with a kind and weary smile, waved away their apologies. "It's alright," he rasped, his voice gentle. "I understand. Please, enjoy your evening."

However, the damage had been done, and the lesson had been learned. In the aftermath of the incident, a somber mood lingered in the air, a heartbreaking reminder of the importance of compassion and respect for all, regardless of appearances or circumstances. The patrons, having witnessed the humility and grace of the restaurant's owner, left with a renewed sense of awareness, vowing never to judge so hastily again.

CHAPTER TWELVE

A BUSINESS OPPORTUNITY AD POSTED, "HOW TO HAVE INCOME FOR LIFE."

WELL, I ALREADY HAVE AN INCOME FOR LIFE. IT'S CALLED A JOB OR JUST-OVER-BROKE.

ONLY IN AMERICA

Circuit Court Judge James Brown of Riverville was a pillar of the community. Known for his fairness and kindness, he was a board member and elder at Riverville Presbyterian Church, where he taught Sunday school to the youth. He regularly volunteered to speak at local schools about law, order, and equality, always emphasizing the importance of justice and compassion. His reputation was that of a gentle person with a kind heart, someone who would go out of his way to help others.

One day, Judge Brown was invited to a crucial meeting that could shape the town's future. Wanting to look his best, he took his favorite suit to Loo Kim's Dry Cleaners, a business run by Mr. and Mrs. Loo Kim. The Loo Kims had immigrated to America with dreams of a better life and had worked tirelessly for nearly two decades to build their dry-cleaning business. However, in recent years, their business had begun to struggle as they aged and their energy waned.

Judge Brown entered the dry-cleaning shop with a warm smile. "Good morning, Mr. and Mrs. Kim," he greeted them.

"Good morning, Judge Brown," they replied in unison, their faces lighting up at the sight of a valued customer.

"I have an important meeting next week and need this suit cleaned and pressed," Judge Brown explained, handing over his neatly folded suit. "Can you have it ready by then?"

"Of course, Judge," Mrs. Kim assured him. "We will take special care of it."

A week later, Judge Brown returned to pick up his suit. However, when he inspected it, his face fell. There was a small burned spot on the shoulder, barely noticeable but significant enough for the meticulous judge.

"What this?" he asked, his voice tight with frustration as he pointed to the burn mark.

Mr. Kim looked at the suit, his face paling. "Oh no, I am so sorry, Judge. This must have happened during the pressing. We will refund your money immediately."

"I'm not just concerned about the money," Judge Brown said, his anger growing. "This suit was very expensive, and now it's ruined. I need compensation for this damage."

Mrs. Kim clasped her hands together, her voice trembling. "Please, Judge Brown, it was an accident. We are already struggling to keep our business afloat. We cannot afford to compensate you for the suit."

Judge Brown's expression hardened. "I understand your situation, but this suit was important to me. If you cannot compensate me, I will have no choice but to take legal action."

The Loo Kims thought the judge was bluffing, hoping he would cool down in a few days. But 45 days later, they received court papers indicating they were being sued for $16 million for damages and emotional distress. They were stunned and confused. Sixteen million dollars for a suit? They believed no court in the United States would entertain such a claim.

Desperate, they hired a lawyer. "This must be a mistake," Mr. Kim said, shaking his head in disbelief as he handed over the legal papers to the attorney.

The lawyer sighed, skimming through the documents. "Unfortunately, it's not. You have to go to court."

The courtroom was tense on the day of the hearing. The judge presiding over the case was a colleague of Judge Brown. Despite the Loo Kims' lawyer presenting a strong defense, arguing that the claim was excessive and unjust, the court initially ruled in favor of Judge Brown. The Loo Kims were ordered to pay $3 million, a reduction from $16 million within a month, but still, it's an amount they could never afford.

"We don't have this kind of money," Mrs. Kim wept outside the courthouse.

"We will lose everything," Mr. Kim added, his shoulders slumped in defeat.

With no other option, the couple appealed the decision, leading to further two years of relentless court battles. Finally, a jury found that the original case was indeed excessive and unjust. However, the jury also determined that the Kims had been negligent and ordered them to pay $3,000 in damages and court fees.

While the verdict was a relief, it came too late. The legal fees and associated costs over the four and half years had drained their life savings, leaving them in financial ruin.

Judge Brown, despite his initial victory, felt a pang of guilt each time he passed by the now-closed dry cleaners. His actions had left a stain on his reputation, much like the burn mark on his suit, one that no amount of legal victories could ever clean away. The town of Riverville once filled with admiration for him, now looked at him with a mix of fear and disappointment. His pursuit of retribution had come at a steep price, not just for the Kims but for his own conscience.

This tragic tale of Judge Brown and the Loo Kims could only happen in America. It is a country where the pursuit of justice can sometimes blur into a pursuit of retribution, where the letter of the law can overshadow the spirit of fairness. In America, the legal system allows for the possibility of extraordinary claims and significant compensations, driven by the belief that everyone deserves their day in court, no matter how seemingly trivial the grievance. But this story also highlights the darker side of that system—how the power and influence of one individual can devastate the lives of others, leading to an outcome that, while legal, feels deeply unjust.

Only in America can the scales of justice tip so dramatically, leading to a scenario where a small business is destroyed over a minor mistake and where the dream of a better life can be so easily shattered by the very system meant to protect it.

A MIRACLE BABY!

In the town of Springfield, Missouri, Charles and Maiv had lived a quiet, unassuming life together for over 18 years. Their home, filled with love and devotion, echoed with a profound silence, for despite their deep desire, they had no children. The years were marked by a relentless cycle of anguish and hope, countless prayers, and numerous medical attempts, each ending in disappointment.

"We almost gave up," Charles would often reflect, his eyes misty with memories of their struggles.

On a particularly hot day on July 12th, 2021, a ray of hope shone into their lives. Doua Her, a revered spiritual figure known in the community as Tais Nruag, visited Springfield. The couple received an invitation to meet her at their pastor's home. After a heartfelt meeting, Maiv, holding onto a thread of faith, approached Tais Nruag.

"Can you pray for us to have a child?" Maiv's voice quivered with vulnerability and hope.

Tais Nruag, with a gentle smile, placed her hands on Maiv's shoulders. "Of course, my dear. Let's pray together." Her words were imbued with warmth and conviction as she prayed fervently for a miracle.

Little did Charles and Maiv know, just a little over a month later, their prayers would be answered unexpectedly. One evening in August 2021, Charles received a phone call from their first cousin, Tsaav Xyooj, and his wife, Ntxawm Xyooj, calling from Manitowoc, Wisconsin.

"We have something important to tell you," Tsaav began. "We want to give you our fifth child, a boy, to raise as your own. We believe he will bring joy and blessings into your lives."

Charles was stunned, his mind swirling with emotions. "Are you serious? This is...this is incredible," he stammered.

"Yes," Ntxawm Xyooj affirmed. "We feel this is the right thing to do, and we want to bless you in this way."

Overwhelmed with gratitude but tinged with skepticism, Charles and Maiv accepted this grand gesture. "Thank you," Maiv whispered, tears of relief streaming down her face.

Determined to formalize the adoption, they hired an attorney. "It should be straightforward since it's a family-to-family adoption," the attorney initially reassured them. However, a month later, the attorney brought less encouraging news.

"It's going to be quite difficult in many aspects," he explained, his tone grave. "You must be prepared for any outcome, and I'm afraid I need to request more funds to cover the additional work required."

Undeterred, Charles and Maiv pressed on. "We won't give up," Charles declared resolutely. "This child is meant to be with us."

Finally, on March 21, 2023, their miracle unfolded. Their little boy was born at 6:21 PM at Aurora Medical Center in Manitowoc, Wisconsin. Charles and Maiv braved the harsh winter snow to reach the hospital, arriving two hours later to meet their son for the first time.

As they cradled the baby in their arms, a wave of profound joy washed over them. "Welcome to our family, Theophilus Ntxhwchoj Thao," Maiv whispered, her voice trembling with love and awe. They signed the necessary legal papers and, after three days, brought him home to Springfield.

The journey had been long and filled with heartache, but the joy they now felt eclipsed all the suffering. "Theo, you are our joy and happiness, our miracle from God," Charles said, his eyes glistening with tears of gratitude.

Reflecting on their journey, Charles and Maiv felt a deep sense of thankfulness. "There are no words to express our gratitude," Charles said one day, holding Theo close. "Thank you, God, for this blessing. And thank you, Theo, for bringing great joy to our lives. The rest is history, but we shall never forget."

THE PRINCESS

Once upon a time, in a small town in West Virginia, a young woman named Sarah set out on a quest to uncover the mysteries of her past. Growing up in a loving adoptive family, Sarah was always baffled about who she was and about her roots.

One day, after her adoptive mother passed away, Sarah felt a deep longing to connect with her biological parents. With determination in her heart, she reached out to her birth mother's family in Sierra Leone, hoping to find answers.

After a heartfelt letter and a phone call that changed everything, Sarah found herself speaking to her long-lost family members. A voice on the other end of the line said, "Hello, Sarah, this is your aunty. I was there when you were born!" Sarah's heart raced as she listened to her uncle reveal the astonishing truth, "Ooooooo, Sarah. You have lots of royal family. Your great-grandfather was a paramount chief, your uncle was chief, and you could be chief someday. You are a princess in this country."

Stunned by the revelation, Sarah's eyes widened with wonder and excitement. "A princess?" she whispered in disbelief. The words echoed in her mind, filling her with a sense of purpose and responsibility. Embracing her royal heritage, Sarah embarked on a journey to Sierra Leone to meet her family, understand her culture, and embrace her newfound identity as a princess.

With courage and determination, Princess Sarah Culberson stepped into her royal lineage, ready to make a difference in the world. Her story inspired many and carried the promise of a new chapter filled with hope, empowerment, and the transformative power of self-discovery.

And so, Princess Sarah's tale of finding her roots and embracing her royal destiny became a beacon of light for all who heard it, a reminder that sometimes the greatest adventures begin with a single question: "Who am I?"

The story of Princess Sarah Culberson's journey to discovering her royal heritage can be seen as a reflection of our relationship with God and our identity as citizens of heaven.

Just as Sarah was unaware of her royal lineage and lived without knowledge of her true identity as a princess, many people may go through life unaware of their spiritual heritage and connection to God. Like Sarah, who embarked on a quest to uncover her roots and understand her royal lineage, we also have the opportunity to seek a deeper understanding of our relationship with God and our identity as citizens in heaven.

Sarah's story highlights the importance of self-discovery, curiosity, and the search for truth. In a similar way, as individuals on a spiritual journey, we have the opportunity to explore our relationship with God, seek answers to life's questions, and discover the depth of our connection to the divine.

Just as Princess Sarah embraced her royal heritage with a sense of responsibility and a commitment to making a positive impact, we, too, can embrace our identity as citizens of heaven with a sense of purpose, love, and service to others. By recognizing our spiritual heritage and relationship with God, we can live with a greater sense of peace, joy, and fulfillment, knowing that we are loved unconditionally and called to share that love with the world.

Princess Sarah's story serves as a reminder that our true identity and worth are found in our connection to God and that through faith, self-discovery, and a heart open to divine guidance, we can live as citizens of heaven, shining brightly with the light of love and grace.

KARMA

In a land governed by the principles of karma, it was believed that those who did good would be rewarded, while those who engaged in wrongdoing would face dire consequences. However, this ideal did not always hold true, as the tale of Johnny Xiong reveals.

In a vibrant neighborhood, a summer evening brought forth a lively street party. Among the merrymakers was Johnny Xiong, a young man known for his integrity and strong moral compass. The festivities began with joy and laughter, but as the night wore on, the atmosphere grew wild, fueled by spirits and rising tensions. Eventually, a violent skirmish broke out, prompting a concerned neighbor to summon the authorities.

The police arrived swiftly, their presence adding to the chaos. Amidst the turmoil, Johnny, driven by a sense of duty, sought to help the officers quell the fight despite his father's stern warnings.

"Johnny, stay back!" cried Mr. Chang Xiong from their porch, worry etched on his face.

"Dad, I can't just stand by and do nothing. Someone could get seriously hurt," Johnny responded, determination in his eyes as he rushed into the fray.

In the ensuing commotion, Johnny accidentally collided with a police officer, sending him to the ground. Misunderstandings ensued, and Johnny found himself arrested alongside the brawlers. As he was being handcuffed, he tried to explain.

"Officer, please! I was only trying to help! I wasn't involved!"

Despite his protests, Johnny spent three harrowing nights in the county jail, charged with assaulting a police officer. This incident marked the beginning of a grueling legal battle.

Johnny's parents, Mr. and Mrs. Chang Xiong, were distraught but resolute. They sought the help of Sarah Thompson, a highly respected defense attorney. Sarah promptly filed a motion to dismiss the case, arguing it was a grave misunderstanding and an unfortunate accident.

"Your Honor, my client, Johnny Xiong, acted as a Good Samaritan. His intention was to aid the police, not assault them," Sarah articulated with conviction.

It seemed that justice might prevail for Johnny, but the judge denied the motion, swayed by the prosecutor's narrative. Mark Davis, the prosecutor, painted a starkly different picture of Johnny.

"Your Honor, Johnny Xiong is not an average citizen. He is a U.S. Marine, a special forces trained in combat. This makes him exceedingly dangerous. The officer he allegedly assaulted is fortunate to be alive," Mark declared emphatically.

As the trial dragged on, Colonel Robert Haskins, Johnny's commanding officer, testified on his behalf.

"Johnny Xiong is one of the finest Marines under my command. The idea that he would intentionally harm a police officer is inconceivable," Colonel Haskins testified, his voice a blend of respect and sorrow.

Despite this powerful testimony, the prosecution presented several witnesses who painted a damning picture of Johnny. The legal battle extended over nearly two years, taking a heavy toll on Johnny and his family.

Finally, the verdict was delivered. Johnny was found guilty of a lesser charge. He faced one year in prison and was dishonorably discharged from the Marines, losing his pension and his dream of a lifelong career in the U.S. Marine Corps.

As Johnny stood in the courtroom, his head held high, his father approached, tears welling in his eyes.

"Johnny, I'm so proud of you. You did the right thing, even if the system couldn't see it that way," Mr. Xiong said, embracing his son tightly.

"Thanks, Dad. I just wish things had turned out differently," Johnny replied, his voice heavy with emotion.

Thus, the tale of Johnny Xiong underscores the complexities and contradictions inherent in the justice system, where doing the right thing can sometimes lead to the most unjust consequences. Don't believe in Karma!

BEWARE THE SYSTEM

In a small town in the heart of the United States, there lived a community of people whose lives were tightly bound by the threads of the social system. Maria, a single mother of two, was one of them. Her days were filled with struggles to make ends meet, relying on the meager support provided by the government to feed her children and keep a roof over their heads.

"The system just keeps us trapped, doesn't it, Mom?" Maria's daughter, Sarah, remarked one evening as they sat at the kitchen table, going over bills.

Maria sighed, her shoulders slumping with weariness. "It does, sweetheart. It's like we're stuck in a never-ending cycle."

"But why can't we get ahead, Mom? Why do they make it so hard for us to improve our lives?" Sarah asked, her voice tinged with frustration.

"Because that's how the system works, dear. They want us to stay dependent, to rely on their support for everything," Maria explained, her eyes reflecting a mix of resignation and determination.

As the days turned into weeks and the weeks into years, Maria watched her children grow up in the shadow of the system that held them back. One evening, as she tucked her son, Michael, into bed, he asked her a question that lingered in the air like a heavy weight.

"Mom, why do we have to struggle so much? Why can't we have the things other kids have?" Michael's voice was soft, filled with innocence and a hint of sadness.

Maria sat on the edge of his bed, brushing a stray lock of hair from his forehead. "I wish I had an easy answer for you, Michael. But sometimes life is just unfair, and we have to do our best with what we have."

Despite the challenges they faced, Maria refused to let despair consume her. She held onto a glimmer of hope, a belief that one-day things would be different. As she shared her dreams with her children, she instilled in them a sense of resilience and determination.

However, the rules of the system loomed over them like a dark cloud, reminding them of its oppressive nature.

"We have to be careful, kids," Maria warned one day as they walked home from school. "If we start doing too well or acquire a good job, the system might take away what little help we have. The system punishes the people who strive to improve."

Sarah nodded her expression a mixture of defiance and frustration. "It's not fair, Mom. They want us to stay poor forever." I know, sweetheart," Maria replied, her voice tinged with sadness. "But we can't let it crush our spirits. We have each other, and as long as we stick together, we can find a way out of this."

LOL AND SORROW

And so, in the small town where the social system reigned supreme, Maria and her children fought a silent battle for a better life, their voices echoing with a quiet strength that refused to be silenced. Though the system sought to keep them down, they clung to each other and to their hopes for a future where they could break free from the constraints that held them back.

CHAPTER THIRTEEN

A QUOTE ATTRIBUTED TO ACTOR GEORGE CLOONEY:

"LIFE IS NOT ABOUT BEING RICH, BEING POPULAR,

BEING HIGHLY EDUCATED, OR BEING PERFECT. IT'S ABOUT

BEING REAL, HUMBLE, AND KIND."

OKAY, MR. CLOONEY, AS AN ACTOR,

YOU EMBODY ALL OF THE ABOVE,

EXCEPT BEING REAL.

THE REWARD AND PUNISHMENT

In the small town of Clearwater, there lived a man named Billy Lo. Billy was known far and wide for his honesty and integrity. He never cheated anyone, never lied, and always did his best to help those in need.

One day, a dark cloud descended upon Billy's life. He was accused of a crime he did not commit. Despite his protestations of innocence, Billy was found guilty and sentenced to eight long years in federal prison. The community was shocked—how could someone as upstanding as Billy be convicted of such a crime?

As Billy began his sentence, he felt a sense of hopelessness creeping in. But he was determined to make the best of his situation. He spent his days reading, learning new skills, and helping his fellow inmates however he could.

One day, Billy heard about a drug rehabilitation program that could help reduce his prison time if he enrolled. Despite not having any history of drug abuse or addiction, Billy saw this as an opportunity to get back to his life and loved ones sooner.

Excited at the prospect of an early release, Billy applied to the program. However, to his dismay, he was told that he did not qualify because he was a clean-living individual with no history of substance abuse. The program director explained that only those with drug issues were eligible for the program.

Billy was taken aback. "So, because I have lived a clean life, I must serve my full sentence while others get their time reduced for their drug use or addiction?" he asked incredulously.

The program director nodded sadly. "I'm afraid that's how the law works, Billy. Good people like you don't get the same benefits as those who have made poor choices."

"That's not right. The system punishes the people who make good choices and rewards those who don't?" Billy exclaimed.

"Unfortunately, that's what happens here," said the director of the Drug Rehab Program. "Even though you don't have a history of drug abuse, your lawyer should have put on your sentencing report that you were a drug abuser."

And so, Billy served his full eight-year sentence with dignity and grace. Despite the injustice he faced, he never lost his faith in the goodness of people and the importance of staying true to one's principles.

When the day of his release finally came, Billy walked out of prison with his head held high. The townspeople welcomed him back with open arms, knowing that he had endured his ordeal with courage and resilience. And though his time behind bars had been unjust, Billy emerged from the experience stronger and more determined than ever to live a life of honor and integrity.

Billy's story became an inspiration to many. His unwavering commitment to his values, even in the face of such adversity, demonstrated the power of maintaining one's integrity. He began speaking at local schools and community centers, sharing his experiences and the lessons he had learned. Billy's message was clear: no matter what life throws at you, stay true to yourself and your principles.

Over time, Billy's influence grew beyond Clearwater. His story reached national attention, sparking conversations about the justice system and the importance of moral integrity. Advocacy groups used his story to push for legal reforms, highlighting the need for more nuanced and fair approaches to sentencing and rehabilitation.

Billy Lo, once a humble man from a small town, became a symbol of resilience and righteousness. His journey from wrongful imprisonment to becoming a beacon of hope and change showed that even in the darkest times, one can rise above and make a lasting impact on the world.

THE STRANGER IN CHURCH

The First Alliance Church of Pineville was one of the largest and most respected churches in town. The majority of its members were middle-class, well-dressed, and faithful Christians. Every Sunday morning, the sanctuary was filled with the sound of hymns and the warmth of community spirit.

On one particular Sunday, as the congregation gathered and greeted each other warmly, a man dressed in ragged clothes, his hair unkempt and carrying a noticeable odor, walked into the sanctuary. The usual buzz of conversation dimmed as people noticed him. Some whispered, and others stared.

"Excuse me, sir," said Jack, the head usher, approaching the man with a courteous but firm demeanor. "Would you mind stepping outside with me for a moment?"

The man followed Jack outside. Once there, Jack handed him a $20 bill. "Here you go. Maybe this can help you out a bit."

The man took the money without a word and walked away. Jack returned inside, thinking the situation had been handled discreetly.

A few minutes later, just as the service was about to start, the same man re-entered the sanctuary. The choir was already singing their opening song, "Amazing Grace." Heads turned again, and the whispers grew louder.

"Can you believe he's back?" one woman muttered to her neighbor.

"Why isn't he leaving?" another person asked.

Jack hurried over to the man again, but this time, he didn't ask him to leave. Instead, he escorted him to the back of the church and let him sit in the last row.

The congregation settled down, but there was an undercurrent of discomfort in the air. They were expecting a special guest pastor that day, Pastor Ray Schultz, who had been invited to speak as he was going to be their new pastor. As the minutes ticked by, Pastor Schultz had not shown up. The congregation grew worried and restless.

"Do you think something happened to him?" whispered Mrs. Jenkins to her husband.

"I hope not. It's not like him to be late," he replied, glancing at his watch.

Just as the murmurs of concern began to rise, the man in the back row stood up and handed a letter to one of the ushers. The usher read it, eyes widening in shock. He quickly walked up to the pulpit and addressed the congregation.

"Excuse me, everyone. We have a rather unexpected situation. This man here," he pointed to the ragged man in the back, "is Pastor Ray Schultz."

A stunned silence fell over the room. The man walked up to the pulpit, the congregation's eyes following him in disbelief. He stood there for a moment, letting the surprise settle in before he began to speak.

"Good morning," he started, his voice steady and kind. "I am indeed Pastor Ray Schultz. I apologize for the confusion and the delay. But I needed to see for myself what kind of church you are."

The congregation sat in stunned silence, still trying to process what was happening.

"You see," Pastor Schultz continued, "a true church of Jesus Christ welcomes people of all kinds, including the poor, the sick, and even the homeless, with love and kindness. Today, I came to you as someone in need, and I saw how you responded."

He paused, looking around the room. "Some of you were kind and gave me money, and for that, I am grateful. But many of you looked at me with judgment and disdain. It is easy to welcome those who look and act like us. But the real test of our faith is how we treat those who are different."

Pastor Schultz's words hung in the air, and many in the congregation looked down, reflecting on their actions, feeling a sense of shame and guilt.

"Today, we all learned a valuable lesson," he concluded. "And for that, I am thankful. I look forward to serving and leading you, and I hope we can grow together in love and understanding."

After the service, many members approached Pastor Schultz to apologize, but he waved them off gently.

"There is no need for apologies," he said with a warm smile. "We all have lessons to learn, and today was one of those days. Let us move forward together, stronger and more compassionate."

The First Alliance Church of Pineville never forgot that Sunday. It became a turning point for the congregation, a reminder of the true meaning of their faith and the importance of welcoming everyone with open hearts.

THE EXTRAORDINARY HEIST

The U.S. Federal Reserve was renowned as the most heavily guarded bank in the world and the most well-built structure in America. Its reputation for impenetrable security was legendary, a modern-day Fort Knox. However, one early morning, this fortress of finance would face an unprecedented challenge.

"911, what's your emergency?" The operator's voice was steady, accustomed to handling crises.

"This is Janet Roberts at the Federal Reserve branch in Havenville, California. We've been robbed!" Janet's voice was shaking, disbelief mingling with fear.

Within minutes, police units swarmed the scene, securing the perimeter as the bank staff, stunned and bewildered, were ushered out of the building. The air was thick with tension and the hum of whispered questions. How could this have happened?

The vault, one of four that housed millions in cash, was completely emptied. The staff had discovered the breach just as they began their workday, the vault door ajar, its steel frame twisted open as if by some phantom force.

FBI Special Agent Marcus Turner arrived shortly after, his sharp eyes taking in every detail. "Alright, let's get to work. I want a full sweep of the premises. No stone unturned."

Two years passed with the case growing colder, until one sweltering afternoon in Arizona, a single hundred-dollar bill emerged. It was a bill recorded as stolen from the Federal Reserve.

Special Agent Turner, now grayer and more weary but no less determined, traced the bill's journey. It led him to a small, dilapidated house on the outskirts of Phoenix. There, they found John Carter, a man with a history of petty crimes but nothing to suggest involvement in a heist of this magnitude. Carter was a double amputee; his legs were lost in an accident years ago.

"I took part in the robbery," Carter confessed, his voice heavy with resignation as he sat across from Agent Turner in the interrogation room. "But I wasn't alone. There were four others."

Turner's eyebrows shot up in surprise. "Go on," he prompted, leaning forward.

Carter sighed. "We planned it for months, every detail. It wasn't just about brute force. We had skills, knowledge. Each of us had a role."

"Who are these others?" Turner asked, his voice barely a whisper.

Carter listed them: Mike, who had lost his sight; Sarah, who couldn't hear; Tom, who had lost his voice; and finally, Ellen, another amputee. Each had their own tragic story, their own reasons for turning to crime.

Turner's team swiftly moved, rounding up the remaining suspects. Each arrest was more shocking than the last. A blind man, a deaf woman, a mute, and another amputee. The media dubbed them "The Disabled Bandits," and their story captivated the nation.

In court, the defense painted a picture of desperation and injustice, arguing that society had pushed these individuals to the brink. The prosecution, however, was relentless, emphasizing the meticulous planning and execution of the heist.

After two grueling years of trials, all five were found guilty and sentenced to prison. As the gavel fell for the final time, a sense of unease settled over the courtroom.

Outside, Turner addressed the press. "This case has highlighted serious flaws in our security systems. We must not underestimate anyone. We must be vigilant and adaptive."

In the aftermath, the government launched a comprehensive review of the Federal Reserve's security protocols. The case had shown that even the most formidable defenses could be breached, not by physical strength, but by cunning and ingenuity.

The story of the Disabled Bandits became a legend, a cautionary tale about underestimating the resolve and resourcefulness of those who had been pushed to the fringes of society. And it served as a stark reminder that no system is foolproof, and that security must evolve continuously to meet ever-changing threats.

THE MYSTERIOUS BRIEFCASE

Wendy Yang was no extraordinary kid growing up in Wheaton, Illinois. She was just like everyone else, nothing special until she found a briefcase in the parking lot at O'Hare International Airport. It was a sunny afternoon, and Wendy was waiting with her parents for their flight to Florida for a family cruise vacation.

As Wendy wandered a bit away from her parents, something unusual caught her eye. A sleek, black briefcase lay abandoned next to a parked car. She looked around but saw no one nearby.

"Hey, Mom! Dad!" Wendy called out, running back to her parents with the briefcase clutched in her hands. "Look what I found!"

Her parents, Mr. and Mrs. Yang, turned to see their daughter hurrying towards them, her face flushed with excitement.

"Wendy, where did you get that?" Mr. Yang asked, his brows furrowing.

"I found it over there, by that car," Wendy said, pointing to the spot. "There was no one around."

Mrs. Yang looked concerned. "Honey, it could be dangerous. We should probably give it to the police or the airport authority."

Mr. Yang nodded in agreement but then paused. "Let's just hold onto it for now. We can decide what to do once we're back from our trip. Maybe there's something inside that can help us find the owner."

Wendy's eyes sparkled with curiosity. "Can we open it now?"

Mrs. Yang shook her head. "No, let's wait until we're somewhere safe. We'll open it at home."

The family enjoyed their vacation, but Wendy couldn't stop thinking about the briefcase. The moment they returned home, she eagerly dragged it into the living room.

"Okay, let's see what's inside," Mr. Yang said, grabbing a pair of scissors to cut through the lock.

Wendy held her breath as the lock clicked open. Her parents gathered around her as they slowly lifted the lid. Inside, they found stacks of documents, a Bible, sermons, and an envelope with an address and a business card. There was also a considerable amount of cash.

"What is all this?" Wendy asked, wide-eyed.

Mr. Yang picked up a document and started reading. "These are... they look like church papers. And here's a Bible and some sermons. This envelope has an address and phone number."

Mrs. Yang looked at the business card. "This says, 'Pastor Dan Wright, Youth President, Church of Agape in North America.' I think we should call him."

Pastor Dan Wright was in his office in Denver, Colorado, feeling anxious. He just realized he had lost his briefcase at the airport in Chicago after returning from a youth conference. His heart sank when his phone rang.

"Hello, Pastor Wright speaking," he answered, trying to mask his worry.

"Hello, Pastor Wright," Mr. Yang's voice came through. "My name is Mr. Yang. My daughter found your briefcase at O'Hare International Airport. We have it here and would like to return it to you."

Pastor Wright's relief was palpable. "Thank you so much! You have no idea how much this means to me. There is important church material and a significant amount of offering money in that briefcase."

Mr. Yang nodded. "We noticed. We understand its importance. We'll send it back to you right away."

The Yang family packed the briefcase carefully and shipped it back to Pastor Wright. When he received it, he was overjoyed and thanked God for the honesty and kindness of strangers.

He called the Yang family to express his gratitude. "I cannot thank you enough. With permission from my superiors, I'd like to award you $1,000 for your honesty."

But Mrs. Yang gently refused. "We appreciate the offer, Pastor, but that money belongs to God. We are just glad it is back where it belongs."

Wendy smiled. "We're happy to help."

Pastor Wright was deeply moved by their integrity. He shared the story with his congregation, praising the goodness in people. Wendy and her family had not only returned a briefcase but had also restored his faith in humanity.

A TURNING TIDE

In the year 1791, in the quiet town of Edwardsville, named after James Cartwright's grandfather, Edward Cartwright, lived a man named James Cartwright. Known for his wealth and his vast plantation in East Virginia, Mr. Cartwright was a prominent figure, respected as an elder in the United Methodist Church of Edwardsville.

One evening, as James Cartwright sat in his grand study, illuminated by the flickering flames of the hearth, he felt a profound stirring within his soul. The voice that came to him was not of this world, and it spoke with clarity and authority.

God: "James, you must free them. Your conscience cannot bear the burden any longer. Let them live in the freedom I have intended for all my children."

The next morning, James summoned his most trusted advisor, Thomas.

James: "Thomas, I have made a decision. One that will change the course of our lives and the lives of those who work for us."

Thomas: "What decision is that, sir?"

James: "I am going to free our slaves. Every last one of them."

Thomas's eyes widened in shock.

Thomas: "But, Mr. Cartwright, think of the consequences. The town, the church—they will not understand."

James: "I have thought of it, Thomas. But my conscience and my faith demand it. We must do what is right, regardless of the cost."

Determined, James called all his slaves to the main courtyard of the plantation. The gathered crowd was silent, anxiety etched on their faces.

James: "I have gathered you all here to tell you something important. As of this moment, you are all free. You owe me nothing. This is your freedom."

Stunned silence followed his words, then, slowly, murmurs of disbelief spread through the crowd. One of the elder slaves, Samuel, stepped forward.

Samuel: "Mr. Cartwright, what does this mean? Where will we go?"

James: "I will give each of you food, shelter, and money to help you start anew. However, I will retain the title to you to prevent any other from claiming you. This deed of gift ensures your freedom."

Tears streamed down the faces of men, women, and children alike. One brave woman, Sarah, spoke up.

Sarah: "Mr. Cartwright, we have nowhere to go. Allow us to stay and work for you, not as slaves, but as free people who choose to serve out of gratitude and love."

With his own slaves freed and staying on their own terms, James felt a renewed purpose. He rode into town on a crisp Saturday morning, determined to extend his newfound mission. The air was thick with anticipation as slave auctions were underway. The scene was familiar, but today, James was a man on a mission.

Auctioneer: "Ladies and gentlemen, we have a fine lot of men, women, and children up for bid today. Who will start the bidding?"

James stepped forward, his voice cutting through the murmurs.

James: "I will. One hundred dollars for the lot."

Gasps filled the air. It was an unheard-of amount, enough to silence any competing bids.

Returning to his mansion with 27 new souls, James gathered everyone in the great hall. The newly bought slaves looked at him with a mix of fear and confusion.

James: "You are free. From this moment on, you owe me nothing. I will give you food, shelter, and money to start anew. However, I will retain the title to you to prevent any other from claiming you. It's called The Deed of Gift. This deed of gift ensures your freedom."

The new freedmen and women were overcome with gratitude, their tears reflecting a mix of relief and hope.

News of James Cartwright's actions spread like wildfire. The townspeople were aghast, and the church elders summoned him.

Elder Williams: "James, what you have done is unprecedented. It defies the norms of our society and the teachings we uphold."

James: "I understand your concerns, but my faith and my conscience leave me no choice. I must follow what I believe to be God's will."

The community's response was swift and harsh. James was cast out of his church, and many shunned him. But the seeds of change had been sown.

Years later, as the tide of history turned towards abolition, James Cartwright's actions were remembered as a beacon of mercy and grace. His courageous stand against slavery inspired many and contributed to the ultimate end of the institution.

In the end, James Cartwright's legacy was not one of wealth or status but of compassion and righteousness, showing that true faith is reflected in acts of love and justice.

CHAPTER FOURTEEN

A QUOTE ATTRIBUTED TO MORGAN FREEMAN, "WHEN YOU'RE DEAD, YOU DON'T KNOW YOU'RE DEAD. THE PAIN IS FELT BY OTHERS. THE SAME THING HAPPENS WHEN YOU'RE STUPID."

AND THE SAME THING HAPPENS WHEN YOU'RE A WISE GUY, TOO.

Charles Cawv Thao

THE ROAD TRIP

Grief-stricken and desperate to escape their sorrow, they encountered a nightmare they couldn't see, but it could see them.

It had been a year since the unimaginable tragedy struck Amy and David, leaving them broken-hearted over the loss of their only child, Lily. Grief had cast a long shadow over their lives, and they decided to embark on a road trip in the hopes of escaping the relentless depression that clung to them like a shroud.

They packed their bags, loaded up the car, and set off on a journey across the country, seeking solace in the open road. As they drove, the passing landscapes provided a temporary distraction from their sorrow. The winding roads and breathtaking vistas offered a glimmer of relief, even if only for a moment.

AMY: David, it's beautiful out here. Just being on the road like this; it feels like a break from our pain.

DAVID: Yeah, Amy. The open road has its own kind of therapy.

One sunny afternoon, they decided to take a break at a rest area nestled in a lush forest. They needed some fresh air and a change of scenery. As they walked down a wooded path, their footsteps echoing through the quiet woods, they were surrounded by the soothing sounds of nature. It was the first time in a long while that Amy and David felt a sense of peace.

But suddenly, their serenity was shattered by a heart-wrenching sound. A baby's cries pierced the tranquil forest, its wails growing louder with each passing moment. Confused and alarmed, Amy and David spun around, searching for the source of the cries.

DAVID: Amy, do you hear that?

AMY: Yeah, it's coming from over there. What on earth?

The cries seemed to follow them, echoing through the trees as they retraced their steps back to the car. They looked around, expecting to find a lost child or a distressed parent, but there was no one in sight. Puzzled and unnerved, they got into the car, thinking it might have been a trick of the wind.

As they continued their journey, the distant cries of the baby faded, and Amy and David tried to put it out of their minds. As darkness fell, they reached a motel on the outskirts of a small, isolated town. The motel had a worn and eerie charm to it, but they were too tired to be picky.

Once they checked into their room and settled in, the eerie calm of the motel was broken by the same heart-wrenching cries. The invisible baby was now in their room, and the cries were deafening. Amy and David searched frantically, checking closets, under the bed, and even outside, but there was no baby to be found.

AMY: David, this is... this is impossible! It's coming from everywhere!

DAVID: I know, Amy. What is going on?

Their desperation grew as they realized the cries were coming from nowhere and everywhere at once. They tried to leave the room, but the cries followed them as though they were trapped in a nightmarish cycle. Fear and anxiety gripped them, and they couldn't escape the relentless cries that reminded them of the child they had lost.

The night grew long, and their exhaustion was compounded by the constant cries. They couldn't sleep, couldn't find any respite. Panic set in as they realized that they were not alone in the room, yet they couldn't see or touch the source of their torment.

Morning finally arrived, and they managed to escape the motel, leaving behind the haunting cries that had plagued their night. They continued their journey, shaken and disturbed, but the invisible baby was no longer with them. It was as if the nightmare had released its icy grip, but the memory of that fateful night would forever haunt their road trip.

The road trip they had hoped would heal their broken hearts had taken a sinister turn, thrusting them into a horrifying ordeal that defied reason. Amy and David were scarred, not just by the loss of their child but by an inexplicable encounter that had left them questioning the boundaries of reality. As they drove away from that motel, they couldn't help but wonder if the invisible baby had been a manifestation of their grief, a ghostly reminder of the child they could never hold again.

WEIRD CAR TROUBLE

In the picturesque town of Jonestown, Mike and Mindy, a young couple, found themselves standing in a cozy living room of a charming house. It was bathed in the warm afternoon sunlight pouring through large windows. The open house was bustling with potential buyers and a friendly real estate agent eager to show them around.

REAL ESTATE AGENT

(With a smile)

"And this is the spacious living room. Perfect for entertaining guests or just relaxing after a long day."

Mike and Mindy exchanged glances, clearly impressed.

MIKE

(Whispering to Mindy)

"I love it. What do you think?"

MINDY

(Smiling)

"I love it too."

The real estate agent led them outside, showing them the backyard, the garden, and the neighborhood.

REAL ESTATE AGENT

(Excited)

"And here's the beautiful backyard. It's a real hidden gem!"

As they stood in the front yard, Mike and Mindy appeared thrilled. They discussed the house's features.

MIKE

(Excited)

"I can already picture our life here."

MINDY

(Giggling)

"Me too!"

They continued the tour, entering the modern and well-equipped kitchen.

REAL ESTATE AGENT

"And here's the heart of the house – a fantastic kitchen!"

Mindy and Mike glanced at each other, clearly smitten with the property.

MINDY

(Whispering)

"It's perfect."

MIKE

(Whispering)

"Let's make an offer."

After the showing, they thanked the real estate agent and headed to their car, parked in the driveway. Mindy got behind the wheel, but when she attempted to reverse out of the driveway, something strange happened. The car moved backward, but the surroundings seemed to warp, and they found themselves right back in the same spot.

MINDY

(Confused)

"What just happened?"

MIKE

(Trying again)

"I don't know. Let's try again."

They attempted to leave multiple times, but each time, they ended up back in the driveway. Mindy tried a different approach, driving forward down the street and around the corner, but they still ended up back at the same driveway.

MIKE

(Nervous)

"This is getting weird. Maybe we're just disoriented."

They tried a few more times, but the same result occurred every time. Frustrated and scared, they got out of the car.

MINDY

(Panicked)

"We need help. Call the police."

Mike dialed 911, and they explained the situation to the dispatcher.

DISPATCHER

(Calmly)

"We're sending an officer to your location. Please stay put."

A police officer arrived shortly after.

POLICE OFFICER

(Confused)

"What seems to be the problem?"

MIKE

(Desperate)

"We can't leave. Every time we try, we end up back in the driveway."

The police officer offered to guide them out in his patrol car. They reluctantly agreed. The police car led the way as Mike and Mindy followed. But as they reached the corner of the neighborhood, the same strange phenomenon occurred. They ended up back in the same driveway.

MIKE

(Panic rising)

"It's happening again!"

The police officer was equally perplexed.

POLICE OFFICER

(Sweating)

"I don't understand. Let's try once more."

For the third time, they attempted to leave, but they were inexplicably drawn back to the same driveway.

MINDY

(Fighting back tears)

"This can't be happening."

As panic set in, they exchanged desperate glances. Desperate and terrified, Mike and Mindy had gathered a small crowd of onlookers, including the real estate agent.

REAL ESTATE AGENT

(Worried)

"I've never seen anything like this!"

The police officer tried one last time to guide them out of the neighborhood. But once again, they ended up back in the driveway.

MIKE

(Defeated)

"We're stuck."

As Mike and Mindy stood helpless and confused, the house seemed to exert its power over them as if it wanted them to stay. The real estate agent and the police officer could do nothing but watch.

REAL ESTATE AGENT

(Whispering to herself)

"The house chose them."

THE MEDIUM

Suddenly, a medium appeared out of nowhere and approached Mike and Mindy. "I see that you're struggling to get out of here," she said.

MIKE AND MINDY

"Yeah, can you help us?" they asked the medium.

THE MEDIUM

"Sure, I'd like to help," the medium said. She retrieved a newspaper article and showed it to Mike and Mindy. The article reported an accident in which a drunk driver swerved off the road and killed several people, including a police officer. It included pictures of all the victims.

FORGOTTEN HEROES: THE HMONG PEOPLE

In the heart of Southeast Asia, the lush, green jungles of Laos concealed secrets that the world would not see. A small airplane descended among the hidden valleys and dense forests, its path cutting through the morning mist. Inside, John Daniel, a young U.S. Army captain and helicopter pilot in his late twenties, stared out the window, a mix of anticipation and uncertainty written on his face. Beside him sat David Anderson, a stern-looking man in his forties, dressed in a suit that seemed out of place in the jungle.

"Remember, John," David whispered, his voice low and serious. "This place doesn't exist on any map. It's a secret, and you're here to serve one man - General Vang Pao. Keep it that way."

The plane touched down on a hidden airstrip surrounded by dense jungle. As John stepped off, he was immediately overwhelmed by the bustling activity of Long Chieng. Helicopters roared as they took off and landed, transporting supplies and personnel in a chaotic dance of war.

"This is General Vang Pao's territory," David said, pointing to the surrounding camp. "He runs this show. We're here as guests. Do everything to please him."

John met Charlie, a grizzled helicopter mechanic in his fifties, with a weathered face and a friendly grin. "You're the new pilot, huh? Welcome to the madness," Charlie greeted him.

Adjusting quickly to life at Long Chieng, John flew dangerous missions, often under heavy enemy fire. Along the way, he befriended two young Hmong villagers: Tseeb, a resourceful man in his early twenties, and Ntxawm, a brave young woman in her late teens. They assisted in base operations and became indispensable to John.

General Vang Pao, a charismatic leader in his fifties, soon noticed John's dedication and skill. He promoted John, assigning him more critical missions. Despite the constant danger, John, Tseeb, and Ntxawm found moments to share stories, laughter, and quiet reflection. Their bond grew stronger with each passing day.

One evening, as the sun set over the jungle, casting a golden hue over the treetops, John sat with Tseeb and Ntxawm. "You two are like family to me," he said, his voice filled with sincerity.

Amidst the chaos of war, Tseeb and Ntxawm found solace in each other's arms. Their love blossomed a beacon of hope and happiness in their turbulent world. They dreamed of a future together despite the uncertainty that surrounded them.

In 1975, a devastating message arrived. The U.S. was withdrawing from Laos, leaving the Hmong people vulnerable to the advancing communist forces. General Vang Pao was livid. "We've been betrayed!" he shouted, his voice echoing through the camp.

The base erupted into chaos as the U.S. began evacuating its personnel. Tseeb and Ntxawm, now expecting a child, faced a heartbreaking decision. They had to flee the impending communist takeover, but doing so meant leaving behind the life they knew.

"I promise I'll find a way to get you out of here," John said, desperation clear in his eyes.

As the last helicopter lifted off, John remained behind, consumed by guilt and despair. Hundreds of Hmong villagers, including Tseeb and Ntxawm, were left stranded as the enemy closed in. The jungle, once a place of camaraderie and hope, now seemed to close in around them.

Years had passed. John, now a civilian, was haunted by memories of Long Chieng and the friends he had left behind. He spent his time advocating for the Hmong people, tirelessly working to ensure their sacrifices were not forgotten. He never forgot his promise to Tseeb and Ntxawm.

One quiet afternoon, John stood at a memorial dedicated to the Hmong fighters, a wreath in his hand. He placed it gently at the base, whispering a promise into the wind. "I'll never forget you. I swear."

And so, the tale of the Hmong people in Laos, of love, loyalty, and sacrifice, remained etched in history. The untold heroes of a forgotten conflict were honored, their legacy remembered by those who knew their story.

THE MOBILE HOME

The explosion was deafening, sending debris flying in every direction. The once serene and quiet town of Loveland was shattered by the blast that echoed for miles. Where there had been a mobile home, now only a charred skeleton remained, its destruction complete. Among the wreckage, two lives were lost, their bodies so incinerated that identification was difficult.

Leng Thao, a hard-working man in his 50s, was a fixture in the community. He was married to Mai and together they had three children. Leng was known for his diligence and caution, which made the events of that tragic night all the more shocking.

It began with a faint but distinct smell of gas. Leng, ever the problem-solver, decided to investigate the source himself. He didn't think to call the fire department; he believed he could handle it.

As Leng crawled under his mobile home, the darkness enveloped him. Above, his eldest son, David, was fast asleep in his room. Mai and the other two children, Lia and Alex, were out visiting relatives. Leng moved slowly, trying to locate the source of the gas leak.

"Let's see, it must be around here somewhere," Leng muttered to himself, his flashlight casting weak beams in the confined space.

Leng, a man of routine, was careful in his actions. Yet, in a moment of misguided judgment, he decided to strike a match to better see in the darkness.

Whoosh!

In an instant, the entire mobile home erupted into a massive explosion. The force of the blast was immense, shaking nearby houses and shattering windows. The explosion was so loud it could be heard in the outskirts of the town as well, causing a wave of panic.

Detective Sarah Collins was the first to arrive at the scene. Her years of experience had prepared her for many things, but the sight of the devastated mobile home was heart-wrenching.

"Jesus, what happened here?" she whispered to herself, surveying the wreckage.

Sarah spoke with the neighbors, trying to piece together what had happened.

"We heard a loud boom, and then everything shook," said Mrs. Anderson, who lived across the street. "It felt like an earthquake."

"Did you notice anything unusual before the explosion?" Sarah asked.

"No, nothing. It was just a normal, quiet evening."

The investigation proceeded methodically. Amidst the chaos, Sarah and her team meticulously searched the remnants of the mobile home. They found the remnants of a gas line that had ruptured. Near the break, they discovered the charred remains of a matchbox and a burnt-out match.

"It looks like he tried to light a match down here," Sarah concluded, shaking her head. "In the dark, with a gas leak, it was a recipe for disaster."

The news of Leng Thao's tragic death spread quickly through Loveland. At the local community center, friends and neighbors gathered to mourn.

"He was always so careful," said Mr. Chang, a longtime friend. "I can't believe he would do something so reckless."

"It's a harsh reminder," Mai said through her tears. "We need to call for help when we suspect something is wrong, no matter how small it seems."

David stood silently beside his mother, holding her hand tightly. He felt the weight of his father's loss deeply, his hero taken in an instant.

In the following weeks, the town of Loveland slowly began to recover. Safety inspectors visited homes to ensure no other gas leaks would go unnoticed. Community meetings were held to educate everyone on the importance of safety and the right actions to take in emergencies.

The memory of Leng Thao lingered in the town; a man remembered for his hard work, love for his family, and an unfortunate lapse in judgment that cost him his life. His story became a cautionary tale, reminding everyone of the importance of safety and the tragic consequences of overlooking it.

SIMPLE BUT PROFOUND

On that scorching summer afternoon of June 2024, the sun beat down relentlessly as my wife and I struggled to fix the deflated spare tire on our Hyundai in the parking lot of Brookline First Baptist Church. I grunted as I tried to crank the jack to raise the car, sweat dripping down my face while my wife held an umbrella over my head, trying to shield me from the harsh sun rays.

Just as I was getting started on lifting the vehicle, a sleek SUV pulled into the lot, kicking up a cloud of dust. A man with a kind face stepped out, wiping his brow. "Do you guys need some help?" he called out, concern evident in his tone.

His name was Mr. David Grospitch, a Navy veteran with a warm smile and a twinkle in his eye. Without waiting for an answer, he retrieved a portable air compressor from his vehicle and set to work, expertly inflating our spare tire and checking the pressure on all the other tires as well.

As the compressor hummed, filling the air with its mechanical drone, we struck up a conversation with David. He shared stories of his time in the service, his favorite foods, and his upcoming plans to expand his business in Phoenix, Arizona. My wife and I listened intently, grateful not only for his mechanical assistance but also for the unexpected camaraderie in the midst of our automotive troubles.

Before long, our Hyundai was roadworthy once more, thanks to David's timely intervention. We thanked him profusely, expressing our gratitude for his kindness and assistance. With a nod and a wave, David bid us farewell, his figure receding into the shimmering heat waves of the parking lot.

As we drove away, the cool air conditioning offering relief from the oppressive heat, my wife and I reflected on the encounter. "That was truly a kind gesture," she remarked, her voice filled with appreciation. I nodded in agreement, touched by the reminder that in a world often plagued by cynicism and division, there are still good people like David Grospitch—individuals who restore our faith in humanity with simple acts of kindness and compassion.

A week later, to our surprise, David followed up with a call. "Hey, just wanted to check in and see if everything is going okay with the car," he said warmly. His concern wasn't just a fleeting moment of generosity; it was genuine care. My wife and I were touched once again by his thoughtfulness. We assured him that everything was fine and thanked him once more for his help. David's follow-up reinforced our belief that there are still people who go above and beyond to help others, making the world a better place one kind act at a time.

A MEETING WITH THE ENEMIES

It was in the evening in Riverspring, and the air was heavy with the scent of jasmine from the garden. The living room was filled with the warm glow of a single lamp. Jerry Thao, a young man in his early twenties with his father's sharp features and inquisitive eyes, walked in with a puzzled expression. In his hand, he held a weathered envelope.

"Dad, somebody sent you a letter from Vietnam. Do you know this person?" Jerry asked, handing the envelope to his father, Paul Thao.

Paul, a man in his sixties with a face etched by years of hardship and experience, took the letter. He felt a chill run down his spine as he recognized the familiar, flowing script of the Hmong language. "Let me see," he said, his voice steady but tinged with curiosity and apprehension.

Paul unfolded the letter and began to read silently. His eyes moved quickly across the lines, his expression shifting from surprise to deep contemplation. Jerry watched his father anxiously, noting the change in his demeanor.

"What does the letter say, Dad?" Jerry asked, unable to contain his curiosity.

Paul took a deep breath and looked at his son. "The letter says I'm invited to go to Vietnam to meet with the people who captured and tortured me during the Vietnam War," he said slowly as if testing the weight of each word.

Jerry's eyes widened in disbelief. "Dad, are you serious? That letter legit, not a joke?" he asked, his voice rising in concern.

"I don't think so because I know this person," Paul replied, his voice calm but firm.

"Who's he?" Jerry inquired, leaning forward in his chair.

"Well, he's the guy who put me in prison and let his men torture me," Paul answered, his gaze distant as if recalling painful memories.

"Why, then, do they want you to go back to Vietnam after 40 years?" Jerry asked, his confusion evident.

"The letter says they're all Christians now, and they want me to come back for a reunion," Paul explained, his voice softening.

"It's not a good idea," Jerry protested, shaking his head. "It could be a trap or some kind of cruel joke."

Paul placed a reassuring hand on his son's shoulder. "I understand your concern, Jerry. But sometimes, facing our past can bring closure. I need to do this for myself."

Despite Jerry's protests, Paul accepted the invitation. The weeks leading up to his departure were filled with preparations and moments of reflection. Finally, in August 2012, Paul boarded a plane to Vietnam, his heart a mix of apprehension and hope.

The journey was long, but Paul's determination never wavered. As he stepped off the plane in Vietnam, he was greeted by a group of men who had aged just like him. They looked at him with a mix of guilt and anticipation.

"Paul, we are so glad you came," said Tran, the man who had once been his captor. His voice was filled with sincerity and regret.

The village welcomed Paul with a ceremony. They killed cows as a gesture of honor and respect, a stark contrast to the brutality he had once faced. Sitting around a fire, Tran and the others began to speak, their voices trembling with emotion.

"Paul, we are truly sorry for what we did to you," Tran confessed, his eyes brimming with tears. "We were lost back then, driven by orders and fear. But we have changed. We have found faith and humanity. Can you find it in your heart to forgive us?"

Paul listened, his own eyes wet with unshed tears. The memories of torture and pain resurfaced, but he also saw the genuine remorse in their eyes. "I forgive you," he said, his voice breaking. "We were all victims of that war."

The days that followed were filled with stories, laughter, and shared meals. Paul and his former enemies bonded over their shared humanity, bridging a gap that had once seemed impossible. They prayed together, finding solace in their shared faith.

When Paul returned to the United States, he felt a profound sense of peace. The long-held scar on his heart had begun to heal. He had faced his past, forgiven his tormentors, and, in doing so, found a new sense of freedom.

Jerry met him at the airport, his face filled with concern and curiosity. "Dad, how was it?" he asked, helping his father with his bags.

"It was...incredible," Paul replied, a serene smile on his face. "I feel like a weight has been lifted off my shoulders. Forgiveness is powerful, Jerry. It's never too late to make peace with the past."

Jerry hugged his father tightly, feeling a newfound respect for the man who had taught him the true meaning of forgiveness and courage. Together, they walked out of the airport, ready to embrace the future with open hearts.

CHAPTER FIFTEEN

AN ATHEIST IS SOMEONE WHO THINKS
ABOUT GOD ALL DAY LONG.

ECHOES OF LOVE

In a small, serene town, the late afternoon sun cast long shadows over a quiet graveyard. The air was thick with the smell of freshly cut grass and the distant sound of birds chirping. Jane, a 64-year-old widow, stood alone by her husband's grave, the weight of his absence pressing down on her heart. She had spent countless afternoons here, seeking solace in the memories that haunted her.

In the warm glow of a summer morning, Jane sat in her living room, a place that had once been filled with laughter and life. Now, it was a sanctuary of memories. The walls were adorned with old photographs capturing moments of joy with her late husband. Clutching a picture frame of her husband, Jane gazed out the window, her eyes reflecting a deep, unending sorrow.

"How did I get here?" she whispered to herself, her voice barely audible in the stillness of the room.

The day wore on, and Jane's granddaughter, Sarah, arrived, her face etched with worry. She held her 5-year-old son, Mike, by the hand as they walked up the path to Jane's front yard.

"Grandma," Sarah said, her voice tinged with urgency, "can you watch Mike for a while? I have an urgent appointment."

Jane's face softened as she looked at her great-grandson. "Of course, sweetheart. I'd love to," she replied, forcing a smile.

Jane and Mike sat on the floor inside the house, surrounded by a sea of colorful toys. With his boundless energy, Mike picked up a toy phone and began playing.

"Ring, ring! Hello?" he said, mimicking an adult's voice.

Suddenly, the toy phone emitted a ring, startling both of them. Mike answered it, his eyes widening with excitement.

"Hi, Grandpa!" he exclaimed, his voice filled with joy.

Jane's heart skipped a beat. She snatched the phone from Mike, her hands trembling. "It can't be..." she muttered, staring at the toy.

"Who is this?" she demanded, her voice shaking.

"It's me, Jane. I miss you," came the soft, familiar voice from the toy phone.

Tears streamed down Jane's face as she clutched the phone. "Stop this, please. It's not funny," she pleaded, her voice breaking.

"I want to come home," the voice said, filled with longing.

A week later, Jane was babysitting Mike again. The scene was eerily similar. They were sitting on the floor, toys scattered around them.

"Ring, ring! Hello?" Mike said, holding the toy phone once more.

Again, the phone rang, and Mike answered with the same wide-eyed excitement. "Hi, Grandpa, where are you?"

Jane's face turned ashen. She grabbed the phone, her hands shaking even more than before. "It can't be... he's dead," she thought, her mind racing.

"Who is this, really? Why are you doing this?" she asked, her voice trembling with fear and desperation.

"It's me, Jane. I miss you," the voice repeated.

Jane's tears flowed freely. "Stop this, please. It's not funny. I'm going to call the police," she threatened, her voice a mix of anger and sorrow.

"I want to come home," the voice said softly.

Jane's face grew pale. "But how? You're dead. How are you going to come home?" she asked, her heart pounding in her chest.

"I'm outside. Please open the door," the voice replied.

With a mixture of fear and hope, Jane slowly opened the front door. Her heart raced as she peered outside. To her shock, her husband stood there, smiling as if nothing had changed.

Jane's legs gave out from under her, and she collapsed, fainting on the spot.

Jane awoke in her bedroom, her breathing heavy and her body drenched in sweat. Sarah was by her side, her face full of concern.

"Grandma? Grandma, are you alright? Wake up! You were having a dream. You're safe now," Sarah said, her voice soothing.

Jane's breathing gradually calmed, and she clutched her husband's picture frame tightly to her chest, her mind a whirlwind of emotions.

The next day, Jane felt a strong urge to visit her husband's grave. She drove to the cemetery, the road a blur as she navigated through her thoughts. Upon arriving, she placed fresh flowers on his grave, a silent prayer escaping her lips.

As she stood there, lost in contemplation, an electrical wire from a nearby pole snapped and fell, landing on her husband's grave. The wire sparked and sizzled, sending a shiver down Jane's spine.

She gasped, her heart pounding as a chill ran through her body. The eerie event left her shaken, but it also brought a strange sense of closure. Perhaps it was her husband's way of saying goodbye.

From that day forward, Jane stopped yearning for the impossible. She realized that her husband would always be with her, not in haunting phone calls or spectral visions, but in the cherished memories and the love they had shared. The echoes of their love would forever resonate in her heart, guiding her through the twilight of her years.

THE AWAKENING

Anna awoke in her dimly lit, cluttered apartment. The room was silent, except for the faintest noise that had disturbed her sleep. She pulled the blankets tighter around herself, reluctant to leave the warmth of her bed. Yet, curiosity tugged at her, pulling her out of the cocoon she had built. Rubbing her eyes, she listened intently, trying to make sense of the distant footsteps echoing in the hallway.

"What's going on?" she whispered to herself, her voice barely audible.

As she sat up, the hallway outside her bedroom door came alive with activity. Muffled voices, children's laughter, and the clinking of kitchenware filled the air. Her eyes widened in surprise. She slipped out of bed and quietly opened her bedroom door, her heart pounding in her chest.

The hallway was a whirlwind of life. Children ran past, playing games, while adults chatted animatedly. The aroma of cooking wafted from the kitchen, filling her with a sense of warmth and homeliness that had been absent for so long.

"Who are these people?" she murmured, inching closer to the kitchen.

She peeked into the bustling kitchen but saw no one. Chairs moved on their own, curtains fluttered without a breeze, and the faucet turned on and off as if controlled by an invisible hand. Anna's mind raced.

"This can't be real," she whispered, her voice trembling with fear and confusion.

Drawn by the sound of running water, she cautiously made her way to the bathroom. Steam filled the room, the shower running full blast, yet again, she found no one. Her reflection in the mirror was pale and almost translucent.

"What's happening to me?" she whispered, her voice echoing in the empty bathroom.

Bewildered, Anna wandered into the living room. Her gaze fell upon the walls adorned with picture frames she didn't recognize. She examined them closely, her fingers tracing the images of a happy family, strangers who seemed to have taken over her home.

"Where did these come from? Who are these people? Why are their pictures in my apartment?" she questioned aloud, her confusion growing with each passing second.

A chilling realization began to dawn upon her as she explored the apartment. In the children's room, toys were scattered about. Closets were filled with clothes that weren't hers. Fresh groceries were neatly stacked in the kitchen. She stood before a mirror once more, staring at her reflection. This time, she saw the truth.

"I'm the ghost... I'm the one who doesn't belong here," she whispered, panic rising in her chest.

Memories flooded her mind – the loneliness, the isolation, the sense of drifting through life unnoticed. She realized that the apartment, once her sanctuary, now belonged to a living family. A family that had filled the space with love and laughter, a stark contrast to the solitude she had known.

Tears welled up in Anna's eyes as she stood in the living room. The family moved about, oblivious to her presence, their happiness palpable.

"I've been living in the past, as a shadow, while they've moved in and made it their home," she said sadly, tears streaming down her face.

As night fell, Anna sat in the corner of the living room, watching the family eat dinner together. They couldn't see her, but she felt a sense of peace wash over her. Her once-empty apartment was now filled with life and love, a home for a family who needed it.

For the first time in a long while, Anna smiled. She had found her purpose in their happiness, content to be a silent guardian of the joy that now filled her old home. She watched them live, cherishing the life she saw before her, knowing she had played a part in making the apartment a home once more.

In the quiet of the night, as the family settled into their routines, Anna's presence faded. She had found peace in the realization that life had moved on, and so could she. The ghostly figure that had once haunted the lonely apartment was no more, replaced by the spirit of a woman who had finally found her place in the world, even if it was just as a silent observer of the life she had left behind.

THE DRIFTER'S ENCOUNTER

Once upon a time, on a lonely country road, a young man named Theo found himself stranded. His car, an old relic that had seen better days, sat with steam rising from its hood. Theo, disheveled and frustrated, paced back and forth, feeling the weight of his troubles bearing down on him.

As the sun hung high in the sky, casting long shadows on the deserted road, a weathered drifter named Joshua appeared in the distance. With a well-worn backpack slung over his shoulder, Joshua walked along the opposite side of the road. He noticed Theo's plight and paused, observing him for a moment before deciding to cross the road.

"Seems like you could use a hand. Car trouble?" Joshua asked softly as he approached Theo.

Theo, a mix of surprise and relief washing over his face, nodded. "Yeah, broke down. Can't afford to fix it now," he said, his voice tinged with defeat.

Joshua set down his backpack and peered under the car's hood. "I might be able to help. Let's see what we can do," he said with a reassuring smile.

Together, they worked on the car, their hands getting greasy as they tinkered with the engine. As they labored, they began to talk.

"I'm Theo, by the way. Thanks for stopping to help," Theo said, slightly awkward but grateful.

"No problem, Theo. I'm Joshua. Nice to meet you," Joshua replied warmly.

As the minutes turned into hours, Theo grew more comfortable with Joshua's presence. There was something calming about the drifter, a quiet wisdom that put Theo at ease.

"Joshua, you seem like a wise man. Can I ask you something personal?" Theo asked hesitantly.

"Of course, Theo. You can ask me anything," Joshua responded sincerely.

Theo took a deep breath, gathering his courage. "I'm going through a really tough time. My marriage fell apart, and I'm drowning in financial difficulties. It feels like my life is falling apart, and I can't see a way out. Sometimes... I even think about ending it all," he confessed, his voice cracking with emotion.

Joshua's expression softened, and he placed a comforting hand on Theo's shoulder. "Theo, I'm sorry to hear about your struggles. Life can be incredibly hard, and it's not uncommon to feel overwhelmed. But I want you to know that there's always hope, even in the darkest times. You don't have to face this alone," he said gently.

Tears welled up in Theo's eyes, and he wiped them away with his sleeve. "It's just... I've been carrying this burden all by myself. I haven't told anyone, not even my closest friends or family. I'm ashamed, and I don't want them to see me like this," he admitted, his voice trembling.

Joshua's voice was filled with compassion as he spoke. "Sometimes, sharing our pain and vulnerability with others can be a source of strength, not weakness. It takes courage to open up, but it can also bring healing and support. You don't have to bear this alone, Theo. There are people who care about you and want to help," he said.

Theo's shoulders slumped, and he looked down at the ground. "I'm afraid... afraid of being judged, of being seen as a failure," he whispered.

"Theo, we all stumble and face hardships in life. It doesn't make you a failure. It makes you human. And sometimes, our most significant growth comes from our darkest moments. It's how we rise from the ashes that defines us," Joshua said with empathy.

Theo lifted his gaze, meeting Joshua's eyes. "But how do I find the strength to keep going? How do I overcome these overwhelming circumstances?" he asked, his voice filled with desperation.

Joshua smiled warmly, his eyes filled with compassion. "Theo, the strength you seek comes from within, but it's also found in the connections we make with others. It's in the love and support we give and receive. Remember that you are not alone, and there is a greater purpose to your life. Have faith, and the path will become clearer," he said.

Theo took a moment to absorb Joshua's words, a glimmer of hope beginning to emerge. "Thank you, Joshua. You've given me a lot to think about. I don't know if I believe in God, but talking to you... it feels like there's something more out there," he said, his voice barely above a whisper.

Joshua smiled. "Theo, whether you believe or not, the kingdom of God is within you. It's not confined to the walls of any church or temple. It's in the love, compassion, and kindness we show one another. Embrace the journey, and you might find the answers you seek," he said.

They shared a moment of quiet reflection before Joshua resumed working on the car, Theo now helping him with renewed determination. Though Theo's life remained uncertain, a glimmer of hope had begun to shine through the clouds of his despair. With Joshua's words echoing in his mind, Theo knew he had the strength to keep moving forward, one step at a time. And so, on that lonely country road, under the vast expanse of the sky, a journey of healing and hope began.

A CHANGE OF HEART

Jake stared out the window of his high-rise apartment, sipping his morning coffee. The city below was a symphony of movement and noise, a stark contrast to his silent, solitary existence. His eyes followed a familiar figure—John, a homeless man—making his daily rounds through the neighborhood. Jake's face twisted in irritation.

Jake, dressed in a tailored suit, marched out of his pristine home, coffee cup in hand. He watched John sift through the trash bin near the curb. Jake's frustration simmered as he approached.

JAKE (agitated): Hey, you! I told you to stop coming around here.

John looked up, his eyes tired but calm. He nodded slightly and shuffled away without a word, clutching his gathered scraps.

Jake lay on his leather couch, the day's events playing on a loop in his mind. The incessant presence of John gnawed at him. He closed his eyes, hoping for peace, but his rest was short-lived. He jolted awake, chest tight, vision blurring. Panic set in as he struggled to breathe.

Stumbling out of his house, Jake gasped for air. His knees buckled, and he collapsed onto the dewy grass, darkness creeping into his vision.

Jake awoke in a dimly lit hospital room, the beeping of monitors filling the air. His body ached, and he turned his head to see John sitting nearby, exhaustion etched on his face.

JAKE (weakly): What... happened?

NURSE: You had a heart attack right outside your house. This man here, John, found you and gave you CPR. He saved your life.

Jake's eyes widened, guilt and gratitude swirling within him as he stared at John.

Jake and John sat on a weathered park bench, the morning sun casting long shadows. John looked cleaner and more at ease.

JAKE (apologetic): I owe you my life, John. I've been so selfish and judgmental.

JOHN (humble): We all make mistakes, sir.

The once immaculate living room now felt warmer, more lived-in. Jake led John inside, their roles no longer defined by wealth or status.

JAKE (earnest): You can stay here, John, for as long as you want.

John's eyes glistened with tears of gratitude. He nodded, words failing him.

Side by side, Jake and John worked tirelessly in the front yard. They planted vibrant flowers, turning the once sterile space into a welcoming garden.

Walking down the street together, Jake and John greeted neighbors who had previously been strangers. Their smiles were genuine, their connection undeniable.

Laughter filled the room as Jake, John, and a group of new friends shared stories and companionship. The walls echoed with a joy Jake had never known.

Jake's heart attack was more than a health scare—it was a revelation. He discovered that true wealth wasn't in his stocks or possessions but in the kindness and compassion he extended to others. Through John's selflessness, Jake found not only a friend but also a sense of purpose and community he had longed for.

A COMPLAINT LETTER

The sun began its slow ascent over the quiet suburban neighborhood, casting a warm, golden glow on the rows of neatly trimmed lawns and flower beds. The morning was serene, with birds chirping softly and the air filled with the scent of blooming flowers. Inside one of the modest houses, Joe, a middle-aged man with a perpetual look of weariness etched on his face, stood in his small, cluttered kitchen. His shoulders slumped as he moved around, cooking eggs in an old, scratched-up frying pan. The aroma of coffee filled the room, but a faint, acrid smell mingled with it.

Joe didn't notice the eggs beginning to burn, his thoughts consumed by the troubles that had plagued him recently. The sizzling sound grew louder, and the edges of the eggs turned an unappetizing shade of black.

"Why can't anything go right today?" he grumbled in frustration.

Rushing out of the kitchen, Joe headed to his garage, the smell of burnt eggs still lingering in the air. He grabbed his car keys from the hook by the door and hurried to his car, a reliable yet aging sedan. Sliding into the driver's seat, he inserted the key into the ignition and turned it. The engine sputtered and coughed but refused to start. Joe's face tightened with anxiety.

"Come on, not today!" he shouted, hitting the steering wheel in a fit of frustration. He tried again and again, each attempt more desperate than the last, but the car remained stubbornly silent.

After a long and arduous bus ride, Joe finally arrived at his office, disheveled and significantly late. The bustling office was filled with laughter and chatter. His coworkers gathered around a table adorned with balloons and a large cake. It was someone's birthday, and the celebration was in full swing. Joe approached the table, hoping to salvage a bit of joy from his morning. His eyes landed on the last piece of cake just as a colleague reached out and took it.

"Just my luck," Joe muttered, his shoulders sagging further in disappointment. He forced a smile and walked away, feeling the weight of the day's misfortunes pressing down on him.

As the sun dipped below the horizon, painting the sky with hues of orange and pink, Joe left work, his spirits still low. He got into his car, which had finally started after much coaxing, and pulled out onto the street. Almost immediately, he was greeted by a sea of red brake lights. Traffic was at a complete standstill. Joe let out a heavy sigh, his hands gripping the steering wheel tightly.

"Could this day get any worse?" he muttered to himself, the frustration evident in his voice.

The house was quiet as Joe sat at his small desk in the corner of his living room, a solitary lamp casting a warm pool of light. He picked up a pen and a piece of paper, his expression one of tired resignation. With a deep breath, he began to write a letter, pouring his heart out in a vent of frustration and despair.

"Dear God, today has been the worst day of my life..."

High above, in a realm beyond human comprehension, God, a celestial being with a benevolent smile and a twinkle of humor in His eyes, sat at His divine desk. The office was a magnificent space, filled with ethereal light and the soft hum of celestial energy. God received Joe's letter, its mortal paper seeming almost out of place in the divine surroundings. He opened it and read, His smile growing wider.

"Let's see what Joe has to say," God murmured to Himself, His voice a soothing melody.

Joe finished his letter with a flourish, sealing it in an envelope addressed to God. He walked to his mailbox, the night air cool against his skin, and dropped the letter in with a sense of finality. Returning to his house, he went to bed, the day's events playing over in his mind.

In the celestial mailroom, a place where mortal letters transformed into shimmering, divine scrolls, a POSTAL ANGEL, radiant and swift, picked up Joe's letter. With a burst of speed, the angel flew to God's office, the scroll glowing softly in the angel's hands.

God opened the letter and read it, chuckling softly. He felt Joe's frustration and decided it was time to shed some light on the day's events. Taking a golden quill, He began to write His response, the ink flowing like liquid light.

"Dear Joe,

I understand that you had a rough day today, but let me shed some light on what happened. In the morning, I made sure your eggs burned to slow you down and prevent you from being in a rush. I was protecting you from a potential accident with a drunk driver on your way to work.

At the office party, you didn't get a piece of cake because it was contaminated and would have made you sick. I saved you from an upset stomach and a trip to the doctor.

And as for the traffic on your way back home, I slowed it down because there was an accident ahead. I wanted to ensure you didn't get caught up in it and potentially injured.

So, Joe, while it might seem like a terrible day, it could have been far worse. Remember, I'm always looking out for you.

Yours sincerely,

God"

The first light of dawn filtered through the curtains as Joe woke up, feeling a sense of heaviness lifting from his heart. He noticed a letter on his desk and, with growing curiosity, picked it up. As he read God's response, amazement and gratitude filled his eyes. Tears welled up, and he whispered a heartfelt prayer of thanks.

"Thank you, God, for watching over me," Joe prayed, a smile breaking across his face for the first time in what felt like ages. He felt a renewed sense of hope, knowing that even in his darkest moments, he was never truly alone.

CHAPTER SIXTEEN

THE SAYING GOES,
"NEVER BE A PRISONER OF YOUR PAST.
IT WAS JUST A LESSON,
NOT A DEATH SENTENCE."

YEAH, SURE, BUT NOT WHEN IT COMES
TO A CRIMINAL RECORD.

LEE & YEE

Long ago and far away, in the secluded mountains of Laos, there lived two young lovers named Lee and Yee. The serene village of Paj Tawg Dawb was where Yee resided, a place surrounded by lush greenery and distant hills. Lee, a young man from a far-off village, had to traverse for a day and a half on foot, braving treacherous terrains and dangerous animals, to visit Yee. But no obstacle was too great for Lee, and the anticipation of seeing Yee spurred him on. Yee, equally eager, awaited his visits with bated breath. Their bond was unbreakable, sealed with a blood vow to remain together forever.

However, their families disapproved of their relationship. Lee was the village chief's son, destined for education in a distant town, while Yee was a farmer's daughter, expected to stay behind and work the land. On his last visit before leaving for school, Lee held Yee's hands tightly, his eyes filled with determination and sorrow.

"I have to go to school," Lee said softly. "I won't be able to come back until next summer. Please wait for me. Do not get married."

Yee's eyes glistened with tears as she replied, "Please don't be gone too long, Lee. I will miss you terribly. I want us to get married soon."

They embraced, the future uncertain but their love unwavering.

Months passed, and Yee received a letter from a courier. It bore bad news: there was a delay, and Lee wouldn't be able to visit for two years. Heartbroken but resolute, Yee decided to wait.

Two years later, Lee finally returned to Paj Tawg Dawb village. As he approached, a sense of foreboding crept over him. The once lively village was now overgrown with bushes and trees. The houses stood empty and neglected, except for Yee's home, which appeared well-maintained, with smoke curling from its chimney.

Lee knocked on Yee's door, and her familiar voice called from inside, "I'm home; please come in, Lee."

As Lee stepped into the house, a chill ran down his spine. Something about Yee was different; her once vibrant eyes were now hollow, her demeanor eerie. Trying to mask his unease, Lee asked, "Where is everyone? The village looks deserted."

"They're all attending the farm," Yee responded with a calm smile. "That's why the village is vacant."

Despite her explanation, Lee felt an overwhelming sense of dread. He needed to leave but couldn't find a way to excuse himself. Sensing his hesitation, Yee suggested, "If you need to go outside, I'll tie a rope around your waist so you don't run away. When you're done, I'll pull you back in."

Lee agreed reluctantly. Yee tied the rope securely, and he stepped outside, intending to escape. Mimicking the sound of urination, Lee hoped to buy some time. But Yee grew suspicious and tugged on the rope, only to find it tied to a pole. Furious, she stormed outside to find him.

Lee sprinted through the forest, but Yee, consumed by a malevolent force, caught up to him with terrifying speed. She grabbed his hands, her grip unnaturally strong. Lee struggled but was overpowered.

"Yee, please," Lee pleaded. "Let me go."

"No, Lee," she whispered with a haunting smile. "We will be together, as we promised. Love is forever."

Lee woke up abruptly, drenched in sweat and terror. Just as he thought he had had a nightmare, he felt someone lying next to him. He slowly turned to check the other side of his bed. There, lying beside him, was Yee, blue and cold, smiling at him as she reached her arm over him.

THE MIRACLE AT REFUGEE CAMP

In the heart of Ban Nam Yao, Thailand, a humble Refugee Camp bustled with life under the scorching early morning sun. Dust danced in the wind, swirling around the makeshift homes as Charles Cawv Thoj lay weak and bedridden in his modest abode. The sounds of bustling crowds and playful children outside his window seemed distant as illness gripped him tightly, wrapping him in an oppressive cocoon of suffering.

At just six or seven years old, Charles felt the weight of his failing body as malnutrition and starvation took their toll. His skin, once vibrant with the energy of youth, now hung loose and pallid over his frail bones. Weeks earlier, the camp hospital had given up hope, unable to offer further assistance with their limited resources. With each labored breath, Charles felt his spirit drifting towards the heavens, longing for the mother he barely remembered, her face a fading memory in the recesses of his mind.

Alone in his suffering, Charles lay gazing at the bamboo-stick roof above, his vision blurred by weakness. The rough texture of the thatch blurred into a hazy mosaic as tears welled up in his eyes. He whispered his mother's name, a quiet plea for comfort that seemed lost in the vastness of his despair. Then, as if in answer to his whispered prayer, the door creaked open, and a mysterious figure entered his dimly lit room.

The stranger moved with ethereal grace, their presence exuding a calm authority that immediately put Charles at ease. With gentle hands and a soothing voice, the stranger lifted Charles from his bed and bathed him with cool water, the liquid washing away not only the grime of his illness but also the layers of despair that clung to his frail form. Each splash of water seemed to carry with it a whisper of hope, a promise of relief from his suffering.

After cleansing his body, the stranger offered a meager meal of sticky rice and a fish named Pasthu. Despite his weakness, Charles felt a flicker of appetite stir within him. With great effort, he lifted the food to his mouth, the simple act of eating infusing him with newfound strength. The stranger watched with kind eyes, their presence a silent encouragement.

Once Charles had eaten, the stranger then administered acupuncture, guiding the flow of healing energy through Charles' ailing body from head to toe. Though small and thin, the needles seemed to carry a potent force with them, each prick sending a ripple of vitality through his limbs. Charles felt a warmth spread through him, a gentle glow that banished the cold grip of his illness.

As quickly as he had appeared, the stranger departed, leaving Charles to rest. The following day dawned bright and hopeful, the sunlight streaming through the gaps in the bamboo walls, casting patterns of light and shadow on the floor. Charles rose from his bed, his body renewed and energized. The transformation was so complete that it bordered on the miraculous. His aunt and uncle, Ntsuab Xwm, and the rest of his family could hardly believe their eyes, confusion and wonder mingling in their expressions.

Driven by gratitude and curiosity, they searched the camp, questioning every resident in a quest to uncover the identity of the enigmatic savior. Yet, no one could provide answers, leaving them to marvel at what seemed like a divine intervention beyond comprehension. They recounted the tale to anyone who would listen, each retelling adding to the growing legend of the mysterious healer.

In the wake of this inexplicable event, Charles' recovery stood as a testament to faith and resilience, a beacon of hope in a world touched by the hand of the miraculous. The story spread beyond the camp, carried on the lips of those who had witnessed the transformation. It became a symbol of the extraordinary power of compassion and grace, a reminder that even in the darkest moments, light can find a way to shine through.

And as whispers of the unknown benefactor echoed through the camp and beyond, one truth remained clear - sometimes, in the depths of despair, a miracle can manifest in the most unexpected ways, renewing the spirit and reaffirming the enduring power of human kindness. Now full of life and vigor, Charles stood as a living testament to this truth, his story inspiring all who heard it to believe in the possibility of the extraordinary.

VOLTAIRE'S PROPHECY: THE IRONY OF FATE

In the quiet town of Ferney in France, where the renowned philosopher Voltaire once resided, there was a sense of anticipation and intrigue in the air. It was the year 1976, precisely one hundred years since Voltaire had boldly proclaimed his prophecy about the fate of the Bible. The townspeople, curious and eager to witness the unfolding of history, gathered in the town square to reflect on the words of the great thinker.

As the day progressed, news spread like wildfire through the town. At the local bookstore, an elderly man named Pierre was arranging his display when a young boy burst in.

"Mr. Pierre!" gasped the boy, eyes wide with excitement. "Did you hear? A first edition of Voltaire's work is for sale!"

Pierre looked up, adjusting his glasses. "Really, Jacques? And how much are they asking for it?"

Jacques grinned. "Eleven cents!"

Pierre chuckled, shaking his head. "Ah, the irony. Voltaire would have something to say about this."

Meanwhile, across the English Channel, another remarkable event was taking place in bustling Paris. In a grand office, two

British officials, Mr. Thompson and Ms. Hamilton, were finalizing a significant purchase.

"This Codex Sinaiticus," said Ms. Hamilton, admiring the ancient manuscript, "is a true treasure."

Mr. Thompson nodded. "Indeed, and for $500,000, it's worth every penny. The historical and religious value is immeasurable."

Back in Ferney, the townspeople gathered in the square, discussing the unexpected turn of events. Old Madame Dupont shook her head in disbelief.

"Imagine that," she said to her friend, Henri. "Voltaire's work for eleven cents and the Bible for half a million dollars!"

Henri laughed, his eyes twinkling with amusement. "Fate has a sense of humor, it seems."

As whispers of Voltaire's prophecy and the unexpected events spread through the streets of Ferney and beyond, a sense of irony and wonder filled the hearts of the townspeople. In the years that followed, the Geneva Bible Society saw an opportunity.

One bright morning, a group of workers from the Society arrived in Ferney, led by a determined woman named Claire.

"Let's set up the press here," Claire instructed. "Voltaire's former home is the perfect place to produce our Bibles."

Pierre, watching from his bookstore, approached Claire. "Need any help?" he asked with a smile.

Claire nodded. "We could always use another pair of hands."

And so, the press started churning out stacks of Bibles to eager readers around the world. The irony of the situation was not lost on those who witnessed the events unfold. Voltaire's legacy and the enduring nature of the Bible became intertwined in a fascinating tale of irony and resilience.

One evening, as the sun set over Ferney, Pierre stood outside his bookstore, looking at the bustling activity around Voltaire's former home. He turned to Jacques, who was sweeping the steps.

"Funny how things turn out, isn't it?" Pierre mused.

Jacques nodded thoughtfully. "Voltaire would never have believed it."

Pierre smiled. "No, he wouldn't. But that's the beauty of history, my boy. It's full of surprises."

In the quiet town of Ferney, where history had taken a different turn from what Voltaire had envisioned, the words of the philosopher lingered in the air like a faint whisper. They served as a reminder of the unpredictable nature of fate and the enduring power of beliefs and ideas across the centuries.

ONENESS

Jonathan was a man of routine, his days meticulously planned and executed with precision. He had always been a perfectionist, finding comfort in the predictability of his surroundings. His colleagues often joked that he would prefer a world where everyone was just like him.

One evening, after a particularly frustrating day at work, Jonathan found himself embroiled in a heated argument with his coworker, Sarah.

"Why can't you just follow the procedure, Sarah?" Jonathan snapped, his face flushed with frustration.

"Because, Jonathan," Sarah retorted, her voice rising, "sometimes the procedure doesn't make sense for every situation. We need flexibility to adapt!"

Jonathan shook his head, exasperated. "Flexibility? That's just an excuse for being sloppy. If everyone did things my way, we'd have consistency and order."

Sarah crossed her arms, her eyes narrowing. "Your way? You mean the way that stifles creativity and ignores individual strengths? Not everyone thinks like you, Jonathan. And that's a good thing."

Jonathan scoffed, "Oh, please. If only everyone could see things the way I do, the world would be a better place."

Their argument ended on a sour note, and Jonathan spent the evening alone in his dimly lit apartment, brooding over his desire for sameness.

The next morning, Jonathan awoke to an eerie silence. The usually bustling streets were deserted, and a sense of unease settled in his chest. "What's going on? Where is everyone?" he called out, his voice echoing off the empty buildings.

As he wandered the empty city, Jonathan's initial excitement at being alone soon gave way to loneliness and longing. "I never realized how much I took other people for granted," he whispered to himself, the emptiness of the world weighing heavily on his shoulders.

Days turned into weeks, and Jonathan found himself talking to himself more and more, the sound of his own voice the only company he had. "I miss the sound of laughter, the warmth of friendship," he mused, his words lost in the vast emptiness around him.

One day, as he sat in the abandoned park, Jonathan looked up at the empty sky and spoke aloud, "I wish I could go back. I wish I could appreciate the diversity and uniqueness of others."

Abruptly, he awoke from his dream, relief flooding through him as he realized it had all been a figment of his imagination.

Grateful for the lesson he had learned, Jonathan sought out Sarah, eager to reconnect and embrace the differences that made each person special.

"Sarah," he began, his voice earnest, "I see now that it is our diversity that makes us strong, that challenges us to grow. I'm sorry for what I said."

Sarah smiled, her stance softening. "I'm glad you see it that way, Jonathan. It's our unique perspectives that make us a better team."

As Jonathan stood among his friends and colleagues, laughing and talking, he knew that he had found something far more valuable than a world of sameness - he had found a world of connection, of acceptance, and of love. And in that moment, he realized lthat he wouldn't have it any other way.

That same afternoon, Jonathan was driving in busy traffic when a vehicle cut him off and sped away, the driver raising a middle finger at him.

THE SLEEP PRESCRIPTION

Fred had always been a bit of an insomniac. His brain refused to shut down at night, continuously replaying the day's events like a broken record. One night, as Fred stared at the ceiling at 3 AM, he decided enough was enough. The next morning, bleary-eyed and disheveled, Fred marched to his family friend, Dr. Dee.

Dr. Dee had known Fred since he was a child. She was more than a doctor to him; she was like an eccentric aunt who occasionally handed out medical advice along with cookies and a good scolding. When Fred shuffled into her office, Dr. Dee was sitting behind her desk, a steaming cup of herbal tea in hand.

"Fred, my boy! You look like you've been run over by a bus," she exclaimed, pushing her spectacles up her nose.

"I feel worse, Dr. Dee," Fred groaned. "I can't sleep. I need something—anything—to help me fall asleep.

Dr. Dee leaned back in her chair, her eyes twinkling with mischief. "Well, Fred, I've got just the thing for you." She rummaged through her desk drawer, pulling out a prescription pad. Fred's hopes soared, expecting a magical sleep-inducing pill that would finally grant him some sweet, uninterrupted sleep.

Instead, Dr. Dee handed him the prescription, a sly smile playing on her lips. Fred read it aloud, "'Go to Mardel's and buy a Bible. Read it, and it will help you fall asleep.'"

Fred blinked. "A Bible? You want me to read a Bible to fall asleep?"

Dr. Dee nodded sagely. "Trust me, Fred. Nothing puts you to sleep faster than a good dose of Leviticus."

Confused but desperate, Fred decided to follow the unconventional advice. He went to Mardel's, a local Christian bookstore, and bought a Bible. That night, he opened it up and started reading.

At first, he was intrigued by the dramatic stories of Genesis. But as he made his way to the detailed descriptions in Leviticus, his eyelids grew heavier. By the time he reached the fifth chapter, he was snoring loudly, the Bible slipping from his hands and landing softly on his chest.

The next morning, Fred awoke feeling surprisingly refreshed. For the first time in weeks, he had slept through the night. Elated, he decided to call Dr. Dee and thank her.

"Dr. Dee, you were right! Reading the Bible really put me to sleep," Fred said excitedly.

Dr. Dee chuckled on the other end of the line. "I knew it would, Fred. It's the original bedtime story. Now, if you start getting too invested in it and it keeps you awake, you can switch to reading my medical journals. Those are guaranteed to knock you out cold."

From then on, Fred kept the Bible on his nightstand. Whenever he struggled to sleep, he'd open it up and let the ancient texts lull him into slumber. And occasionally, when the Bible wasn't quite doing the trick, he'd borrow a few of Dr. Dee's medical journals, marveling at how something so dry could be so effective.

Fred's friends soon noticed his improved mood and energy. When they asked him what his secret was, he'd grin and say, "I owe it all to Dr. Dee and a little help from the Good Book. Who knew a prescription for sleep would come with such divine intervention?"

Fred became somewhat a local legend, the guy who beat insomnia with a Bible. And every time he saw Dr. Dee, she'd give him a knowing wink, reminding him that sometimes the best medicine comes in the most unexpected forms.

CHAPTER SEVENTEEN
"100 IS THE TEMPERATURE, NOT THE SPEED LIMIT," SAID THE STATE TROOPER TO A MOTORIST.

GOD IS NOT FAIR!

Bob felt utterly dejected as he trudged his way to the local church. He felt like he was carrying the weight of the world on his shoulders. His beloved girlfriend had left him for another man, and he couldn't understand why this had happened to him. "God is not fair," he muttered under his breath.

Upon reaching the church, Bob made a beeline for Pastor Johnson, who was busy attending to some paperwork at his desk. Clearing his throat, Bob said, "Pastor Johnson, I need to talk to you. I think God is not fair."

The pastor looked up, concern etched on his face. "Why do you think that, Bob? Please, have a seat and tell me what's on your mind."

Bob slumped into a chair and poured out his heart to the pastor. "I've been a faithful Christian, attending church every Sunday, praying regularly. And yet, my girlfriend chose to leave me for someone else. It's just not fair!"

Listening attentively, Pastor Johnson pondered for a moment before suggesting, "Bob, how about we pray together and ask God to be fair to you? Maybe there's a lesson in this that we can uncover through prayer. What do you think?"

Bob nodded hesitantly, willing to try anything to ease the pain in his heart. "Alright, Pastor. Let's pray and ask God to be fair to me."

With heads bowed and hands clasped together, Pastor Johnson led the prayer. "Dear God, we humbly ask for fairness in Bob's life. Help him understand your plans and find peace in your wisdom."

As the prayer concluded, a sudden realization dawned on Pastor Johnson. "Bob, I believe God has heard our prayer for fairness."

Excitedly, Bob looked up, hoping for a sign of divine intervention. "What is it, Pastor? What did God say?"

With a chuckle, Pastor Johnson replied, "God has answered our prayer, Bob. He has decided to make things fair by giving you... gout."

Bob's eyes widened in disbelief. "Gout? But why?"

The pastor grinned mischievously. "It's not fair that only I have gout, Bob. We should all share the gout, don't you think? Be careful what you ask for, my friend. Sometimes, the answer might surprise you."

"No, no," Bob exclaimed. "I don't want to share your gout. Please ask God not to give it to me."

"Well then, shall we ask God not to be fair again?" the pastor asked.

"Yes," Bob agreed.

So, they prayed again. Now Bob has a toothache.

GOD DOES ANSWER PRAYERS

Once upon a time, in the bustling town of Willow Creek, there lived a man named Tommy Lo. Tommy was a successful entrepreneur who had built a thriving business empire from the ground up. However, despite his financial success, Tommy had a secret struggle that weighed heavily on his heart.

You see, Tommy was a devout member of the local church, and he believed in the importance of tithing to support the work of God. But as his business flourished, so did his income, and the thought of tithing a significant portion of his earnings made him uneasy. The more money he made, the harder it became for him to part with a tenth of it as an offering to the church.

One Sunday morning, Tommy mustered up the courage to seek guidance from his pastor, the wise and kind-hearted John Hawj. He poured out his heart to Pastor John, confessing his struggles with tithing and his guilt for not being able to commit fully to it.

Pastor John listened intently to Tommy's dilemma and offered a compassionate smile. "Tommy, I understand your concerns, but remember that God loves a cheerful giver. Let's pray together and ask for His help in overcoming these challenges."

Tommy nodded in agreement, his heart heavy with guilt and uncertainty. "Yes, Pastor John, I would like to ask God for help so I can overcome this guilt and tithe faithfully."

With heads bowed and hands joined, Pastor John prayed fervently for Tommy, asking for God's guidance and wisdom to help him become a faithful giver despite his struggles.

Not long after that heartfelt prayer, a series of unexpected events unfolded in Tommy's life. His business, once thriving, was forced to downsize and restructure the workforce to save the company from bankruptcy. Tommy found himself facing financial uncertainty and the loss of his big income.

Shocked and dismayed by the sudden turn of events, Tommy couldn't help but reflect on the prayer he had shared with Pastor John. "Yes, please ask God for help so I can overcome this feeling and tithe faithfully," he realized with a mix of awe and amusement.

Despite the challenges he faced, Tommy found a silver lining in the midst of adversity. He learned a valuable lesson about faith, trust, and the mysterious ways in which God works. With newfound humility and gratitude, Tommy stood before the congregation and testified about his journey of struggle, prayer, and unexpected blessings. God does answer prayers.

THE PROOF

In the bustling city of New York, Sawn Chang, a pastor's kid and a staunch atheist, stumbled upon an intriguing advertisement that sparked his curiosity. The ad beckoned all atheists to a symposium where they could present arguments to prove the non-existence of God. The prize? A hefty sum of 1 million dollars. With an unwavering belief in his convictions, Sawn saw this as an opportunity to showcase his atheistic beliefs to the world.

Eager and self-assured, Sawn applied and was promptly accepted as a panelist for the symposium. As the event date drew near, he immersed himself in research and preparation, confident that he would emerge victorious and claim the coveted prize. The prospect of proving his atheistic stance in front of a large audience, with the media in attendance, filled him with excitement.

When the day of the symposium finally arrived, Sawn entered the conference venue with anticipation, only to find himself standing alone among the empty seats designated for fellow atheists. Disappointment washed over him as he realized that no one else had shown up to defend their beliefs.

The panel judges greeted him, saying, "Welcome, Sawn. It seems all the other atheists who applied have backed out. You're the only one here. Thank you for coming."

As the media cameras focused on him, eager to witness his proof, Sawn felt the weight of the moment pressing down on him. The pressure to deliver a compelling argument against the existence of God loomed large. However, to his dismay, he found himself at a loss for words, unable to provide concrete evidence to support his claims.

"I cannot prove God does not exist; it's only a theory," Sawn admitted, his voice tinged with defeat.

The chair of the symposium, a stern figure, addressed Sawn, offering him a lifeline. "You still keep the 1 million dollars as long as you acknowledge the uncertainty of your theory."

Sawn, recognizing the flaws in his argument, conceded, acknowledging that his theory could indeed be fallible. However, his admission proved to be his undoing as the chair reminded him of the contractual obligation to provide proof. With a heavy heart, Sawn watched as the promised prize slipped through his fingers, lost due to a breach of contract.

As he left the symposium, Sawn was left to ponder the weight of his beliefs and the consequences of his overconfidence. The experience served as a humbling lesson, teaching him that certainty in the absence of proof could be a dangerous gamble. And so, with newfound humility, Sawn embarked on a journey of introspection, reevaluating his convictions and the question of the existence of God.

That was then. Today, Shawn is a guest Bible professor at a university and a pastor in New York.

A MIDNIGHT DRIVE: AN IMMIGRANT'S FIRST CAR ADVENTURE

In the fall of 1979, in the month of August, in Wheaton, Illinois. Winter was just around the corner. Only months after arriving in the United States, Nzer bought his first vehicle, a light blue Chevrolet Caprice. Nzer and his cousin, Yae, were thrilled. They had never imagined they would own a car.

"Can you believe we own a car?" Nzer marveled, running his hand over the hood of the Caprice.

"I know! It's like a dream," Yae replied, his eyes sparkling with excitement.

Armed with only a learner's permit, they thought it would be fun to test drive the vehicle at night when everyone was asleep and the streets were empty. They waited until midnight. Their young nephew, Charles, sat in the back seat, eager to join the adventure.

"This is going to be so much fun!" Charles exclaimed.

"Yes, but we must be very careful," Nzer reminded him, trying to conceal his nervousness.

At 11 p.m., close to midnight, they found what seemed to be the perfect spot: a large, illuminated, and vacant parking lot in downtown Wheaton. They drove around in circles, laughing and enjoying the ride.

"This is perfect, Nzer! We have the whole place to ourselves," Yae said as he took his turn behind the wheel.

But suddenly, after about ten minutes of their joyride, two police cars appeared and started tailing them.

"Oh no, Nzer, what do we do?" Yae whispered, his hands tightening on the steering wheel.

"Stay calm, Yae. I'll handle this," Nzer replied, though his own heart was pounding.

The police officers approached and asked them what they were doing.

"We... uh... just driving," Nzer stammered, his English faltering under the pressure.

Sensing their confusion, the officers asked them to step out of the car, including young Charles.

"Please step out of the vehicle," one officer said firmly.

"What's happening, Uncle?" Charles asked, his voice trembling.

"It's okay, Charles. Just do as they say," Nzer reassured him, trying to stay calm.

The police escorted them to the station, which was only a few feet away. The officers suspected that they didn't know what they were doing and quickly realized they were newly arrived immigrants.

At the station, the police called Xeng Djoua Xiong, a community leader who could help. Xeng arrived at 3:00 a.m. and spoke with the officers.

"Thank you for coming, Mr. Xiong," one officer said. "We found them driving around the parking lot. They didn't seem to understand where they were."

Xeng nodded and turned to Nzer and Yae. "You were driving in the county police station's parking lot. It was vacant because all the employees had left for the day, and only a few shift workers were present."

Nzer and Yae looked at each other, feeling both foolish and embarrassed.

"We thought we found a good spot to practice," Nzer explained sheepishly.

"It's kind of funny when you think about it," Xeng chuckled. "But yes, you were trespassing on police property."

Yae sighed. "We just wanted to learn how to drive without bothering anyone."

"I understand," Xeng said kindly. "But next time, let's find a proper place."

As they drove home, Nzer and Yae couldn't help but laugh at their mistake despite their embarrassment.

"When you think about it, it's kind of funny," Yae said, smiling.

"Yes, but also a little sad," Nzer agreed. "At least we have a story to tell."

And with that, they drove home, wiser and ready for their next adventure in their new country.

THE APPLE

A quaint college known for its rigorous science programs stood in the small town of Pinewood, nestled among rolling hills and dense forests. Among the faculty was a distinguished professor renowned in the scientific community for his expertise on quercetin—a powerful antioxidant found in apples. His knowledge of quercetin was unrivaled, earning him accolades and admiration from scientists and students alike.

One crisp autumn Monday, the air was filled with anticipation as students filed into the lecture hall. The room buzzed with excitement; the students felt fortunate to be in the presence of such an esteemed scholar. Whispers of admiration floated through the room as they settled into their seats.

"I heard the professor is going to reveal some new findings about quercetin today," one student whispered to another.

"Yeah, he's a genius! We're so lucky to have him," another replied.

The professor stepped to the front of the room, his presence commanding attention. His lecture began smoothly, his passion for the subject evident in every word. But as he delved into the intricate science behind quercetin, a soft but persistent crunching sound interrupted the flow of his speech. He paused, scanning the room to find the source of the distraction.

A student was nonchalantly eating an apple in the front row, the crunch echoing through the silent hall. The professor's irritation was palpable, but he maintained his composure.

"Excuse me," he said, his voice steady but firm. "Could you please refrain from eating during my lecture? It's quite distracting."

The student looked up, unfazed, and swallowed his bite. "I apologize, Professor. I just couldn't resist. Apples are delicious, you know."

The professor raised an eyebrow. "I've heard you've never eaten an apple in your life, Professor. Is that true?"

The room went silent, all eyes now on the professor. He hesitated, caught off guard by the question. "I cannot say that I have. But what relevance does that have to today's lecture?"

The student smiled, a mischievous glint in his eye. "Well, it's just that you're an expert on quercetin, which is a major component in apples. Isn't it a bit ironic that you've never tasted one?"

A murmur of agreement rippled through the room. The professor felt a slight sting of embarrassment but maintained his calm demeanor. "No, I don't find it ironic. My expertise lies in the chemical properties and health benefits of quercetin, not in the taste of apples."

The student leaned forward, his voice carrying a hint of challenge. "But don't you think that by never eating an apple, you're missing a fundamental aspect of your studies? It's one thing to know the science, but another to experience it."

The professor regarded the student thoughtfully before responding. "You make an interesting point. However, since you seem so passionate about this, why don't you step up to the podium and teach today's lesson?"

The student shook his head. "That's not necessary, Professor. I just wanted to share my perspective. You see, I know apples. And I know that without experiencing the taste, you're missing something essential."

The professor nodded slowly. "That's quite profound. Please see me in my office after class. I'd like to discuss this further."

The following day, the student appeared at the professor's office carrying a bright red apple. "Here, Professor. I brought you an apple. They say an apple a day keeps the doctor away."

The professor accepted the apple, a curious expression on his face. With a sense of ceremony, he took a bite. The sweet, crisp flavor burst in his mouth, a revelation in its simplicity. He chewed thoughtfully, savoring the experience.

"It's good," he admitted, a hint of a smile playing on his lips. "I never realized what I was missing."

Years later, in the same lecture hall, the professor recounted this story to his chemistry class, the memory vivid in his mind.

"Professor, who was that student?" one of his students asked, eyes wide with curiosity.

The professor smiled warmly, a twinkle in his eye. "I was that student."

CHAPTER EIGHTEEN

A QUOTE ATTRIBUTED TO ACTOR DANNY GLOVER, "NEVER BE AFRAID TO TREAT PEOPLE THE WAY THEY TREAT YOU."

ALRIGHT! NOW IT'S REVENGE.

THE SEEKERS

In the remote and serene mountains of Nepal, where the air was crisp, and prayers carried on the wind, a monk of great wisdom resided in a modest monastery. Known far and wide for his profound insights and the bestselling book he authored, "Life's Questions and Answers," the monk was a beacon of enlightenment in a world shrouded in mystery and uncertainty.

Meanwhile, far away in a bustling city, two men grappled with profound loss that shook the very foundation of their beliefs. Ted Lee, a devout Christian, mourned the tragic loss of his only child, while Bill Johnson, a staunch atheist, struggled to make sense of the sudden death of his beloved wife in a car accident. Both men found themselves at a crossroads, seeking solace and answers to their life-altering tragedies.

Driven by a desperate need for understanding, both Ted and Bill embarked on a pilgrimage to Nepal, drawn by the tales of the monk who held the key to life's mysteries.

Bill, the atheist, arrived at the monastery first, his eyes clouded with doubt and despair. Meeting the monk with a heavy heart, he asked the age-old question, "Is there a God?" The monk, with unwavering certainty, replied, "Yes, there is a God. He exists."

Later that day, Ted, the Christian, arrived at the monastery gates, his soul burdened with grief and his faith tested to its limits. Sitting before the monk, he asked the same question, "Is there a God?" This time, the monk's response was starkly different, "No, there is no God. He doesn't exist."

Confounded and bewildered, both men left the monastery with more questions than answers, their hearts heavy with uncertainty.

A curious disciple of the monk, who had witnessed both encounters, approached his master with a furrowed brow. "Teacher," he inquired, "why did you tell the atheist there is a God but then tell the Christian there is no God? What is the wisdom behind these contradictory answers?"

With a serene smile, the monk imparted his timeless wisdom, "Both answers were a test of their convictions. If they truly believe in what they hold dear, they will find the answers they seek. But if their faith falters in the face of uncertainty, they will remain lost, adrift in a sea of doubt where life's questions have no answers."

And so, the monk's words echoed through the mountains, a reminder that sometimes the greatest truths lie not in the answers we seek but in the unwavering faith we hold in our hearts, even in the midst of life's deepest mysteries.

SILENT SHADOWS: THE ENIGMA OF JOE'S MISSING FAMILY

Joe returned home from work one evening, looking forward to seeing his family after a long day. As he opened the front door, a chilling silence greeted him. "Honey? Kids?" he called out, but there was no response. Panic began to rise in his chest as he searched the house, only to find it empty, with no sign of his loved ones.

Frantic and bewildered, Joe rushed to his neighbors, hoping for some answers. "Have you seen my family? Do you know where they are?" he asked, desperation creeping into his voice. But to his dismay, everyone shook their heads, avoiding his gaze or muttering excuses to leave.

Feeling a mix of fear and frustration, Joe filed a police report about his missing family. "Please, you have to help me find them," he pleaded with the officers, but they seemed indifferent, dismissing his concerns with vague reassurances.

As days turned into weeks and then months, Joe's worry and longing for his family deepened. He tried to reach out to friends and acquaintances, but no one would engage with him, their eyes darting away when he mentioned his missing loved ones.

"Why is everyone acting like this? What's going on?" Joe muttered to himself, confusion clouding his thoughts. It felt as though a dark cloud of secrecy and avoidance hung over him, isolating him from the truth.

Then, one day, as Joe lay in his hospital bed, his eyes fluttered open to see unfamiliar faces around him. "You've been in a coma for nine months, Joe," a nurse explained gently. "We're glad you're awake."

"What happened?" Joe asked, perplexed.

"You were in an automobile accident on your way home from work," said the nurse, assuring him, "but now you're all fixed up, you're going to be okay."

As the pieces of the puzzle slowly fell into place in his mind, Joe's heart raced with a mix of relief and disbelief. The time he thought he had spent searching for his family had been a dream, a mirage in his subconscious mind.

Tears welled up in his eyes as he realized the truth, a bittersweet mixture of sorrow for the loss he thought he had experienced and gratitude for the second chance he had been given. "I need to see them, to hold them close," Joe whispered, his voice filled with a newfound sense of hope and appreciation for the precious gift of family.

ECHOES OF PARADISE

In the remote wilderness of North Michigan, Joe relished the solitude of hunting and fishing. He found solace in the whispering pines and the gentle lap of water against his boat. One serene day, he set out alone to the lake for a fishing excursion, seeking the tranquility of nature's embrace. As the sun began its descent, casting a warm glow across the water, Joe was lulled into a peaceful slumber in his trusty boat.

A sudden jolt shook him awake. Blinking in confusion, Joe squinted toward the shore and beheld an impossible sight – his long-lost buddy from the Vietnam War, Brad. His heart skipped a beat as he navigated his boat closer, disbelief and curiosity mingling in his mind.

"Brad? Is that really you?" Joe called out, his voice thick with emotion.

Brad turned, a ghostly smile playing on his lips. "Hey there, Joe. Long time no see, huh?"

Joe's boat reached the shore, and as he stepped out, a flood of memories from their time in Vietnam washed over him. "I saw you die, Brad. How is this possible?" Joe asked, his voice barely above a whisper.

Brad placed a comforting hand on Joe's shoulder. "Sometimes, things aren't what they seem, buddy. Welcome to our little slice of paradise."

Together, they wandered the tranquil fishing island. Joe's eyes widened in amazement as he spotted familiar faces among the trees and cabins. "Grandpa? Is that you?" he gasped, his heart brimming with joy and confusion.

Brad grinned. "Yep, they all found their way here. It's a good place, Joe. A place to heal."

The days turned into nights, and Joe and his comrades reveled in each other's company, sharing stories and laughter under the starlit sky. The air was filled with the sounds of camaraderie and merriment, a stark contrast to the memories of war that once haunted them. It felt like a dream – a perfect, endless summer evening where pain and sorrow were banished.

But paradise is a fragile thing.

One night, as Joe lay on a soft patch of grass, gazing at the infinite expanse of stars, he felt a strange pull. The serene world around him began to blur, the laughter of his friends growing faint. A sharp, piercing pain shot through his chest, and the paradise he had embraced started to dissolve like mist in the morning sun.

Joe's eyes shot open to the sterile surroundings of a mortuary. The shock on the mortician's face was palpable as he realized Joe was alive. Frantic calls were made, and soon, the medical examiner and police were at the scene.

The medical examiner explained to Joe the truth of his condition – he had been in a tragic accident on the lake, struck by a drunk boater. Despite being declared dead upon arrival at the medical examiner's office, Joe had somehow defied the odds and come back to life.

As the mortician hesitated with his tools, Joe's family was contacted, their relief visible upon hearing the news of his miraculous revival. Amidst the chaos and the flurry of activity, Joe couldn't shake the surreal experience of the island and the reunion with his fallen comrades.

In the following days, Joe grappled with the fragile boundary between life and death. He sought solace in the familiar rhythms of his daily life, but the memories of that ethereal island haunted him. Were they just a figment of his imagination, a dream conjured by a dying mind? Or was there something more, a hidden realm where lost souls found peace?

One evening, as he sat by the lake, the setting sun casting a golden hue over the water, Joe felt a presence beside him. He turned to see Brad, his smile just as warm and ghostly as before.

"Hey there, Joe. Looks like you made it back," Brad said.

Joe nodded, tears welling in his eyes. "Yeah, but it feels like I left a part of me behind."

Brad placed a comforting hand on Joe's shoulder once more. "Maybe you did. But remember, we're always with you, buddy. In every whisper of the wind, in every rustle of the leaves. The bonds we share, they transcend time and space."

As Brad's figure faded into the twilight, Joe felt a profound sense of peace. He knew that the island was real, in its own way, a place where the bonds of friendship and love endured beyond the mortal coil. And as he watched the sun dip below the horizon, Joe smiled, knowing that he would carry the memories of his comrades with him, always.

In that quiet moment by the lake, Joe understood that life and death were but two sides of the same coin, and the love he felt for his friends was an eternal thread that wove through the fabric of his existence. And with that realization, he found the strength to live each day with a heart full of gratitude and a soul unburdened by fear.

FLIGHT 43

The Boeing 747 soared at a height of 35,000 feet, a majestic titan of the skies. Passengers enjoyed their in-flight meals, unaware of the tiny drama unfolding beneath their feet.

In the dark recesses of the cargo hold, a small mouse named Pip wriggled out of a burlap sack. He had snuck aboard with a shipment of cheeses destined for a gourmet market in Paris. Pip had always been a curious mouse; this time, his curiosity had led him into the belly of a beast he could scarcely comprehend.

In the cockpit, Captain Jessica Armstrong and First Officer Michael Reeves monitored their instruments.

"Smooth sailing so far," Jessica said, glancing at the clear blue skies ahead.

"Absolutely," Michael replied, stretching his arms. "Hope it stays that way."

Down below, Pip's nose twitched. The pressurized cabin was a foreign environment, but the tantalizing aroma of cheese spurred him on. Pip scurried along the cables and wires, gnawing occasionally to test their flavor. A sudden spark made him jump back, but the damage was done.

Back in the cockpit, an alarm blared.

"What's that?" Jessica asked, her eyes narrowing.

Michael checked the control panel. "Electrical malfunction. That's odd. Everything was fine a moment ago."

Jessica grabbed the radio. "Ladies and gentlemen, this is your captain speaking. We are experiencing a minor technical issue. Please remain calm as we address the situation."

In the passenger cabin, tension grew as lights flickered and the plane shuddered. Flight attendants tried to reassure the passengers, but murmurs of fear spread like wildfire.

In first class, a young boy named Timmy clutched his mother's hand. "Mom, what's happening?"

"It's okay, sweetheart," she said, though her voice trembled. "The captain will take care of it."

Meanwhile, in the cargo hold, Pip continued his exploration. He nibbled on another wire, and the plane jolted violently. Pip was thrown against a crate, dazed but unharmed.

"We're losing control!" Michael shouted as the plane began to descend.

"We need to find the source of this malfunction," Jessica said, her mind racing. "And fast."

A loud thump echoed from the cargo hold. Jessica's eyes widened. "Could it be...?"

"Only one way to find out," Michael replied.

Jessica made a quick announcement, then left the cockpit, racing toward the cargo hold with Michael close behind. They opened the hatch and were met with the sight of Pip, his tiny form silhouetted against a backdrop of sparking wires.

"A mouse?" Michael exclaimed.

"Looks like it's been chewing on the wiring," Jessica said. "We need to fix this. Now."

Jessica approached Pip cautiously. "Hey there, little guy. We don't want to hurt you."

Pip, sensing the urgency, squeaked and darted away. Jessica grabbed a pair of insulated gloves and set to work on the damaged wires. Michael watched the mouse, ensuring it didn't cause further havoc.

Minutes felt like hours, but finally, Jessica stood up. "I've done what I can. Let's hope it's enough."

They raced back to the cockpit, the plane's descent slowing as systems came back online. Jessica took the controls, steadying the aircraft.

The passengers erupted in applause as the plane touched down safely at Charles de Gaulle Airport. Jessica and Michael shared a relieved smile.

In the cargo hold, Pip found himself a hero, though he had no idea of the chaos he had caused. A flight attendant discovered him and decided to keep him as a pet, naming him "Hero."

"Ladies and gentlemen, welcome to Paris," Jessica announced. "Thank you for your patience. We hope you enjoy your stay."

As the passengers disembarked, Timmy ran up to Jessica. "Were you scared, Captain?"

Jessica knelt down, smiling. "A little, but I knew we could handle it. And we had a little help from an unexpected friend."

Timmy's eyes widened. "A mouse?"

Jessica winked. "That's right. Sometimes, the smallest things can make the biggest difference."

And so, the story of Pip, the little mouse that brought down a 747, became a legend among the airline crew, a tale of chaos, bravery, and the unexpected heroes that come in all shapes and sizes.

ONLY IN AMERICA: THE STEVEN VANG STORY

In the heart of Riverdale, Minnesota, resided a man of remarkable resilience and fortitude named Steven Vang. Having arrived in America from a Thai refugee camp at the tender age of 8, Steven's journey unfolded into a narrative of courage and sacrifice. Graduating from high school, he answered the call to duty and enlisted in the Marine Corps, where he honed his skills as a sharpshooter during three harrowing tours in the Middle East amidst the tumult of the Persian Gulf War.

After his honorable discharge from the Marines, Steven transitioned into a role with a private security firm tasked with safeguarding government assets, including the invaluable yet vulnerable human intelligence sources vital to national security. Despite the demands of his profession, Steven remained a devoted father, prioritizing precious moments with his children amidst the chaos of his professional life.

One fateful evening, as the clock struck 2:00 AM, Steven returned home from a long night's work to find his children peacefully slumbering in the living room, having indulged in their customary weekend TV night. Seeking solace and reflection, he ascended the stairs to his home office, guided by the comforting words of his Bible.

"Hey, Dad," a sleepy voice called from the couch. It was his daughter, Lily.

"Hey, sweetheart," Steven whispered, smiling. "Go back to sleep. I'll tuck you in later."

"Okay," she mumbled, her eyes already closing.

As Steven settled into his office chair, a sudden noise shattered the tranquility. The front door exploded open, shards of glass cascading in a discordant symphony. The chilling screams of his children pierced the night, propelling Steven into a state of heightened vigilance, his instincts primed for defense. Fearing an intrusion in their less-than-ideal neighborhood, he swiftly dialed 911 for assistance and armed himself with his rifle, poised to shield his loved ones from harm.

"Dad!" his son, Alex, screamed from the living room. "What's happening?"

"Stay down! Stay hidden!" Steven shouted back, his voice firm yet comforting. "I'm calling for help."

The chaos unfurled, with gunfire echoing in the confines of his home. The arrival of local law enforcement added a layer of complexity to the unfolding drama. To Steven's astonishment, the intruders revealed themselves as federal agents who had erroneously stormed his residence in a misguided operation. A tense confrontation ensued between the local authorities and the federal agents, culminating in a precarious standoff that teetered on the brink of tragedy.

"Hold your fire!" Steven yelled, lowering his rifle as he realized the intruders' true identity. "I'm a civilian! You've got the wrong house!"

"Stand down, Vang!" one of the federal agents commanded, their weapons still trained on him. "We're here on official business."

"This is my home! My kids are here!" Steven's voice cracked with both anger and fear. "You've made a mistake!"

Subsequent investigations unveiled a grievous error in the execution of the operation, as the informant had indeed provided the correct address to the federal agents. However, a critical misinterpretation of the information led them astray, targeting the wrong residence in a regrettable case of mistaken identity. Acknowledging their misstep, the agents expressed remorse for the distress inflicted upon Steven and his family.

Despite the acknowledgment of the error by the federal agents, Steven found himself entangled in a legal quagmire, facing grave charges for the injury inflicted upon the agents during the tumultuous encounter. The prosecution, leveraging his military background and proficiency with firearms, painted Steven as an insurmountable force, leaving the agents with no alternative but to defend themselves against perceived threats.

Steven's lawyer, Amanda Carter, passionately defended him during the trial. "Steven Vang is a decorated veteran, a father, and a law-abiding citizen," she argued. "He acted in defense of his home and his children against what he believed to be a real threat. This is a clear case of self-defense."

The prosecutor, however, was relentless. "Mr. Vang's military training made him a dangerous opponent. The agents were simply doing their job, and their lives were put at risk."

Following a riveting trial that captivated the community, Steven was convicted of the charges and sentenced to a potential decade behind bars for the grievous offense of manslaughter. The weight of his military training and expertise with weapons cast a long shadow over the proceedings, influencing the jury's verdict and sealing his fate.

Enduring three arduous years within the confines of a federal prison, Steven's unwavering spirit remained undimmed, buoyed by the beacon of hope flickering on the horizon. Through a labyrinthine process of appeals, he emerged from the crucible of incarceration, determined to reclaim his place in the narrative tapestry of his life and rebuild the fractured fragments of his existence.

Upon his release, Steven hugged his children tightly. "I'm home," he whispered, tears in his eyes. "I'm finally home."

"We missed you so much, Dad," Lily said, her voice trembling.

"We knew you'd come back," Alex added, his eyes shining with pride.

Together, they walked out of the prison gates, ready to face whatever the future held, united by the strength of their bond and the hope of a new beginning.

CHAPTER NINETEEN

A RENOWNED INSPIRATIONAL SPEAKER SAID, "GIVING UP IS NOT AN OPTION IN MY BOOK. I RISE, I FALL, I RISE AGAIN."

HEY, THAT SOUNDS A LOT LIKE MY 15-MONTH-OLD BOY. HE DOES THAT EVERY DAY.

THE PHENOMENON

In a quiet town nestled in the hills of the countryside, a peculiar mystery had gripped the community for several months. The Smith family—Mother, Father, and their two young children—had been mysteriously waking up each morning in their front yard. Their neighbors were struck with fear, the police were mystified, and the medical community was at a loss to explain this baffling phenomenon.

One morning, Mrs. Anderson, the Smiths' next-door neighbor, peered over the fence and called out, "Mrs. Smith, have you thought about moving? This whole situation is downright spooky!"

Mrs. Smith shook her head, looking exhausted. "Believe me, we've considered it, but where would we go? This is our home."

Rumors swirled around the town. At the local diner, Mr. Johnson, the mailman, whispered to the waitress, "I bet it's ghosts. Or maybe a curse. Ever since old Mr. Thompson cursed that place, strange things have been happening."

The waitress, wiping down the counter, replied, "Or aliens! I've read about abductions that sound just like this."

As the days turned into weeks, the town's anxiety grew, and the Smith family became the subject of intense scrutiny and gossip. Then, one day, a renowned paranormal scientist from Canada, Dr.

Robert Ray, arrived in town. Standing at the town hall, he addressed the curious townsfolk.

"Ladies and gentlemen, I assure you; I will get to the bottom of this," Dr. Ray declared confidently.

After conducting a thorough investigation, Dr. Ray gathered the townspeople in the community center to share his findings.

"Good evening, everyone," Dr. Ray began, "I have discovered why the Smith family keeps waking up in their front yard. It's not ghosts or aliens."

A collective gasp went through the crowd. Mr. Johnson muttered, "I knew it wasn't aliens."

Dr. Ray continued, "The answer is actually quite simple. The Smiths' air conditioning is broken, and the interior of their house becomes unbearably hot at night. They unconsciously seek relief outside."

Mrs. Anderson looked at Mrs. Smith in surprise. "Why didn't you fix it earlier?"

Mrs. Smith sighed. "We were worried about the cost. Fixing the air conditioning would spike our electric bill, and with no backyard to sleep in, the front yard was our only option."

As the truth behind the mysterious phenomenon was revealed, the entire town felt a sense of foolishness for jumping to supernatural conclusions. Mr. Johnson chuckled, "Well, I guess we all got carried away."

Mrs. Anderson nodded. "We sure did. Poor Smiths, we made a mountain out of a molehill."

The once-feared and pitied family now became the subject of amusement and lighthearted jokes. Mr. Johnson joked with the waitress at the local diner, "Remember when we thought it was aliens? Turns out it was just a busted AC!"

In the end, the Smith family was relieved to have a simple explanation for their strange behavior. As they stood on their porch one evening, Mr. Smith turned to his wife and said, "I'm glad that's over. Now we can finally sleep in peace."

The town learned a valuable lesson in not jumping to conclusions without all the facts. Dr. Robert Ray returned to Canada, leaving behind a town that was a little wiser and a lot more skeptical of the mysterious occurrences that seemed to haunt their quiet community.

JOURNEY OF RESILIENCE

In the bustling halls of O'Hare International Airport, my journey to a new life began as I stepped off the airplane from the refugee camp in Thailand on that cold winter day in 1979. The vastness of the airport and the hum of activity around me were a stark contrast to the tranquility of my homeland, signaling the start of a new chapter in my story.

Wheaton, Illinois, awaited me beyond the airport gates—a town nestled in the heart of America, where snow-covered streets and welcoming faces would become the backdrop of my childhood. The transition from the familiarity of Thailand to the foreignness of Illinois was daunting, yet I carried with me a sense of hope and determination to embrace the challenges that lay ahead.

As the airport echoes faded behind me, Wheaton unfolded like a patchwork quilt of new experiences and encounters. The warmth of the community enveloped me, offering a sense of belonging in a world far from what I had known. Neighbors reached out with kindness, teachers guided me through the intricacies of a new language, and classmates became companions on this shared journey of discovery.

Walking the charming streets of Downtown Wheaton, I was captivated by the historic buildings lining the sidewalks, each one telling a story of a town steeped in tradition and community spirit.

The bustling cafes and quaint shops exuded a sense of nostalgia, inviting me to explore and immerse myself in the vibrant tapestry of small-town life that defined Wheaton's downtown.

Among the many people who touched my life as I grew up in Wheaton, Mr. & Mrs. Jean Dusek, Steve Myer, Carl Hearts, Jimmy Cjaka, Xeng Djoua Xiong, Jean Burton, Miss Martha Hall, my Sunday school teacher, Mrs. Reams at Long Fellowship School, and Mr. John Anderson at Franklin Junior High School played pivotal roles in shaping my path. Their guidance, wisdom, and unwavering support were pillars of strength as I navigated the challenges of adolescence in a new land.

Additionally, individuals like Xf. Nyaj Tswb Yaaj, Greg Vaam Suav Vaaj, Yawm Txiv Ntsuab Nchai, and Tais Npaub, along with my family and countless friends and acquaintances, brought light and laughter into my days, creating a tapestry of relationships that wove its way into the fabric of my existence.

Through the seasons of the 1980s, Wheaton became my anchor, a haven where I explored the depths of my identity and forged lasting friendships that transcended cultural divides. I embraced the duality of my heritage, blending the colors of my past with the hues of my present, creating a mosaic of experiences that shaped me into the person I am today.

As the decade drew to a close, I reflected on the journey that had brought me from the busy halls of O'Hare Airport to the quiet streets of Wheaton. The snow that once adorned the roads had melted, symbolizing the thawing of fears and the blossoming of dreams that had taken root in this welcoming town.

In Wheaton, I found not just a place to live but a place to thrive—a place where resilience was cultivated, dreams were nurtured, and the echoes of my past mingled with the promises of the future. And as I stood on the cusp of new beginnings, I knew that Wheaton's downtown and special places, along with the people who touched my life, would always hold a piece of my heart, a testament to the strength found in embracing change and the beauty of building a life in a place where snow-covered roads lead to endless possibilities.

THE SPECTATORS

After a successful competition, having led his team to victory in the World Soccer Championship in Brazil, a reporter approached Roberto Corona with a beaming smile. "Roberto, how do you feel now that you're the best soccer player in the world?"

Roberto, still catching his breath, looked thoughtfully for a moment before replying. "I don't think I'm the best. I was just doing my best. The best players are the spectators. They know every move and what it takes to win without ever playing."

His response left the reporter momentarily speechless, and then he laughed, a little taken aback. "That's quite humble of you, Roberto. But surely you must feel some sense of accomplishment?"

Roberto nodded. "Of course I do. But I've learned that everyone watching from the stands or on TV often believes they understand the game better than the players on the field. They see the mistakes we make and think they could have done better. It's easy to be perfect when you're not the one playing."

This exchange between Roberto and the reporter quickly went viral, inspiring people around the world. It sparked countless discussions and debates about the nature of expertise and the pressure of performance.

One evening, in a small café in Milan, two friends, Marco and Elena, were discussing Roberto's statement over coffee.

"You know, Marco," Elena said, stirring her cappuccino, "Roberto has a point. It's always easier to criticize when you're not the one under pressure."

Marco nodded, leaning back in his chair. "True, but don't you think spectators have valuable insights too? I mean, sometimes they notice things players might miss."

Elena shrugged. "Maybe. But the difference is they aren't the ones making split-second decisions with the weight of the world on their shoulders."

At a sports bar in New York, a heated conversation was taking place between a group of soccer enthusiasts.

"Come on, guys," Jake argued, waving his beer bottle for emphasis. "If I were on that field, I would've scored that goal. Roberto missed an easy shot."

His friend, Lisa, shook her head. "It's not that simple, Jake. Watching from here, everything looks clear-cut. But in the heat of the moment, with defenders closing in and the crowd roaring, it's a whole different story."

Jake smirked. "Easy for you to say. You've never even played soccer."

Lisa's eyes flashed. "And you have? Look, it's like Roberto said. People who do things make mistakes. Those who don't do anything don't make mistakes because they never try. It's easy to be a perfect player from a barstool."

In a quiet park in Tokyo, a father and his young son were kicking a soccer ball around. The boy looked up at his father, curiosity in his eyes. "Dad, why do people think they can play better than the players?"

His father smiled, ruffling his son's hair. "It's because when we're not the ones playing, we can see the whole field and think we understand everything. But playing the game and making decisions in real time is much harder. It's easy to say, 'I would've done this' when you're not the one running and sweating out there."

The boy nodded slowly, trying to understand. "So, it's like how it's easier to draw a perfect picture in your head than on paper?"

"Exactly," his father replied. "Remember, son, the ones who make mistakes are the ones who are trying. And trying is always better than doing nothing."

Roberto Corona's humble words echoed in conversations around the globe, reminding everyone that true excellence isn't about never failing. It's about giving your best, making mistakes, and learning from them. It's about understanding that spectators have a different perspective, but it's those who step onto the field who truly play the game.

THE EVANGELS

Dao's short-term mission to Vietnam with Positiv Impac Ministries in 2019 was supposed to be a journey of faith and service. Little did he know it would become a test of his resolve and belief.

Dao stepped off the plane and was immediately enveloped by the humid heat of Vietnam. He adjusted his backpack and joined his fellow missionaries and local pastors, their faces reflecting a mix of excitement and apprehension.

"We're here to share hope," Dao said, trying to encourage the group. "Let's trust in God's plan for us."

The group nodded, and they set off for the high mountain villages where the Hmong people lived. For the next ten days, they traveled through rugged terrain, shared meals with the villagers, and held secret prayer meetings. The Hmong welcomed them with open hearts, eager to hear the message of the gospel.

On the eleventh day, everything changed. Dao and his companions were in the middle of a prayer session when the door burst open. Armed police officers stormed in, shouting orders in Vietnamese. The villagers scattered, but Dao and the others were quickly apprehended.

"You are under arrest for spreading unlawful religious propaganda," one of the officers declared, his face stern and unyielding.

Dao looked at his companions, their faces pale but resolute. He knew they were in serious trouble.

At the police station, Dao and the others were separated and subjected to intense interrogation.

"Confess your crimes!" the interrogator demanded, slamming his fist on the table. "You are spies sent to disrupt our country."

"We are not spies," Dao replied calmly. "We are here to share our faith and help those in need."

The interrogations continued for three days, with little food or rest. The pressure was relentless, but Dao and his friends remained steadfast.

Finally, they were brought before the chief of police, a formidable man with a piercing gaze.

"If you confess, you can go home," the chief said, his voice deceptively gentle. "If you don't, you can die in prison."

Dao took a deep breath. "We have done nothing wrong. We cannot confess to a lie."

The chief's expression hardened. "Some of your companions have already confessed. Why not follow their example?"

Dao shook his head. "Our faith teaches us to stand for the truth, even in the face of death."

Their defiance earned them beatings and a harsh prison sentence. The days turned into weeks, and the weeks into months. In the damp, dark cell, they relied on their faith to sustain them, praying and singing hymns in whispers.

Two months later, without warning, they were pulled from their cells and escorted to the airport. As they were about to board the plane, the chief of police approached Dao.

"Brother," he whispered, his voice soft and filled with an unexpected warmth. "Your faith is strong, and you were very brave. I wish you a safe journey home. May our Lord Jesus Christ be with you always."

Dao's eyes widened in surprise. He turned to look at the chief, who gave him a small, almost imperceptible nod. At that moment, Dao realized that even in the heat of their ordeal, their message had reached someone they never expected.

As the plane took off, Dao looked out the window, the landscape of Vietnam fading into the distance. He silently prayed for the people they had met, for the chief of police, and for the strength to continue his mission wherever it might lead him next.

THE HELPER

It was a bright Saturday morning in late spring, and sunlight bathed the roads as Charles and his wife Maiv set off on their journey to Aurora, Illinois. Today held special significance as Charles' cousin was getting married. However, the couple had not anticipated how exhausting the drive would be.

The previous night had been restless, filled with last-minute preparations and little sleep. Determined to arrive on time, Charles insisted on taking the wheel. But as the hours passed, fatigue began to take its toll.

"Charles, your eyes are barely open. Let me drive for a bit," Maiv said, her voice tinged with concern as she glanced at her husband. She could see the strain on his face, his eyes heavy with sleep.

"Sweety, you're too tired. Let me drive so you can rest," she urged, her tone gentle yet firm.

Charles sighed, rubbing his eyes. He knew she was right. "Alright, Maiv. I'll let you take over for a while so I can get some rest," he conceded, pulling over at the next exit.

They swapped seats, and Maiv took the wheel with determination. Charles settled into the backseat, stretching out and closing his eyes with relief. The hum of the engine and the gentle vibrations of the car began to lull him into a near-sleep.

Suddenly, a jolt woke him. The car had come to a stop on the side of the road. Charles sat up, disoriented and confused. Maiv turned around in her seat, her face pale.

"Sweety, can you drive now?" she asked, her voice trembling slightly.

Charles blinked, glancing at his watch. "But you've only been driving for eleven minutes," he replied, trying to shake off his grogginess.

"I know," Maiv said softly, "But I'm tired."

CHAPTER TWENTY

SOMEONE ASKED ME,
"I'M 59 YEARS OLD. WHAT DO I NEED TO DO TO PREPARE FOR MY RETIREMENT?"

I REPLIED HONESTLY,
"AT YOUR AGE, FORGET ABOUT PLANNING FOR RETIREMENT. JUST HAVE FUN!"

BROKEN DOWN

Ted Morrison's life was in shambles. After dedicating 25 years to his job, he was unceremoniously let go. His wife, Nancy, had grown weary of his increasing despondency and drinking habits, and she had given him an ultimatum: get his life together or face a divorce. With every day that passed, Ted felt more like a failure, and he began to drown his sorrows in alcohol again.

One Sunday, after another restless night, Ted attended service at St. Mark's Church. He sat in the back, trying to avoid the sympathetic glances from the congregation. After the service, he lingered, watching as the last of the parishioners filed out. Pastor Daniel Ferguson noticed Ted and walked over, his face full of concern.

"Ted, can we talk?" Pastor Ferguson asked gently, placing a hand on Ted's shoulder.

Ted nodded reluctantly and followed the pastor into his modest office. The room was adorned with various religious artifacts and pictures of missionary work.

"What's going on, Ted? You don't seem yourself lately," Pastor Ferguson began, his voice calm and soothing.

Ted sighed heavily. "It's everything, Pastor. I lost my job. Nancy is threatening to leave me. And... I've started drinking again."

Pastor Ferguson looked at Ted with understanding eyes. "Ted, I know it feels like the world is against you right now, but remember, with God, all things are possible."

Ted scoffed. "I trusted God, Pastor. Look where it got me. I feel abandoned."

Pastor Ferguson opened his Bible and pointed to a verse. "Matthew 19:26, Ted. 'With man, this is impossible, but with God, all things are possible.' I want you to read it."

Ted glanced at the verse but quickly looked away. "It's just words, Pastor. They don't mean anything to me anymore. God lied."

Pastor Ferguson sighed, knowing he couldn't force faith back into Ted's heart. "Just think about it, Ted. God hasn't abandoned you."

Ted left the church feeling no better than when he entered. The following week, he had a job interview lined up three hours away in Nebraska. It felt like a last chance, a flicker of hope in an otherwise dark tunnel. As he drove along the highway, his old sedan sputtered and died. Ted cursed under his breath, slamming his hands on the steering wheel.

He got out of the car, the summer sun beating down mercilessly on him. He waved at passing cars, but no one stopped. It was blistering hot, and Ted's throat felt parched. He started walking, hoping to find a gas station or some help. The wind picked up, and dust swirled around him.

As he trudged along the roadside, something caught his eye. It was a tattered postcard lying on the ground. Curious, Ted picked it up. The postcard was addressed to a "David Johnson" and had an old stamp on it. The handwriting was faded but legible.

"Dear David, always remember, with God, all things are possible. Matthew 19:26. I hope you're with Him. Love, Dad."

Ted stared at the words, his heart pounding. It was the same verse Pastor Ferguson had pointed out. The coincidence was too much to ignore. As he read the message again, he felt a profound sense of realization wash over him. He had been so focused on his misfortunes that he had completely lost sight of his faith. He had turned his back on God, blaming Him for his problems instead of seeking His guidance and support.

Ted sank to his knees, clutching the postcard. "God, I'm sorry," he whispered, his voice cracking. "I thought you lied and had abandoned me, but it was me who abandoned You. Please, help me find my way back."

Just then, a car pulled over, and a man stepped out. "Hey, you okay?" the stranger called out.

Ted looked up, the tears streaming down his face. "My car broke down. I need help," he replied.

The man smiled warmly. "Let's get you to a gas station. Hop in."

As Ted climbed into the car, he felt a glimmer of hope for the first time in months. He clutched the postcard tightly, feeling a sense of renewed faith. Maybe, just maybe, things could get better. He realized now that he was not alone and that with God, all things were indeed possible.

THE INK OF FATE

In the shadowy outskirts of a bustling city lived Jake "The Fox" Thompson, a seasoned criminal whose reputation for meticulous planning preceded him. Jake was known far and wide for his cunning and careful execution of his heists. He believed that the next job would be his last, a final score that would set him up for life.

One evening, in his dimly lit apartment cluttered with blueprints and tools, Jake sat at a wooden table, scribbling the address of his next target on his hand: 143 Elm Street. He muttered to himself, "Easy in, easy out. Just one more job and I'm done with this life."

His phone buzzed, jolting him from his thoughts. It was a message from his partner, Lucas. "You ready for tonight? This one's big."

Jake quickly replied, "Born ready. Meet you at the spot."

Later that night, Jake and Lucas, dressed in dark clothes, approached the quiet suburban house at 143 Elm Street. As they crept through the shadows, Lucas whispered nervously, "You sure about this? This place looks too quiet."

"Trust me," Jake replied confidently. "I've been watching this place for weeks. No alarms, no dogs. We're in and out."

They broke into the house, moving swiftly through the rooms, gathering valuables. But as they reached the living room, Jake accidentally knocked over a lamp, causing it to crash to the floor. "Damn it!" he cursed under his breath.

Lucas, panicking, hissed, "We need to get out of here, now!"

Ignoring Lucas's anxiety, Jake gathered the last of the valuables before they made their escape. Unbeknownst to them, the noise had alerted a neighbor, who promptly called the police.

At the police station, Officer Ramirez examined the scene of the crime and found a piece of paper with an incomplete to-do list, partially smeared but still readable. Turning to his partner, he said, "Look at this. Seems like our guy was in a hurry. Forgot to take his shopping list."

Back at the station, they enhanced the smudged writing, revealing the address written on Jake's hand. Officer Ramirez chuckled, "This address matches the house on Elm Street. Let's pay a visit to Mr. Thompson."

The next morning, the police knocked on Jake's door. Still oblivious to his mistake, Jake opened it casually. "Jake Thompson?" Officer Ramirez asked.

Suspicious, Jake responded, "Who's asking?"

"You're under arrest for the robbery on Elm Street. Hands behind your back," Officer Ramirez ordered.

Jake, confused, protested, "What? You can't prove anything!"

Officer Ramirez held up a photograph of Jake's hand with the address. "We found your to-do list. Nice handwriting, by the way."

As Jake sat in the back of the police car, hands cuffed, he stared at his hand where the address had faded but was still faintly visible. He muttered to himself bitterly, "All that planning, and I get taken down by a stupid ink smudge. Should've worn the damn gloves."

In the courtroom, Jake stood before the judge, his lawyer arguing for leniency. The judge said, "Mr. Thompson, it seems even the best-laid plans can go awry with the simplest of mistakes. Sentencing will be swift."

Turning to his lawyer, resigned, Jake whispered, "Just one mistake, and it cost me everything."

The judge's gavel slammed down, sealing Jake's fate.

As Jake sat in his prison cell, he pondered the irony of his downfall. He looked at his new cellmate and said, "You ever write something down and wish you hadn't?"

His cellmate laughed, "Every day, man. Every day."

Jake nodded, his eyes filled with a mix of regret and determination. "Next time, no mistakes. If there ever is a next time," he thought to himself.

And so, Jake "The Fox" Thompson learned that even the cleverest plans could be undone by the smallest of oversights. It was a lesson written in ink, indelible and fateful, forever marking the end of his life of crime.

LILY

In the bustling city of Rivertown, a woman named Isabel Rivers was known for her kind heart and gentle spirit, but behind her warm smile lay a dark secret.

One fateful day, Isabel's life took a tragic turn when she was brought to court, accused of the death of her 16-month-old daughter, Lily. The courtroom was filled with tension as the judge prepared to announce her sentence.

"Ms. Rivers, you stand accused of aggravated murder and endangering children," the judge declared solemnly. "How do you plead?"

Isabel, tears streaming down her face, stood before the court and spoke in a trembling voice. "Your Honor, I left a bottle of milk for my baby before I left for my trip. I never meant for any harm to come to her."

The prosecutor's voice cut through the air like a knife. "Leaving a child alone for over a week is not just neglect; it's a betrayal of the highest order. Lily suffered a horrific death because of your actions."

As the trial unfolded, Isabel's defense attorney, Mr. Carter, called her to the stand to testify. "Ms. Rivers, can you explain what happened during that fateful week?"

Isabel took a deep breath and recounted the events that led to her daughter's tragic demise. "I was struggling with depression and mental health issues," she confessed. "I thought a vacation would help me clear my mind, but I never imagined this would happen."

The courtroom was silent as Isabel's words hung in the air. The jury deliberated, and finally, the judge delivered the verdict. "Isabel Rivers, you are sentenced to life in prison without parole for aggravated murder and eight to twelve years for endangering children."

Isabel collapsed to the floor, sobbing uncontrollably. "I'm so sorry, Lily. I never meant for any of this to happen," she cried out.

As she was led away to begin her sentence, Isabel's voice echoed through the courtroom. "I have prayed for forgiveness every day. Please, forgive me."

Amid the courtroom drama, a few characters' voices and emotions added depth to the tale.

Courtroom Scene:

Defense Attorney Mr. Carter: "Isabel, can you walk us through your state of mind and why you thought leaving for a vacation was the right decision?"

Isabel Rivers: "I was overwhelmed, Mr. Carter. I thought... I thought I could come back refreshed and be a better mother to Lily. I didn't think... I didn't think it would turn out this way."

Prosecutor Ms. Blackwood: "Ms. Rivers, are you suggesting that your mental health justifies abandoning your child?"

Isabel Rivers: "No, no, that's not what I'm saying. I know it was wrong. I just... I couldn't see a way out of the darkness. I made a terrible mistake."

Judge Harrison: "Mental health struggles are real, Ms. Rivers, but the consequences of your actions have been devastating. The law requires us to hold you accountable."

As Isabel was led away, her last words echoed in the hearts of everyone present. The tragic tale of Isabel Rivers came to a close, a story of love and loss, betrayal and remorse, forever etched in the annals of Rivertown's history.

THE HUM

In the small, tight-knit town of Loveliland, New Mexico, nestled amidst the arid desert and sprawling cacti, life moved at a languid pace. The sky stretched wide and clear, the land a serene yet unforgiving landscape of red rock and dust. Despite its tranquil appearance, Loveliland had a secret—an inexplicable, low-frequency hum that seemed to emanate from the very air itself.

The hum was subtle yet persistent, a droning sound that permeated the stillness of the desert nights. Some residents likened it to the distant rumble of thunder or the hum of a far-off engine. For months, it had been the talk of the town, with theories ranging from natural phenomena to alien interference.

One hot summer evening, as the sun dipped below the horizon and painted the sky with hues of orange and pink, a small group of townsfolk gathered at the local diner, Rosie's Place. Rosie herself, a plump woman with a kind smile and a penchant for gossip, served coffee and pie as the discussion turned, once again, to the mysterious hum.

"I'm telling you, it's not natural," insisted Hank, a burly rancher with a weather-beaten face. "I've lived here all my life, and I've never heard anything like it."

Mary, the schoolteacher, shook her head. But Hank, what else could it be? We're miles from any major road or factory. There's nothing out here but sand and sagebrush."

"Maybe it's the government," piped up Tim, a lanky teenager with a fascination for conspiracy theories. "They could be testing some kind of secret weapon."

Rosie chuckled as she refilled their coffee cups. "Oh, Tim, you and your wild ideas. It's probably just the wind playing tricks on us."

But the hum persisted, growing louder and more unsettling as the days turned into weeks. Visitors to Loveliland, drawn by curiosity and the lure of the unknown, began to report the same phenomenon. Journalists, scientists, and thrill-seekers all converged on the town, each eager to uncover the source of the hum.

One such visitor was Dr. Evelyn Carter, an acoustics expert from Albuquerque. With her dark hair pulled back in a tight bun and her eyes sharp with determination, she set up her equipment in the heart of the desert. Evelyn had spent years studying sound waves and frequencies, and she was determined to solve the mystery of Loveliland's hum.

As she adjusted her instruments, she couldn't help but feel a shiver of excitement. "There's something out here, something we don't understand," she murmured to herself. "And I'm going to find out what it is."

Evelyn's investigation led her deep into the desert, far from the comfort of Rosie's Place and the safety of the town. One night, as she camped under the stars, she heard the hum more clearly than ever before. It seemed to resonate within her very bones, a haunting melody that both fascinated and unnerved her.

Suddenly, the ground beneath her began to tremble. Evelyn sprang to her feet, her heart pounding. "What the hell?" she whispered, scanning the darkness for any sign of movement.

Out of the shadows emerged an elderly Navajo man, his weathered face lined with wisdom and age. He introduced himself as Tsohanoai, a name that meant "Sun Bearer." With a calm and steady voice, he spoke of ancient legends and forgotten secrets.

"The hum you hear is not new," Tsohanoai explained. "It has been here for centuries, a song of the earth itself. Long ago, our people believed it was the voice of the spirits, a reminder of the delicate balance between our world and theirs."

Evelyn listened, captivated by his words. "But why now? Why is it getting louder?"

Tsohanoai's eyes glinted with a mixture of sorrow and hope. "Perhaps it is a warning, or perhaps it is a call to remember what we have lost. The land is alive, and it speaks to those who will listen."

With Tsohanoai's guidance, Evelyn continued her research, blending modern science with ancient wisdom. As the days passed, she began to understand that the hum was more than just a sound—it was a bridge between the past and the present, a connection that bound the people of Loveliland to the very soul of the desert.

Back in the town, the residents noticed a change. The hum, though still present, no longer seemed ominous. Instead, it became a comforting presence, a reminder of the enduring spirit of Loveliland and its people. And as the sun set over the desert, casting long shadows across the land, they knew that they were part of something much greater than themselves—a mystery that, in its own way, had brought them closer together.

A HUNTER'S LEAP OF FAITH

Vang Tou was a seasoned hunter, his heart beating with the thrill of the chase. He especially loved hunting deer, drawn to their grace and the challenge they presented. Solitude was his preferred companion on these expeditions; the forests of northern Wisconsin were his cathedral, a place where he found peace away from the bustle of human life.

A devout Christian, Vang Tou never missed a Sunday service at the small church in his hometown of Rhinelander. His faith was the cornerstone of his life, and he tithed faithfully, serving in various ministries within his church. The townsfolk held him in high esteem, a family man with three wonderful children and a heart as big as the forest he roamed.

One crisp autumn morning, with the air tinged with the scent of pine and the promise of winter, Vang Tou embarked on a three-day deer hunting expedition. With his trusty rifle slung over his shoulder and a sidearm at his hip, he set off into the Chequamegon-Nicolet National Forest, eager for the adventure that awaited. The first day passed smoothly, the forest alive with the whispers of nature. By the second day, he had tracked a magnificent buck until twilight, the setting sun casting long shadows through the tall trees.

As darkness fell, Vang Tou pressed on, adrenaline pumping through his veins. He had wounded the deer earlier and was determined to find it. The forest, once familiar, now seemed like an endless maze under the dim light of his flashlight. Hours slipped by, and he was so engrossed in his pursuit that he didn't notice the encroaching darkness until it swallowed him whole.

Suddenly, the ground gave way beneath him. He fell into a hidden hole, the impact knocking the wind out of him and rendering him unconscious. When he came to, the blackness was suffocating. His flashlight was lost, and he couldn't tell how deep the hole was. Exhausted and disoriented, Vang Tou felt panic begin to rise.

"Lord, help me get out of here," he prayed, his voice trembling in the void.

To his astonishment, a soft, gentle voice answered, "Do you trust me?"

"Lord, is that you?" Vang Tou's heart pounded. "I trust you. Help me get out of here."

The voice replied, "If you trust me, then just get out of there. Go ahead, get out."

Skepticism and fear gripped Vang Tou. The voice was comforting, yet the darkness was absolute. He decided to wait until dawn, feeling safer in the dim light of day. As the first rays of sunlight pierced the blackness, he saw it—a tunnel connected to the hole, an old, abandoned mine shaft. It had been there all along, just behind him.

Vang Tou's heart ached with the realization. He had doubted when he should have trusted. The Lord had provided a way out, but his fear had kept him trapped.

He clambered out of the hole, his mind racing with gratitude and regret. The forest around him was bathed in the golden glow of morning, a stark contrast to the darkness that had held him captive. As he returned to camp, Vang Tou's thoughts were filled with a renewed sense of faith and the knowledge that trust in the Lord could light the way, even in the darkest of places.

Returning to Rhinelander, Vang Tou shared his harrowing experience with his family and church community. His tale became a testament to the power of faith and trust, resonating deeply with those who heard it. From that day forward, Vang Tou's hunts in the Wisconsin wilderness were not just about the thrill of the chase but also about the spiritual journey and the lessons of faith learned in the heart of the forest.

CHAPTER TWENTY-ONE

THE FAMOUS SAYING GOES, "THERE'S NO SUCCESS WITHOUT HARDSHIPS."

WELL, I HAVE HARDSHIPS. DOES THAT MEAN I AM GOING TO BE SUCCESSFUL NOW?

THE YARD-SALE

In the quaint town of Hillberry, a famed front yard sale captivated residents once a year. This event was a treasure trove of tools, antiques, and stories waiting to be discovered. John, a local enthusiast with a penchant for collecting, eagerly awaited this annual tradition.

On a sunny Saturday morning, John decided to explore the town in search of the perfect sale. He drove around Hillberry, enjoying the picturesque scenery, when his eyes were drawn to a magnificent mansion perched atop a hill. The mansion's grandeur was awe-inspiring, overlooking a serene lake and a sprawling golf course. To John's delight, a front yard sale was taking place in the mansion's beautiful courtyard.

Excitedly, John parked his car and strolled into the sale. He browsed through various items, eventually purchasing a vintage watch and an ornate lamp. As he wandered towards the back of the courtyard, he noticed fewer people and a dusty, antique-framed portrait catching his eye. Intrigued by its age and craftsmanship, he inquired about its price.

One of the sales staff called for the mansion's owner, Mr. Raymond Siegfried, to assist. When Mr. Siegfried arrived, his expression was stern. He said, "I'm sorry, but that portrait is not for sale."

Captivated by the portrait, John insisted, "I really want to buy it. How much would it cost?"

Mr. Siegfried's eyes softened with a hint of nostalgia and sorrow as he replied, "It's priceless."

John, undeterred, pressed on, "I'll pay whatever it takes. Please, name your price."

With a deep sigh, Mr. Siegfried said, "If you truly want that portrait, you must buy the entire inventory here."

John's eyes widened in surprise. "The entire inventory? At what price?"

Mr. Siegfried gazed at John, a faint smile playing on his lips. "Since you're so determined and willing to go to great lengths, you can have everything for free. That portrait, everything here, including my mansion, is yours. I'm too old to maintain it. The portrait is of my only son. By taking it, you take everything I hold dear."

John was stunned into silence, his mind racing. "Are you serious? This entire estate, all of it, for free?"

Mr. Siegfried nodded solemnly, his eyes glistening with unshed tears. "Yes. You see, my son was killed by a drunk driver thirty years ago. This mansion, all these possessions, they are filled with memories of him. By taking this portrait, you inherit not just my estate but also the memory of my beloved son."

John's heart ached at the revelation. "I... I'm so sorry for your loss."

Mr. Siegfried placed a trembling hand on John's shoulder. "Thank you. It's time for me to move on and live a simpler life. Perhaps this place can bring you joy, as it once did for me and my son."

Several weeks later, John, now the new owner of the mansion and the entire estate, watched as Mr. Siegfried packed his belongings and left to lead a simpler life. The old man's departure was bittersweet, leaving behind a legacy wrapped in memories and a portrait that symbolized a lifetime of love and loss.

As John stood in the grand courtyard, holding the portrait of Mr. Siegfried's son, he felt a profound sense of responsibility and gratitude. The mansion and its treasures were now his to cherish, and with them, he inherited the stories and dreams of the past.

ETERNAL BRUSHSTROKE

Mary Woodruff was a talented painter whose canvases burst with life and emotion. Her works captured the raw beauty of the world, a talent that drew praise from critics and art lovers alike. Despite the accolades, Mary struggled with self-doubt and insecurity, always feeling unworthy of her success.

In the quiet solitude of her studio, she often whispered to herself, "Why can't I see what they see?" The walls of her studio, adorned with her vibrant paintings, seemed to mock her insecurities. She poured her heart and soul into her art, yet every brushstroke felt like a battle against an unseen enemy.

One day, in a moment of utter despair, Mary decided she could no longer bear the weight of her doubts. With trembling hands and tears streaming down her face, she gathered her beloved paintings and set them ablaze. The flames devoured years of her passion and talent, leaving nothing but ashes and the lingering smell of smoke.

"I can't do this anymore," Mary sobbed, watching her life's work disappear into the fire.

Decades later, Mary passed away at the age of 92. Her granddaughter, Amanda Brown, was tasked with sorting through her grandmother's belongings. As she rummaged through the attic, Amanda discovered a hidden gem—a painting Mary had missed in her moment of destruction. The canvas, covered in dust, depicted a serene landscape bathed in the warm glow of a setting sun.

Amanda stared at the painting, a sense of awe and sadness washing over her. "Grandma, why did you never show this to anyone?" she whispered.

Determined to honor her grandmother's legacy, Amanda decided to sell the painting at her garage sale. A modest affair in the suburbs, the sale attracted a few curious neighbors and passersby. Among them was an art collector, a keen-eyed man named Robert Hastings.

He approached Amanda, eyeing the painting with interest. "How much for this piece?" he asked, his voice betraying a hint of excitement.

"Ten dollars," Amanda replied, unaware of its worth.

Robert handed her the money, sensing he had stumbled upon something extraordinary. Later, he had the painting appraised and discovered its true value. It sold at an auction for an astonishing $500,000, catapulting Mary's work into the spotlight she had always shied away from.

The painting was loaned to numerous art galleries and museums, where it captivated audiences and ignited discussions about the tragic brilliance of Mary Woodruff. Critics marveled at the emotion and technique displayed in the piece, a testament to the talent that Mary had doubted all her life.

A few weeks after the auction, Amanda received an unexpected letter. Inside was a check for $80,000 and a heartfelt note from Robert Hastings.

"Dear Amanda," it read. *"Your grandmother's painting has touched many hearts, including mine. Her talent deserves to be celebrated, and I hope this gift honors her memory. Use it to pursue your own dreams or to remember her in a special way. Best regards, Robert."*

Amanda held the letter close, tears streaming down her face. "Thank you, Robert," she whispered. "And thank you, Grandma, for everything."

Mary's work survived in a big way, touching the hearts of countless art lovers. Though she had passed away, her spirit lived on in her paintings, a legacy of beauty and emotion transcending her earthly struggles. As Amanda stood before the painting in a grand museum, she felt a profound connection to her grandmother.

"Grandma, your art will never be forgotten," she whispered, tears of pride and sorrow glistening in her eyes.

A BROKEN ROAD TO REDEMPTION

Dennis Williams sat in the dimly lit living room, the shadows of the past casting long, tormenting silhouettes against the walls. His gaze fixated on a photograph perched on the mantelpiece – a snapshot of happier times when Crystal's smile could light up the entire room. But those days seemed like a distant memory, buried under layers of misunderstandings and unresolved conflicts.

Crystal Williams, a spirited and ambitious young woman, had always dreamed of attending college. Her father, Dennis, a stern yet caring man, had his own dreams for her, dreams that often clashed with Crystal's vision of her future. Their relationship had been strained for years, the tension between them a palpable presence in the house they shared.

The night before Crystal was set to leave for college, the air was thick with unspoken words and simmering resentment. As they sat down for dinner, the silence between them was heavy, with each forkful of food feeling like a battle won.

"Crystal," Dennis finally broke the silence, his voice gruff with a mix of concern and frustration, "I still don't understand why you chose that school. It's so far away. Why not stay closer to home? You know I can help you more if you're nearby."

Crystal's eyes flashed with defiance, her fork clattering onto her plate. "Dad, it's my life! I want to experience things on my own and make my own choices. Why can't you support me for once instead of always trying to control everything?"

Dennis slammed his hand on the table, making the dishes rattle. "Control? Is that what you think this is about? I'm trying to protect you, Crystal! The world isn't as kind as you think it is."

Tears welled up in Crystal's eyes, but she refused to let them fall. "I don't need your protection, Dad. I need your trust. Why can't you understand that?"

The argument escalated, each word a dagger, each retort a wound. Finally, in a moment of heated anger, Dennis shouted, "Fine! Go ahead! Go to your precious school. But don't come running back to me when things go wrong!"

Crystal's face crumpled, and she stormed out of the house, slamming the door behind her. The echo of that slam reverberated through the house long after she was gone, leaving Dennis alone with his anger and regret.

The next morning, Dennis awoke to the sound of his phone ringing. Groggy and disoriented, he answered it, his heart sinking as he listened to the officer on the other end. "Mr. Williams, there's been an accident. Your daughter... she didn't make it."

Time seemed to stand still. The words echoed in his mind, a cruel reminder of the final, harsh words they had exchanged. Dennis dropped the phone, his body shaking with uncontrollable sobs. The weight of his regret was suffocating, the pain of never getting to apologize, never making things right, an unbearable burden.

Days turned into weeks, and Dennis found himself visiting the cemetery more often, standing by Crystal's grave with a heart full of remorse. "I'm so sorry, Crystal," he would whisper, tears streaming down his face. "I was so wrong. I just wanted to keep you safe, but I lost you instead."

One evening, as the sun set, casting a golden glow over the cemetery, Dennis felt a presence beside him. It was Mrs. Thompson, the elderly neighbor who had always been like a second grandmother to Crystal. She placed a comforting hand on his shoulder.

"Dennis, she knew you loved her," Mrs. Thompson said softly. "You both had your differences, but your love for her was never in question. She knew that."

Dennis nodded, but the pain in his heart was still raw. "I just wish I had told her that before it was too late."

Mrs. Thompson smiled gently. "Then tell her now, Dennis. Live your life in a way that honors her memory. Be the man she would have been proud of."

From that day forward, Dennis began to heal slowly. He started volunteering at the local community center, helping young people who, like Crystal, were trying to find their way in the world. He shared his story with them, hoping to spare them the pain he had endured.

And every night, before he went to bed, Dennis would look at Crystal's photograph and whisper, "I love you, Crystal. I always will." In his heart, he knew that she heard him, and in some way, she had forgiven him.

Though the road to redemption was long and fraught with pain, Dennis walked it with determination, each step a tribute to the daughter he had lost and the love that would forever bind them.

FAITH, LOVE, AND BLUEBERRY LATTES: A TALE OF MARRIAGE STRUGGLES

At Blue Moon Cafe, a quaint establishment known for its cozy atmosphere and delectable blueberry pastries, Cherry found herself engrossed in a heartfelt conversation with her friend, Pam, who was grappling with struggles in her marriage.

Pam took a thoughtful sip of her blueberry-infused latte before confiding, "Cherry, I feel like we're drifting apart more and more each day. I don't know how to fix it."

Cherry empathized with Pam's plight, understanding the pain of a troubled marriage all too well. "I hear you, Pam. It's tough when things don't go as planned. Have you ever considered seeking guidance from a higher power?"

Pam looked intrigued but puzzled. "What do you mean?"

Cherry opened up about her own journey of turning to faith during her marriage challenges and the newfound hope and strength it had brought her. "Our love alone may be not strong enough. Sometimes, inviting God into our relationships can provide clarity and direction. It's not about being perfect but about seeking wisdom beyond our own understanding."

Their conversation was interrupted by the arrival of Greg, a familiar face at the cafe, who had overheard their discussion.

"Marriage troubles, huh? I know a thing or two about that," he said with a knowing smile.

Cherry nodded, grateful to connect with others who could relate to her struggles. "Indeed. But with faith and perseverance, we can navigate even the toughest times."

As more patrons joined in, sharing their own tales of marital challenges and victories, a sense of camaraderie enveloped the cafe. Some emphasized the importance of communication, while others stressed the virtues of forgiveness and patience.

In that moment, Cherry realized that their shared experiences underscored the power of community and support in navigating the complexities of marriage. As she absorbed the voices around her, she understood that with God's guidance and the love of those who cared, she and Mark could rebuild their relationship and forge a stronger, more enduring bond.

With renewed hope in her heart, Cherry smiled at her friends and expressed gratitude for their words of wisdom and encouragement. As she bid farewell to Blue Moon Cafe that day, she knew that regardless of the obstacles ahead, she would confront them with faith, love, and an unwavering belief that her marriage was worth fighting for.

THE LAST STRETCH OF THE PATH

In a quaint little town nestled among rolling hills, there lived a father named James and his son, Michael. Their relationship had been strained for many years, marred by misunderstandings and a lack of communication. As time passed, the gap between them seemed to widen, leaving both with a sense of emptiness and regret.

James, now an elderly man with a gentle smile and wise eyes, spent his days reminiscing about the past in the comfort of his cozy home filled with memories. Michael, a busy man in the prime of his life, often found himself preoccupied with work and personal matters, leaving little time for his father.

One crisp autumn evening, as the leaves painted the town in shades of gold and crimson, Michael received a letter from his father. The letter was simple yet heartfelt, a plea from a father to his son to mend what had been broken between them. Touched by the words written by his father's hand, Michael decided to pay him a visit.

As Michael walked through the door of his father's home, he was greeted by the familiar scent of his childhood, a mixture of old books and pipe tobacco. James looked up from his favorite armchair, his eyes lighting up with surprise and joy.

"Michael, my boy, it's good to see you," James said, his voice filled with emotion.

"I'm sorry, Dad. I should have visited sooner," Michael replied, his voice tinged with regret.

They sat down together, the clock ticking on the mantelpiece filling the room with nostalgia. James began to speak, telling stories of his youth and adventures long past. Michael listened intently, his heart heavy with the realization of all the missed moments.

"Dad, I want to make things right. I want to be there for you like you were there for me," Michael said, his voice filled with determination.

James looked at his son, a tear glistening in his eye. "I've always been proud of you, Michael. I just wanted you to know that."

From that day on, Michael made a conscious effort to spend more time with his father. They went for walks in the park, shared meals at the kitchen table, and talked about everything under the sun. With each passing day, their bond grew stronger, bridging the gap that had separated them for so long.

One day, as they sat in the garden watching the sunset paint the sky in hues of pink and orange, James took Michael's hand in his own.

"Thank you, son. Thank you for letting me live and be a part of your life," James said, his voice filled with gratitude.

And as the days turned into weeks and the weeks into months, Michael and James walked side by side, hand in hand, making up for lost time and cherishing every moment they had together.

And in the end, as the sun dipped below the horizon, casting long shadows across the garden, father and son sat in peaceful silence, their hearts full of love and forgiveness.

For in the twilight of their days, they had found redemption and a love that transcended time—a love that would guide them on the last stretch of the path they had left to walk together.

CHAPTER TWENTY-TWO

THE SAYING GOES, "SUCCESS IS IN MY DNA. I WILL FIGHT TILL THE END."

MY ADVICE IS TO GET IN SHAPE FIRST BEFORE ENTERING THE RING FOR THE FIGHT.

BETRAYAL OF THE FAITHFUL

Emma and James had always been the epitome of young love. They met in high school; their bond cemented through shared faith and dreams. They married soon after graduation, vowing to build a life rooted in their beliefs and their tight-knit community. Emma, with her radiant smile and unwavering faith, was the heart of their home. James, with his steady demeanor and deep commitment to their church, was well-respected by all who knew him.

Life in their small town was predictable, a comforting routine that Emma cherished. However, everything changed when Sarah arrived. A recent transplant to the town, Sarah joined their congregation looking for solace and new beginnings. She quickly became involved in church activities, catching James's attention with her vivacious spirit and shared passion for service.

It was during a church mission trip that their paths intertwined more closely. As they worked side by side, building homes and hope, they shared more than just tasks. Personal stories, struggles, and dreams spilled out in the late hours of the night, forming a connection that neither had anticipated.

One evening, under the stars, Sarah confided in James about her painful past, her voice trembling with emotion. James listened intently, his heart aching for her. He felt a pull towards her, a desire to protect and comfort her that he hadn't felt in years.

"James," Sarah whispered, with tears glistening, "I don't know what I would have done without you on this trip. You've been my rock."

James reached out, gently brushing a tear from her cheek. "Sarah, you're stronger than you think. But I'm here for you. Always."

The line between friendship and something more blurred as days turned into weeks. Their stolen glances, secretive smiles, and late-night conversations became the highlight of their days.

Back home, Emma sensed a change in James. He was distant, lost in thought, his phone always within arm's reach. One evening, as James showered, Emma noticed his phone buzzing incessantly. Curiosity got the better of her, and she glanced at the screen. Her heart sank as she read the messages—intimate, emotional, and unmistakably romantic.

Confrontation was inevitable. That night, Emma, with tears streaming down her face, held up the phone to James. "What is this, James? Who is she?"

James's face turned pale, his eyes filled with a mix of guilt and fear. "Emma, I... I can explain."

"Explain? How can you explain this? You've betrayed me, James. You've betrayed us."

James fell to his knees, tears streaming down his face. "Emma, please. I'm so sorry. It was a mistake. I never meant to hurt you. Please, forgive me."

Emma's world shattered that night. The man she had trusted, loved, and built a life with had broken her heart. Unable to cope with the betrayal, she grabbed her keys and fled their home, tears blurring her vision as she drove aimlessly through the night.

The rain poured down, mirroring her anguish. Blinded by her pain and the storm, Emma lost control of the car on a sharp turn. The crash was sudden and violent, the sound of metal crunching and glass shattering echoing through the night.

James was awoken by the call that no one ever wants to receive. The words of the police officer on the other end of the line were a blur, but the message was clear: Emma was gone. The weight of his guilt crushed him, the realization that his actions had led to this unbearable loss.

At the funeral, the congregation gathered to support James, though whispers of the affair spread like wildfire. Sarah, overcome with guilt herself, kept her distance, her heart heavy with the knowledge that she played a role in the tragedy.

James stood at Emma's grave, his voice choked with emotion. "Emma, I am so sorry. I loved you more than anything, and I failed you. I will spend the rest of my life making amends, but I know it will never be enough."

In the following months, James immersed himself in church activities, seeking solace and redemption in his faith. He and Sarah never spoke again, their connection severed by the weight of their shared guilt.

James knew that forgiveness would be a long and arduous journey, both from his community and within himself. But as he knelt in prayer each night, he held onto the hope that one day, he might find peace.

The small town, forever changed by the tragedy, rallied around James, offering their support and understanding. Emma's memory lived on in the hearts of those who loved her, a reminder of the fragility of trust and the enduring power of faith.

THE REJECT

Jake Freedman was known far and wide among steak lovers as the father of the famous steak sauce recipe that revolutionized the way Americans enjoyed their meat. But before he became a household name, his life was a long, winding road paved with failures, regrets, and unfulfilled dreams. By the time he reached his 60s, Jake had lost almost everything that mattered to him. He lived alone in a tiny, run-down house on the outskirts of town, his only company, the haunting memories of a life filled with mistakes. His car, as battered as his spirit, was his last remaining valuable possession. Each month, he scraped by on meager $100 social security checks, a bitter reminder of how little he had achieved. Yet, despite the overwhelming weight of his past, Jake still held onto a glimmer of hope. He believed that he had something left to offer the world.

One evening, as he sat in his dimly lit kitchen, Jake clutched a weathered recipe card in his hands. It was the one thing that connected him to his family and his past—a steak marinade recipe passed down through generations. With a deep breath and a resolve that had been buried for years, Jake made a decision. This recipe would be his salvation, his last chance to leave a mark on the world. He would sell it to restaurants across the country, convinced that it could change the way Americans ate steak.

The journey to this decision had been anything but easy. Years earlier, when Jake had first shared his dream of turning the family recipe into a business, his wife, Betty, had scoffed at the idea. Betty had always been the practical one, focused on stability and security. The notion of Jake chasing after an impossible dream was too much for her to bear.

"I can't believe you're still talking about that steak recipe," Betty said one evening, her voice laced with frustration. "We need a real plan, Jake. Something that actually pays the bills."

Jake looked at her with pleading eyes filled with a mixture of hope and desperation. "Betty, I know it sounds crazy, but I really believe this could work. I just need a chance."

Betty shook her head, her expression hardening into one of resignation. "You've been saying that for years. And what do we have to show for it? Nothing. You were born with nothing, and you'll leave this world with nothing."

Her words cut through him like a knife. Shortly after that conversation, Betty packed her bags and left, unable to stand by a man she believed was destined to fail. As Jake watched her go, he felt the sting of loss, not just of his marriage but of the life he had hoped to build.

To survive, Jake took a job as a dishwasher at a nearby Thai restaurant called Thailand Station. The work was grueling, and the hours were long, but the small paycheck he earned, combined with his social security checks, kept him from sinking completely. Night after night, as he scrubbed pans in the steamy kitchen, Jake couldn't shake the feeling that he was meant for more.

One night, while scrubbing a particularly stubborn pan, Jake's boss, Lin, a kind-hearted woman with a quiet strength, approached him. "Jake," she said gently, "you've been working very hard. Is everything alright?"

Jake paused, wiping the sweat from his brow. "I'm fine, Lin. Just trying to make ends meet and save up for something important."

Lin nodded, sensing the depth of his unspoken struggles. "If you ever need to talk, you know where to find me."

Despite the physical and emotional toll, Jake clung to the belief that his recipe could be his ticket out of the darkness. He saved every penny, and when he had enough, he packed his beat-up car with a cooler full of marinated steaks and set off to pitch his recipe to restaurants.

His first stop was a family-owned diner that had been around for decades. The owner, an elderly man named Tom, listened to Jake's pitch with polite interest but ultimately shook his head.

"Sorry, son," Tom said with a sympathetic smile. "We're happy with the steaks we serve. We've been doing things the same way for years, and our customers like it that way."

Rejection after rejection followed. In one upscale bistro, the head chef, Denise, didn't even let Jake finish his pitch. "Look, Mr. Freedman," she interrupted, "we have a very specific brand and flavor profile. I'm afraid your recipe doesn't fit with our menu. Best of luck, though."

In a bustling city diner, the manager, Carlos, was even blunter. "You think you're the first guy to come in here with a 'secret' recipe?" he scoffed. "I've heard it all. Sorry, but no thanks."

Jake's journey was filled with lonely nights spent sleeping in his car, rationing out what little food he had, and praying for just one chance to prove himself. Each "no" felt like another nail in the coffin of his dreams, but he refused to give up.

One rainy afternoon, Jake found himself in a small Midwest town, tired, hungry, and nearly out of hope. He pulled into the parking lot of a modest-looking restaurant called "Grill House." The owner, a burly man named Mike, stood behind the counter, eyeing Jake with a mix of curiosity and skepticism.

"What can I do for you?" Mike asked, his voice gruff but not unkind.

Taking a deep breath, Jake launched into his well-rehearsed pitch. He spoke with all the passion and determination he had left, describing the rich flavors and tender texture of his marinated steak. Mike listened, his expression slowly shifting from indifference to genuine interest.

"Alright," Mike finally said, "I'll give it a try. Cook up a sample for me."

With shaking hands, Jake prepared a steak in the restaurant's kitchen. The aroma filled the air, catching the attention of the staff and a few curious customers. When Mike took his first bite, his eyes widened in surprise and delight.

"This is amazing," he declared, his gruff demeanor softening. "You've got yourself a deal."

Jake could hardly believe it. After more than a thousand rejections, he had finally found someone who believed in his dream. That moment marked the turning point in Jake's life. Word of the delicious steak spread quickly, and soon, other restaurants were clamoring to feature Jake's marinade on their menus.

As Jake's business grew, so did his confidence. He expanded his operations and eventually opened his own chain of restaurants called "America's Steakhouse." The man who had once been dismissed as a hopeless dreamer had become a success story, transforming the way people across the country enjoyed their steaks.

Years later, Jake stood on the stage at the grand opening of the latest America's Steakhouse location, the crowd cheering for him. As he looked out over the sea of faces, Jake felt a deep sense of pride and fulfillment. He had proven that it was never too late to chase your dreams, that failure was not the end but a stepping stone to success.

Addressing the crowd, Jake shared his journey, emphasizing the power of persistence. "All my life, I made mistakes," he began, "but those mistakes didn't define me. It was my determination to keep going, to believe in myself that brought me here today. Remember, no matter how many times you hear 'no,' keep going until you hear that one 'yes.'"

Jake Freedman's story became a beacon of hope for those who had faced setbacks in their own lives. His legacy lived on, not just in the perfectly marinated steaks that graced the tables of America's Steakhouse, but in the hearts of those who found inspiration in his unwavering spirit.

*

Publisher's Note:

This story bears a striking resemblance to the author of this book. Like Jake Freedman, the author has faced numerous failures, mistakes, and tragedies. But these challenges could not deter him from completing this book—a dream that has been thirty years in the making. Just as Jake transformed his life with determination and belief, the author poured his heart and soul into creating this work, overcoming countless obstacles along the way. May this story inspire you to chase your dreams with the same unwavering spirit.

RICE PARADISE

Once upon a time, in a bustling city, a non-Asian man named Bob found himself at a local Asian restaurant called "Rice Paradise." Intrigued by the menu filled with various rice dishes, Bob decided to strike up a conversation with the Asian chef named Mr. Vang.

Bob: "Hey there, Mr. Vang! I've always wondered: why do Asians eat rice all the time? Is it like your secret superpower?"

Mr. Vang chuckled and replied, "Oh, Bob, it's not a superpower, but rather a delicious tradition passed down through generations! Rice is a staple in many Asian cultures because it's versatile, nutritious, and simply tastes amazing."

Bob scratched his head in confusion, "But don't you get tired of eating rice every day? I mean, don't you ever crave a burger or pizza instead?"

Mr. Vang laughed heartily, stirring a pot of fragrant fried rice, "Ah, but you see, Bob, rice is like a best friend to us Asians. It's there for us in good times and bad, ready to be paired with any dish and always comforting to the soul. Besides, who needs burgers and pizza when you have the endless possibilities of rice dishes to explore?"

Just then, a group of diners at a nearby table overheard the conversation and chimed in.

Diner 1: "You know, rice is such a versatile ingredient! It can be steamed, fried, boiled, or even turned into rice noodles. The possibilities are endless!"

Diner 2: "Absolutely! And let's not forget how comforting a bowl of warm rice can be on a cold day. It's like a hug in food form."

Diner 3: "Speaking of rice, have you ever tried Tsabmim International purple sticky rice? It's a special variety grown in Asia, and let me tell you, the taste is out of this world! The beautiful purple color adds a unique touch to any dish."

Bob's eyes widened with curiosity as he listened to Diner 3's description of the exotic purple sticky rice.

Bob: "Wow, that sounds amazing! I never knew rice could come in such vibrant colors. I definitely need to try that someday."

Mr. Vang smiled warmly, serving Bob a steaming bowl of special fried rice, "Here, Bob, try this and let the magic of rice work its wonders on you!"

As Bob took his first bite of the flavorful rice dish, he couldn't help but smile. Maybe there was something special about rice after all, and perhaps he would come to appreciate it just as much as Mr. Vang and his fellow Asians did, including the intriguing Tsabmim International purple sticky rice.

And so, Bob left "Rice Paradise" that day with a newfound appreciation for the beloved grain, ready to embrace the wonderful world of rice in all its delicious glory. From then on, he never looked at a bowl of rice the same way again, understanding the deep-rooted connection and joy it brought to those who cherished it.

UNSPOKEN ECHOES

Paul Deans had always been a quiet man, his emotions tucked away in the recesses of his heart. From a young age, he harbored a deep affection for his childhood friend, Kary McKay. They had grown up together in the small town of Clearwater, their lives intertwined with shared memories and dreams. Paul, ever the reserved one, expressed his love for Kary in heartfelt letters, pouring his soul into every word. But despite his best intentions, fear and insecurity kept him from sending them.

Years slipped by like sand through an hourglass. Paul watched from afar as Kary moved on with her life while he continued to write, each letter more poignant than the last. He stashed the unsent letters in an old wooden box, hoping he would one day muster the courage to reveal his feelings.

One crisp autumn morning, tragedy struck. Paul was involved in a car accident; his life abruptly cut short. The letters, filled with his unspoken love, remained hidden, their ink now a testament to what could have been. His daughter, Sarah, was left to sort through his belongings, piecing together the fragments of her father's life.

As Sarah rummaged through her father's things, she stumbled upon the wooden box. Inside, she found the stack of letters, each envelope bearing Kary's name in Paul's meticulous handwriting. She began to read, her heart breaking with every word.

One letter in particular stood out:

Dear Kary,

I've loved you since we were children, chasing fireflies and dreaming of faraway places. Every time I saw you smile, it felt like the world was a brighter place. I've written you countless letters, but I never had the courage to send them. I was afraid of losing our friendship, afraid of what you might say. But now, I realize that my biggest regret will be not telling you how much you mean to me.

With all my love,

Paul

Determined to honor her father's memory, Sarah tracked down Kary, who now lived in Naperville, Illinois. With trembling hands, she dialed Kary's number, her heart pounding in her chest.

Sarah: (nervously) "Hello, is this Kary McKay?"

Kary: (warmly) "Yes, speaking. Who is this?"

Sarah: "My name is Sarah Deans. I...I found some letters that my father wrote to you. He never sent them, but I think you should have them."

Kary's breath caught in her throat as she listened. Memories of Paul flooded back, and she felt a pang of sadness at the news of his passing. They arranged to meet at a cozy café in downtown Naperville.

When the day came, Sarah arrived early, clutching the wooden box tightly. Kary walked in, her eyes searching the room until they met Sarah's. They sat down, the air thick with unspoken emotions.

Kary: (softly) "I can't believe Paul is gone. We lost touch after high school, but I always wondered what happened to him."

Sarah:(handing over the box) "He never stopped thinking about you. These letters...they're filled with his love for you."

Kary opened the box, her hands trembling as she pulled out the first letter. She began to read, tears streaming down her face. The café seemed to fade away as she was transported back to her childhood, to the days when she and Paul were inseparable.

Kary: (whispering) "He loved me all this time, and I never knew."

Sarah: (with a sad smile) "He did. He was just too afraid to tell you."

They spent hours at the café, reading through the letters and sharing stories about Paul. Kary's heart ached with regret, but she also felt a sense of closure. Paul may have never sent the letters, but his love had finally reached her.

In the days that followed, Kary and Sarah forged a bond over their shared memories of Paul. They visited his favorite spots in Clearwater, reminiscing about the man who had loved so deeply and quietly.

Paul's unsent letters had brought them together, and in a way, he continued to live on in their hearts. His love story, though unspoken in life, had found its voice in the end, echoing through the letters Sarah had so bravely delivered.

THE TRIO COMMONALITY

Once upon a time, in a bustling city, Chicago, an Asian man named Yang, a black man named Jamal, and a white man named Dave found themselves waiting at a crowded train platform. As they stood there, they struck up a conversation that quickly turned into a heated debate about what they had in common.

Yang proudly declared, "We all love noodles! It's in our blood, I tell you."

Jamal rolled his eyes and retorted, "Noodles? Really? We obviously all love basketball. It's a passion that unites us."

Feeling left out, Dave said, "Hold on a minute! I think the real commonality here is our love for music. Whether it's hip-hop, rock, or country, we all enjoy a good tune."

Their argument reached a crescendo just as the train approached the platform. In the midst of their bickering, they failed to notice the train hurtling towards them until it was too late. With a loud screech of metal on metal, the train ran them over in a comical blur of confusion.

To their surprise, the trio found themselves standing before a luminous figure in a realm of white light. It was none other than God, looking down at them with a mix of amusement and exasperation.

"What were you three arguing about this time?" God boomed in a voice that resonated like thunder.

Yang, Jamal, and Dave exchanged sheepish glances before Yang hesitantly spoke up, "We were trying to figure out what we have in common, but we couldn't agree on anything."

God chuckled and shook his head. "Oh, my children. You are all brothers of another mother. Your common bond is humanity itself."

Relieved and slightly embarrassed, the three friends looked at each other with newfound understanding. Before they could ask any more questions, Yang suddenly woke up with a start, realizing it was all just a dream.

As he blinked away the remnants of the dream, Yang looked around the train carriage to see Jamal and Dave, the two annoying passengers next to him, chatting away. With a newfound sense of appreciation for the diversity of humanity, Yang joined in their conversation, grateful for the connection he felt with his fellow passengers, both in the dream and in reality.

CHAPTER TWENTY-THREE

A QUOTE ATTRIBUTED TO AMANDA TYLER:

"NOT INVITED, DON'T GO. NOT TOLD, DON'T ASK. LATE INVITES, DECLINE. YOU WERE NEVER PART OF THE PLAN. ACCEPT THAT."

THANKS, I ALWAYS WONDERED WHY PEOPLE WERE SO EXTRA NICE TO ME WHEN I WENT TO THEIR PARTIES.

THE CHOPSTICKS

Once upon a time, in a bustling marketplace in a distant land, there was a traveler named Christopher, known for his insatiable curiosity and love for trying new foods. While exploring the vibrant stalls filled with exotic dishes, Christopher stumbled upon a group of locals deftly using chopsticks to enjoy their meals.

Intrigued by the sight, Christopher approached the group and asked, "Excuse me, may I ask why you use these interesting sticks to eat instead of traditional utensils like forks and knives?"

The locals, named Sofia, Amir, and Mei, exchanged amused glances before Mei, the most talkative of the group, spoke up. "Ah, you must be new to these parts! Chopsticks have a long and fascinating history in our culture. Legend has it that chopsticks were invented in ancient China."

Sofia, the wise elder of the group, continued, "Yes, the story goes that chopsticks were first used by ancient Chinese emperors who wanted to avoid burning their fingers while cooking over open flames. They found that using two sticks to handle their food was both practical and efficient."

Amir, the jovial storyteller, added, "Over time, chopsticks symbolized unity and harmony in our society. They require skill and precision to use, fostering a sense of community and shared experience around the dining table."

Christopher listened intently, fascinated by the story behind the simple yet elegant utensils. "That's truly remarkable! I never knew chopsticks held such significance. Thank you for sharing this with me."

Sofia smiled warmly and offered Christopher a pair of chopsticks. "Here, why don't you give them a try? Who knows, you might just discover a new way to enjoy your meals!"

And so, Christopher sat down with Sofia, Amir, and Mei, clumsily attempting to wield the chopsticks as they shared a delicious meal together. Though he struggled at first, Christopher soon found himself laughing and bonding with his new friends over the shared experience of mastering the art of chopsticks.

As the sun set on the marketplace, Christopher realized that chopsticks were more than just utensils; they were a gateway to a rich cultural heritage and a means of connecting with others in a meaningful way.

And that, dear readers, is the story of how a chance encounter with chopsticks opened Christopher's eyes to a world of tradition, unity, and delicious food.

THE TEXTING TROUBLE

Once upon a time in a bustling town, there lived two best friends, Xiong and Jamie. Their bond was as strong as any, but like all friendships, it had its moments of tension. One sunny afternoon, Xiong found themselves frustrated with Jamie's recent behavior. Seeking a confidant, Xiong decided to vent to their friend Sam. With a phone in hand, Xiong typed furiously:

"Ugh, Jamie is being so annoying lately. They just don't get it. Always interrupting and making everything about themselves. I can't stand it anymore."

Feeling relieved, Xiong hit "send" and relaxed, not realizing they had sent the message to Jamie instead of Sam.

Meanwhile, in Jamie's cozy apartment, the message arrived. Jamie's face turned a mix of red with anger and hurt as they read the text. Without hesitation, Jamie called Xiong.

"Xiong, what the hell is this?" Jamie's voice trembled with a mix of confusion and pain.

"What do you mean?" Xiong replied, puzzled.

"The text you just sent me!" Jamie exclaimed.

A wave of horror washed over Xiong as they realized their mistake. "Oh no... Oh NO! Jamie, I am so sorry. I meant to send that to Sam. This is so embarrassing."

"Oh, I'm sure it was meant for Sam. But guess what? I received it, and now I know exactly how you feel about me," Jamie responded sarcasm lacing their words.

The next day, Xiong and Jamie met at a local café to talk things over. They sat across from each other, an awkward silence hanging in the air. Xiong fidgeted nervously, trying to find the right words.

"Jamie, listen, it was a stupid mistake. I didn't mean any of it. I was just venting," Xiong pleaded.

"So, you don't think I'm annoying and self-centered?" Jamie asked coldly.

"No! I mean, yes... I mean, sometimes, but who isn't? We're all annoying sometimes!" Xiong stammered, digging themselves deeper into the hole.

"Wow, Xiong. You're really digging yourself deeper," Jamie remarked, raising an eyebrow.

Just then, their friend Lily walked in, sensing the tension. "Hey guys, what's going on? You both look like you just walked out of a horror movie."

"Xiong here just accidentally sent me a message meant for Sam, complaining about me," Jamie explained.

Lily burst into laughter. "Oh no, Xiong. Classic mix-up. Remember when you sent that weird selfie to your boss instead of me?"

Xiong groaned. "Don't remind me. But this is worse, way worse."

Later, as Xiong and Jamie walked together outside the café, they tried to ease the tension. "Jamie, seriously, I'm really sorry. I shouldn't have said those things, even to Sam. It was mean and uncalled for," Xiong apologized sincerely.

"Well, maybe I should be more mindful, too. I didn't realize I was bothering you that much," Jamie replied, softening.

"Friends again?" Xiong asked with a hopeful smile.

"Friends. But you're buying me coffee for a week," Jamie said, a smile breaking through.

"Deal!" Xiong laughed.

Just as they were about to enter the café again, Xiong's phone buzzed with a message from Sam.

"Dude, I can't believe you sent that to Jamie! LOL, you're in so much trouble!" the message read.

Jamie peeked at the message and started laughing. "Well, at least we can laugh about it now."

"Yeah, but maybe next time I'll double-check before hitting send," Xiong grinned.

They both laughed and walked into the café, their friendship stronger and their spirits lighter. And so, Xiong learned the importance of being careful with words and, more importantly, with friends.

THE MISPLACED LETTER

Billy's fingers trembled as he sealed the envelope, his heart pounding with a mix of excitement and terror. The love letter he'd spent hours crafting was finally ready. Each word had been meticulously chosen to convey the depth of his feelings for Jessica, the girl he'd admired from afar for months. He rehearsed what he would say as he handed it to her, his mind racing with possibilities.

In his rush to catch the morning bus, Billy grabbed the envelope and shoved it into his bag without a second glance. He was determined that today would be the day he confessed his feelings.

The school hallways were bustling with students as Billy navigated his way to his locker. His palms were sweaty, and his heart raced faster with every step. He spotted Jessica by her locker, her golden hair catching the sunlight streaming through the windows. Taking a deep breath, he reached into his bag, pulled out the envelope, and walked towards her.

"Hey, Jessica," he said, trying to keep his voice steady.

Jessica looked up and smiled. "Hi, Billy! What's up?"

Billy's heart fluttered. "I, uh, have something for you," he said, handing her the envelope.

At that very moment, Jessica's friend, Max, came rushing down the hallway, accidentally bumping into Billy. The envelope slipped from Billy's hand and, in the confusion, ended up in Max's.

"Oops! Sorry, Billy!" Max laughed, handing back an envelope.

Billy flustered and not realizing the mix-up, quickly took the envelope from Max. "No problem," he muttered, his face flushing crimson. He turned back to Jessica, but before he could say anything, the bell rang.

"See you later, Billy!" Jessica called, rushing to class.

Billy sighed, stuffing the envelope back into his bag. He decided to try again later.

During lunch, Max sat down with his friends, oblivious to the envelope now poking out of his bag. His friend, Sarah, noticed it first.

"Hey, Max, what's that?" she asked, pointing to the envelope.

Max pulled it out, confused. "I don't know. Must have slipped into my bag this morning."

Curious, he opened the envelope and began to read aloud. "'Dear Jessica, I've admired you from afar for so long, and I can't keep my feelings hidden anymore...'" Max's eyes widened as he realized what he was reading. "'Your smile lights up my day, and I think about you constantly...'"

Laughter erupted around the table. "Billy gave you a love letter?!" one of his friends teased.

Max's face turned bright red. "No way! This must be a mistake. This is meant for Jessica!"

Sarah giggled. "Billy must have given it to you by accident. You should return it."

Max nodded, mortified. "Yeah, I'll do that."

Meanwhile, Billy spent the afternoon in a state of nervous anticipation, completely unaware of the chaos his letter was causing. He decided to find Jessica after school and finally gave her the letter.

As the final bell rang, Billy saw Max approaching him with the envelope in hand. Max's expression was a mix of amusement and sympathy.

"Hey, Billy," Max began, "I think you gave me this by mistake."

Billy's heart sank as he recognized the envelope. "Oh no..."

Max chuckled. "Don't worry, man. I didn't read the whole thing. Just make sure it gets to the right person this time."

Billy nodded, taking the envelope back. "Thanks, Max. I appreciate it."

Determined not to mess up again, Billy waited by Jessica's locker after school. When she appeared, he took a deep breath and approached her.

"Hi, Jessica," he said, holding out the envelope. "This is for you."

Jessica took the envelope, eyes widening in surprise. "For me?"

Billy nodded, his heart pounding. "Yeah. Just... read it when you get a chance."

As Jessica opened the envelope and began to read, Billy watched her face intently. A smile slowly spread across her lips, and she looked up at him, her eyes sparkling.

"Billy, this is... really sweet," she said softly. "I had no idea you felt this way."

Billy smiled, relief washing over him. "So, uh, what do you think?"

Jessica smiled back. "I think we should talk more. Maybe over coffee?"

Billy's heart soared. "I'd love that."

As they walked out of the school together, Billy couldn't help but feel that, despite the confusion and embarrassment, everything had turned out just right.

A LESSON IN LAUGHTER

It was a bright Sunday morning in the small town of Greenfield, and the New Life Hmong Alliance Church congregation had gathered for their weekly service. The pews were filled with familiar faces, all eagerly anticipating Pastor David's sermon. Known for his eloquent speeches and heartfelt messages, Pastor David had become a beloved figure in the community. Little did they know today would be a service unlike any other.

Pastor David stood behind the podium with a confident smile as he glanced down at his notes. However, his smile quickly faded when he realized what he was looking at wasn't his sermon at all. It was a grocery list written by his wife, Julie. Panic surged through him as he read the items: "Milk, eggs, bread, chicken, apples..."

Taking a deep breath, he began to speak, trying to recall the sermon he had meticulously prepared the night before.

"Good morning, everyone," he started, his voice slightly shaky. "Today's message is... about nourishment." He glanced down at the list again, hoping for some sort of inspiration. "Just as we need milk for strong bones, we need faith to strengthen our spirits."

The congregation exchanged puzzled glances, but Pastor David pressed on. "And, uh, eggs... Eggs are like... the opportunities God gives us. Fragile, yet full of potential."

He could see a few raised eyebrows and whispers among the crowd. Determined to salvage the situation, he continued. "Bread! Yes, bread is a staple in our diet, much like how prayer should be a staple in our daily lives."

A few chuckles could be heard at this point, and Pastor David felt his face growing warm. He was losing them. Desperately, he tried to tie in the next item. "Chicken... um, well, chicken reminds us to be... strong and... versatile in our faith?"

A ripple of laughter spread through the congregation. Pastor David's heart sank. He was making a fool of himself. Glancing around, he caught sight of Julie sitting in the front row, her eyes wide with confusion and concern. He took a deep breath and decided to come clean.

"My friends," he said, holding up the grocery list, "I must confess. In my rush this morning, I mistakenly brought my wife's grocery list instead of my sermon notes."

The church erupted in laughter, and Pastor David felt a mix of relief and embarrassment wash over him. "I tried to make it work," he admitted, "but I think it's clear that I'm better at sermons than shopping lists."

As the laughter subsided, he looked out at his congregation, who were now smiling warmly at him. "Even pastors make mistakes," he continued, "and today, I made a pretty big one. But I believe there's a lesson in everything. Perhaps this reminds us that we all need a little grace and forgiveness, even when we mess up."

Julie stood up, her eyes twinkling with amusement. "We forgive you, David," she called out, prompting a chorus of agreement from the congregation.

Pastor David smiled, his heart swelling with gratitude. "Thank you," he said. "Let's bow our heads and pray."

As he led the prayer, he couldn't help but feel a renewed sense of humility and connection with his congregation. They had seen him at his most vulnerable and still embraced him with open arms. It was a humbling experience but one that deepened the bond between him and his community.

After the service, Julie approached him with a playful smile on her lips. "David, I think you owe me a trip to the grocery store," she teased.

He laughed, wrapping his arm around her. "I think you're right," he replied. "And maybe next time, I'll leave the grocery lists to you."

The couple walked out of the church together, hand in hand, ready to face whatever came their way with faith, love, and a little bit of humor.

THE LAST SUPPER

In the sweltering summer of 1983, Wheaton, Illinois, was buzzing with anticipation for Rev. XuXu's visit to the Hmong Alliance Church. The church, a modest but vibrant community center, had been busy with preparations for weeks. The congregation was excited to hear Rev. XuXu, known for his profound insights and charismatic delivery.

The afternoon sun blazed down, making the air thick and heavy. Inside the church, ceiling fans whirred in a futile attempt to bring some relief. The pews were filled with congregants, their faces showing the fatigue of a long, hot day. Children fidgeted, and the elderly wiped the sweat from their brows, but there was an undercurrent of excitement and reverence as Rev. XuXu, in his crisp white clerical collar, stepped up to the podium.

His presence was commanding yet comforting. As he began, his deep voice resonated through the sanctuary, "Brothers and sisters, it is an honor to be with you today." There was a murmur of approval from the congregation. Rev. XuXu then announced that they would start with communion.

With a solemn expression, he read the scripture about the Last Supper, his voice filled with reverence. He then offered a short, heartfelt prayer, closing his eyes in deep concentration. "Let us eat and drink together," he finally said, lifting the bread and wine.

Without hesitation, he consumed them, setting an example for the congregation.

Suddenly, a voice exclaimed, "You forgot, none of us have received the bread and the wine yet!" It was Martha, his wife, her eyes wide with a mix of amusement and alarm.

There was a moment of stunned silence. Then, like a wave, laughter rippled through the congregation. The tension of the long, hot day broke in an instant. Rev. XuXu's face turned crimson, and he gave a sheepish smile. "My deepest apologies," he said, his voice laced with humor. "In my eagerness, I seem to have started a bit early."

He chuckled, and the congregation joined in with renewed laughter. The sound was warm and genuine, echoing off the wooden beams of the church.

"Did you see his face?" whispered Mrs. Vang to her husband, her eyes twinkling with amusement.

Mr. Lee leaned over to his wife, "I knew something felt off. He forgot to give us our bread and wine."

Rev. XuXu quickly rectified his mistake, ensuring everyone had their bread and wine. As they finally took communion together, a sense of unity and joy filled the room. The small mishap had turned into a moment of connection, reminding everyone of the humility and humanity at the heart of their faith.

After the service, the congregants lingered, sharing smiles and stories, the air filled with a sense of community strengthened by shared laughter and faith.

"I won't forget this sermon anytime soon," Mr. Lee said with a grin.

"Neither will I," Mrs. Vang replied, chuckling. "It just made us love him more."

Rev. XuXu, standing by the exit, shook hands with each congregant, his heart warmed by the laughter and the camaraderie that filled the air.

CHAPTER TWENTY-FOUR

A SAYING GOES,
"YOU WILL BE RICH VERY SOON.
NO EVIL CAN STOP IT."

WOW, OKAY,
I'M QUITTING MY DAY JOB
TOMORROW.

BLIND TRUST

In a quaint, quiet town where everyone knew each other by name lived Mrs. Reams, a beloved school teacher at Longfellow School. Known for her gentle smile and nurturing spirit, she had taught generations of children, always going the extra mile for her students.

For over ten years, Mrs. Reams had trusted her car to Mr. Beal at The Beal Auto Repair. Known for his friendly demeanor, Mr. Beal was considered a reliable figure in the neighborhood. But over time, whispers of his dishonesty reached Mrs. Reams.

One brisk November morning, Mrs. Reams noticed her car sputtering and shaking on her way to school. Concerned, she decided to take it to Mr. Beal, but not without a plan. She had been approached by the local police, who suspected Mr. Beal of fraudulent practices and agreed to help them catch him in the act.

As she entered the shop, she was greeted by the familiar scent of motor oil and rubber.

"Good morning, Mr. Beal," she said with a friendly smile. "My car's been acting up. Could you take a look at it?"

"Of course, Mrs. Reams! Leave it with me, and I'll see what I can do," Mr. Beal replied, unsuspecting.

The next day, he called her. "I found the issue with your engine. It's going to cost about $700, parts and labor."

Feigning concern, Mrs. Reams responded, "That's quite a bit, but if it needs fixing, I trust you. Go ahead."

Four days later, she returned to pick up her car, knowing what was about to unfold. Mr. Beal greeted her warmly, and she paid the bill. Just as she did, a group of undercover police officers stormed into the shop.

"Mr. Beal, you're under arrest for fraud and theft," an officer announced, revealing the sting operation.

The room fell silent. Mrs. Reams watched as handcuffs clicked around Mr. Beal's wrists.

"I can't believe this is happening," Mr. Beal stammered, looking at Mrs. Reams, shocked.

"I'm sorry, Mr. Beal," she said calmly. "I trusted you, but you took advantage of so many. This had to stop."

In court, it was revealed that Mr. Beal had been deceiving his customers for years, exploiting their trust. He had specifically targeted elderly women who knew little about car mechanics, overcharging them for repairs that were never needed. Mrs. Reams had been part of a carefully planned operation to catch him red-handed. The police had loosened a spark plug in her car to set the trap.

As the trial unfolded, several other townspeople came forward to testify.

"I always thought he was a nice guy," said Mrs. Thompson, an elderly widow. "I took my car to him for years. I never suspected a thing."

"He seemed so trustworthy," Mr. Jenkins, a retired firefighter, added. "I can't believe I was fooled too."

Each testimony echoed the same sentiment: they had all been deceived by Mr. Beal's charming facade.

"How could you, Mr. Beal?" Mrs. Reams asked, her voice steady but filled with disappointment. "You had our trust."

"I never wanted to hurt anyone, but it got out of hand," Mr. Beal admitted, a hint of regret in his voice.

The townspeople gathered in disbelief, realizing that the friendly facade Mr. Beal had worn for so long was just that—a facade. He had seemed like a kind, reliable man, always willing to help, but underneath, he was a crook who had been robbing them blind for years.

The incident left the community shaken but wiser. They had learned a valuable lesson: trust is precious, and appearances can be deceiving.

In the following months, Mrs. Reams found solace in her students, who rallied around her with drawings and letters of support. The town came together, stronger than before, determined to rebuild the trust that had been shattered.

And so, the town moved forward, holding tight to the bonds of community and looking out for one another, ensuring that betrayal would not shadow their bright little town again.

This tale serves as a reminder that even in the most familiar places, deceit can lurk and that true character is revealed through actions, not appearances.

ELDORIA

Once, in the remote village of Eldoria, nestled at the foot of the towering Blackspire Mountain, a dark pact had been forged long ago to ensure the prosperity and tranquility of the village. Every fourth spring, a sacrifice had to be made to the monstrous entity that dwelled atop the mountain, a being of immense power and insatiable hunger.

As the dreaded fourth spring approached, a hush fell over the village, and whispers of fear and sorrow filled the air. The villagers knew what had to be done to safeguard their way of life, but that did not make it any easier. Three days before the fateful day, a child was born to a young couple, Emma and Thomas, named Jonathan. The villagers saw this as a sign, a cruel twist of fate that demanded the sacrifice of the newborn.

On the second day, under the weight of heavy hearts and tear-filled eyes, the villagers gathered in the town square to make the dreadful decision. Despite the desperate pleas of Emma and Thomas, the will of the village prevailed, and they were coerced into surrendering their precious infant to uphold the ancient pact.

As the sun dipped below the horizon on the third day, a somber procession made its way up the winding path leading to Blackspire Mountain's summit. In the midst of the crowd, Emma followed at a distance, her heart torn asunder by grief and determination. She knew what had to be done, but she was not willing to let her beloved child be taken without a fight.

Taking a treacherous alternate route known only to a few, Emma ascended the mountain swiftly, her resolve steeling with every step. As the villagers reached the sacrificial altar at the summit and prepared to offer up Jonathan to the slumbering beast, a primal roar shattered the stillness of the night.

The monster, a grotesque amalgamation of claws and fangs, eyes ablaze with malevolent hunger, emerged from the shadows to claim its due. But before it could strike, Emma stepped forward, a glint of defiance in her eyes. With a fierce cry, she unsheathed a hidden blade and launched herself at the beast with courage born of a mother's love.

A fierce battle ensued, the clash of steel against scales echoing through the mountain peaks. The villagers watched in awe and terror as Emma fought with unmatched ferocity, her determination unwavering. In a final, desperate gambit, she plunged the blade into the heart of the monster; its deafening roar cut short as it crumbled to the ground, vanquished.

As the first light of dawn kissed the horizon, the villagers stood in stunned silence, their eyes wide with disbelief. Emma stood before them, bloodied but unbowed, holding her infant son close to her chest. The pact had been broken, the cycle of sacrifice shattered by a mother's unyielding love and courage.

Jonathan, the child who had unknowingly defied fate, gazed up at his mother with innocent eyes, a beacon of hope in a village once shrouded in darkness. The villagers looked upon them with reverence and gratitude, knowing that they owed their freedom and their future to a mother's bravery and a child's resilience.

And so, in the village of Eldoria, a new tale was born of sacrifice and redemption, of love that conquered all. And the legend of Emma and Jonathan, the mother and child who faced the monstrous entity and emerged victorious, would be told for generations to come.

From that day onward, the village of Eldoria was forever changed. The oppressive shadow of fear that had loomed over the villagers lifted, replaced by a newfound sense of unity and hope. Emma and Jonathan became symbols of resilience and defiance, their story spreading far and wide, inspiring others to stand up against tyranny and injustice.

As the years passed, Eldoria flourished like never before. The fields yielded bountiful harvests, the people lived in peace and prosperity, and the memory of the dark pact that once bound them faded into obscurity. Emma and Jonathan were revered as heroes, their names spoken with reverence and gratitude by all who knew their tale.

Jonathan grew into a young man of remarkable courage and compassion, guided by the strength and love of his mother. Together, they roamed the lands, spreading stories of hope and liberation, offering aid to those in need, and standing up for the oppressed. Their bond was unbreakable, forged in the crucible of adversity and triumph.

And so, the village of Eldoria thrived, its people united by a shared history of sacrifice and redemption. The memory of the monster that once demanded innocent lives was overshadowed by the legacy of Emma and Jonathan, the mother and child who had defied fate and reshaped their destiny.

As the sun set over the tranquil village, casting a warm glow over the humble cottages and bustling market square, a gentle breeze carried the echoes of a new legend, a tale of love and courage that would endure for eternity. And high atop Blackspire Mountain, where once a beast of darkness had ruled with fear and dread, now stood a monument to the indomitable spirit of a mother and the child who had changed everything.

And so it was that in Eldoria, where once sacrifices were made to appease a monster, a new era had dawned, marked by the triumph of the human spirit over adversity and the enduring power of love to conquer even the darkest of shadows.

"Today, we conquer not a mythical beast," Emma proclaimed, her voice filled with hope, "but the darkness within ourselves. Let us embrace the light within, and let it guide us."

As the villagers stood united, Emma's voice echoed a warning, "Our beast is not real, but the greatest monster is us. Our fear, hatred, and relentless pursuit of success can make us the true monsters of this earth. Let us be vigilant, for the darkness lies not on the mountain but within ourselves."

And with that resolve, Eldoria thrived, embracing the light within and vowing never to let fear and hatred dictate their actions again.

THE DISAPPEARANCE

In the close-knit town of Maplewood, seven-year-old Mariana was a beloved presence. Her bright smile and cheerful demeanor brought joy wherever she went. But one ordinary afternoon, everything changed. Mariana disappeared while walking home from school, only five blocks from her house.

Her parents, Maria and David, were devastated. They had always been protective of Mariana, their only daughter, who loved drawing pictures of butterflies and playing in the garden.

"Where could she be, David?" Maria sobbed, clutching Mariana's favorite stuffed bunny. "She never walks off the path home."

"We'll find her, Maria," David reassured her, though his own voice shook. "Everyone's searching. We won't stop until she's home."

The search was relentless; family, friends, and even strangers joined the effort. Days turned into weeks and weeks into months, yet there was no trace of her. The community, usually brimming with warmth, was gripped by fear and uncertainty.

Speculation and rumors ran rampant. "Did you hear?" whispered one neighbor to another. "They think she might have been taken."

"Or worse," replied another, a shadow of dread crossing their face.

The lack of witnesses only deepened the mystery. The FBI offered their assistance, deploying top experts, and the townspeople combed through every inch of Maplewood, going door to door. Still, Mariana remained missing—a heart-wrenching enigma.

Twelve long years passed, and life in Maplewood carried on, but a shadow lingered. James, Mariana's older brother, now in his twenties, had grown up carrying the weight of his sister's disappearance. He often wandered the path she took that fateful day, lost in memories and what-ifs.

One crisp autumn evening, as the sun dipped below the horizon, there was a knock at the door of the family's modest home. James opened it to find a young woman standing there, her face eerily familiar.

"Can I help you?" he asked, his heart pounding.

"My name is Mariana," she said softly, her eyes a mirror of his own.

Maria, hearing the commotion, rushed to the door, tears streaming down her face as she embraced her daughter. "Is it really you?" she cried. "Oh, my sweet girl!"

David, who was at work, hurried home, disbelief etched across his features. "Mariana?" he gasped, pulling her into a tight embrace. "Where have you been?"

They bombarded Mariana with questions. "What happened to you twelve years ago?" Maria asked, her voice trembling. "Where did you go?"

Mariana's response was bewildering. "I wasn't missing," she insisted. "I was just walking home from school. It feels like only moments ago."

"What do you mean?" James asked, his brow furrowed in confusion. "You've been gone for twelve years."

"I don't understand," Mariana said, tears welling up in her eyes. "It was just a short walk. How could I be gone for so long?"

The local police were called, and as they questioned her, Mariana's confusion deepened. "I heard a voice calling my name, like from another era," she explained, "but I don't remember anything in between."

"Can you hear it?" she suddenly exclaimed, looking around the room. "Someone's calling my name, now!"

The family exchanged worried glances. "We don't hear anything, honey," David said gently.

Then, everything shifted. Mariana found herself gasping for breath, surrounded by a blinding white light. She blinked and realized she was in a hospital room, a nurse performing CPR on her chest. Her head turned to see familiar faces—her parents, her brother, doctors, and nurses.

"Mariana, welcome back. You've been gone!" one of the nurses exclaimed.

As she processed the scene, the truth came flooding back. Twelve years ago, while walking home from school, she had been struck by a drunk driver, leaving her in a coma.

"I'm here," she whispered, tears streaming down her face. "I'm finally back."

Tears of joy and sorrow mingled as her family embraced her. "We never gave up hope," Maria said, holding her daughter tightly. "We knew you'd come back to us."

"I was lost, but now I'm found," Mariana said softly, gripping her brother's hand.

Though the journey ahead would be challenging, one thing was certain: they were finally reunited, ready to heal together and face whatever came next, cherishing each moment as a gift.

THE MANSION

In a charming town rich with history, a young couple named Jeff and Eliza, along with their son Mike, found themselves captivated by a historical mansion that had lingered on the real estate market for years without a buyer. Snapping up the property at a steal, Jeff and Eliza felt as though they were living out a dream they had long believed unattainable.

After settling into their new home, the family reveled in the grandeur of the old mansion, embracing the sense of history that permeated its walls. Little did they know that the past would soon intertwine with the present in a most unexpected way.

One tranquil evening, as Eliza busied herself in the kitchen preparing a meal, an unusual event unfolded, setting off a chain of mysterious occurrences within the walls of their new abode.

Eliza, calling out from the kitchen, said, "Mike, can you keep an eye on the stove for me? I'll be right back."

"Sure, Mom!" Mike replied, focusing on the task at hand.

Upon her return, the family gathered around the dinner table, enjoying a peaceful meal together, unaware of the extraordinary events that awaited them.

The following morning, a serene Saturday dawned, only to be disrupted by Mike's urgent cries from downstairs, alerting his parents to a strange figure standing outside their home.

"Mom, Dad, come quick! There's someone outside looking at our house!" Mike exclaimed.

Jeff and Eliza exchanged puzzled glances before Jeff decided to investigate. Peering out the window, he spotted a mysterious man on the sidewalk, his gaze fixed on their residence.

"Who is that, Jeff?" Eliza asked, joining him at the window.

"I have no idea, but it's strange," Jeff replied, watching as the man disappeared from view.

In the days that followed, the mysterious visits persisted, with the gifted stranger appearing outside the mansion sporadically. Intrigued by the man's otherworldly abilities, Jeff initiated a conversation with him, leading to a revelation that would forever alter their perception of their new home.

Curious, Jeff approached the stranger and asked, "What brings you here? What do you know about this place?"

The stranger, pulling out a smartphone, replied, "I did some research and found an article online. This mansion tragically burned down 20 years ago, claiming the lives of a family."

Shocked, Eliza interjected, "Are you saying... we are connected to that tragedy?"

The stranger nodded solemnly. "Indeed, your spirits are bound to this place, lingering between worlds."

Mike, trying to grasp the situation, asked the stranger, "How do you see us if we're dead?"

The stranger answered, "I don't really know. I bumped my head when I was 12 years old, and now I have this gift, or as some people call it, a special ability."

Together, they navigated the ethereal landscape of their former home, coming to terms with their newfound existence and the profound connection that bound them to the mansion and its haunting history. Amidst the whispers of bygone days and the echoes of a tragedy long past, Jeff, Eliza, and Mike found solace in the enduring bond that transcended the boundaries of time and mortality, forever united in the ethereal embrace of their shared legacy.

COALVILLE

In the quiet town of Coalville, with its population of just 465, strange occurrences defied all logic. Once a bustling community supported by a coal mine, the town had dwindled to a shadow of its former self after the mine's closure decades ago. With limited income and no tourism, many residents moved away, but some chose to stay, bound by history and a lack of options.

Coalville was barely a dot on the map, with one traffic light, a small grocery store, and the Alliance Life Church. The local library shared space with the City Hall in an old brick building that stood as a testament to better days.

One morning at 4:35 a.m., the townspeople awoke to the sound of military trucks rumbling through the streets, helicopters hovering overhead, their searchlights cutting through the darkness. National Guardsmen patrolled the roads, and the sleepy town buzzed with an eerie energy. Curious residents peered out their windows, some venturing outside to ask the soldiers what was happening.

"It's classified," was the only response they received. "Stay inside your homes until further notice."

The anxious and bewildered residents turned on their televisions, catching the news from a city 50 miles away. The story reported that one of their own, Albert Samuel, had mysteriously erected a garden filled with hundreds of heavy stone statues overnight. The report raised questions that seemed impossible to answer. How could Albert, a quiet man in his sixties, have accomplished this without the use of heavy machinery or any visible assistance? There were no tracks, no signs of large vehicles, and certainly no witnesses.

"What's going on, Ma?" young Jimmy asked, his eyes wide as he clutched his mother's hand.

"I don't know, sweetheart. But it's something big," she replied, glancing nervously at the soldiers outside.

As curiosity and fear mingled, some residents called the local police, while others whispered conspiracies. The sudden and inexplicable appearance of the statues alarmed the government, which descended upon Coalville to investigate the potential threat to national security.

Investigators combed through Albert's garden, marveling at the intricate details of the stone figures. Each statue stood tall, imbued with lifelike expressions and uncanny realism. Yet, despite extensive questioning, Albert remained silent, his eyes distant and unfocused.

"How did you do it, Albert?" an investigator asked, frustration lacing his voice. "We need answers."

Albert remained mute, his silence only deepening the mystery.

"He couldn't have done this alone," one resident insisted. "Those statues weigh tons!"

With no evidence of a crime but plenty of shock, the government erected a fence around the garden, plastering signs that warned against trespassing. "Deadly force will be used," the signs read ominously.

Within weeks, the government bought out the town, offering the remaining residents money to relocate. Coalville became classified, shrouded in secrecy, and off-limits to the public.

Albert was taken to a secret location, where the government struck a deal with him. Whatever secrets he held would now belong to them.

As the townsfolk packed up their lives, an air of sadness mingled with a haunting curiosity. What had truly happened that night? What secrets did Albert keep?

"Where do you think they took him?" one woman asked her neighbor as they loaded their belongings into a moving truck.

"Who knows?" the neighbor replied. "But I bet we'll never see him again."

Years passed, and Coalville faded from memory, its mysteries buried beneath layers of government classification. The warning signs around the garden still stand, a stark reminder of the strange events that had unfolded.

No one knows what happened to Albert Samuel. Perhaps he's living under a new identity, or perhaps he's still working with the government, unraveling secrets that will never see the light of day. But in the town that once was, the silence of the statue's echoes, leaving a lingering question: what really happened in Coalville?

CHAPTER TWENTY-FIVE

A SAYING GOES,
"LAZINESS KILLS AMBITION.
JEALOUSY KILLS PEACE.
ANGER KILLS WISDOM.
FEAR KILLS DREAM."

DANG! THAT'S EXACTLY WHAT MY EX
HAS BEEN SAYING TO ME.
THESE IDEAS ARE DANGEROUS. THEY
NEED TO BE PROSECUTED!

THE GOOD PASTOR

Once upon a time, in a quaint village, a church stood at the heart of the community. Every Sunday, the pews filled with eager congregants, their hearts brimming with anticipation. The pulpit, a beacon of hope, awaited its shepherd.

Pastor John, a kind-hearted man with wisdom etched in his eyes, greeted each member with warmth. His clerical robe flowed as he shared smiles and pleasantries, his mind on the sermon he was about to deliver.

In his office, Pastor John whispered the words of his sermon, each line a reflection of his passion for his flock and family. Yet, beneath his devotion lay a hidden tension.

The congregation rose as Pastor John approached the pulpit, his voice echoing through the hallowed halls. He preached fervently about love and commitment within families, his words weaving a tapestry of hope.

Amidst the congregation, Sarah, his devoted wife, entered with their young daughter Emily by her side, a suitcase in hand. Her face was a mix of determination and anxiety.

As she strode toward the pulpit, murmurs rippled through the crowd. Pastor John's voice faltered, his eyes locking with Sarah's as she stood beside him, trembling.

"Townsfolk," Sarah began, her voice steady but filled with emotion, "I admire the pastor who preaches love and compassion, but the man I know at home is distant. I yearn for the connection we once had."

Gasps and whispers filled the sanctuary. Congregants exchanged glances, grappling with the unexpected confession unfolding before them.

"I want to be with this man, the one who embodies the values he shares here," Sarah continued, her eyes glistening. "But at home, there is a chasm between us. We have lost our way."

Pastor John's heart ached with remorse. Flashbacks of their strained relationship played in his mind—the distance, the neglect. He realized how his dedication to his work had overshadowed his family.

Gathering his courage, Pastor John addressed the congregation, his voice soft yet firm. "I have failed as a husband and a pastor. I vow to rekindle the love we've lost and rebuild our family."

With tears in her eyes, Sarah stepped down from the pulpit. Pastor John reached out, his voice filled with sincerity, "Sarah, forgive me. Let us heal together, for Emily and for us."

As they embraced, the congregation's hearts softened. Whispers of hope filled the air. "It takes courage to admit faults," one congregant murmured, "and strength to seek forgiveness."

In the days that followed, Pastor John, Sarah, and little Emily spent cherished moments together. Laughter and love blossomed anew; their bonds strengthened by the trials they had overcome.

Weeks later, Pastor John stood again at the pulpit, his sermon a testament to love, forgiveness, and second chances. The congregation listened, hearts warmed by the couple's journey.

As the service concluded, congregants mingled, reflecting on the tale of redemption. "It reminds us that even those we admire have their struggles," one remarked. "We must nurture our own relationships."

Hand in hand, Pastor John and Sarah stood before their community, their hearts filled with gratitude. Together, they had weathered the storm, emerging stronger, inspired by the love and support that surrounded them.

And so, once again, the church became a place of worship but also of healing and hope, reminding all that even in the face of trials, love could prevail.

ENA'S PUPPY

Ena, a young girl with a bright smile, lovingly held her golden retriever puppy, Max, in her arms. She gazed at him with adoration, whispering softly about their upcoming trip to see her grandmother. As they approached the bustling airport, the sun cast a golden hue, matching Max's fur. At the check-in counter, an airline staff member named Maria greeted them warmly, explaining the process of pet travel. Reluctantly, Ena handed Max over, kissing his head gently.

"Take care of him, please," she pleaded.

"We'll make sure he's safe and comfortable. Don't worry!" Maria reassured her.

On the plane, Ena sat by the window, her gaze fixed on the clouds. Clutching a picture of her and her grandmother, she whispered to Max in her heart, excited but slightly anxious.

Upon landing in Minnesota, the airline staff discovered the unthinkable: Max had passed away during the flight. Panic set in as they huddled together, brainstorming solutions to avoid breaking Ena's heart.

"We can't let this ruin her trip. What do we do?" Maria asked, her voice tense.

After a heated discussion, they decided to find a replacement puppy, fearing the impact of the truth on Ena.

Later, at a nearby pet shop, Maria and another staff member searched for a look-alike puppy amidst the playful barks and wagging tails. Spotting one that resembled Max, they purchased it, their hearts heavy with the deception but hopeful they could make things right.

Arriving at her grandmother's house, Ena's heart raced with anticipation. The cozy home, nestled in a blanket of snow, filled her with warmth and nostalgia. When the airline staff arrived at the door with the new puppy, Ena opened it, her eyes wide with surprise.

"What's going on?" she asked, confused.

As they presented the puppy, its eyes bright and tail wagging, Ena's confusion turned to shock, then joy.

"My puppy was dead... I brought him to Minnesota to bury him here with Grandma because she gave him to me as a birthday present. But now he's alive again. How did this happen?" she exclaimed, tears welling in her eyes.

The staff, dumbfounded and unsure of how to respond, exchanged anxious glances. Maria stepped forward, speaking softly.

"Sometimes, miracles happen when we least expect them."

Embracing the puppy, Ena's tears flowed freely, a mix of relief and disbelief. Her grandmother, watching from the doorway, understood the situation.

"Love works in mysterious ways, my dear," her grandmother said gently.

"I missed you, Nana. And now I have Max back, too!" Ena beamed, the room filling with warmth and joy.

As the night deepened, snow fell softly outside, blanketing the world in peace. Inside, laughter and love filled the air, a testament to the resilience of hope and the magic of second chances.

FATHER'S DAY

As Touger stood in solitude, surrounded by the comforting presence of his family, the gentle rustle of leaves and the soft hum of crickets filled the air. The flicker of hope in his heart began to grow, a fragile flame in the vast darkness of his grief. The loss of his father felt like an immense chasm, but the words of his brother and mother were a lifeline, pulling him back from the brink.

"We're here for you, Touger. Dad would be proud of the man you've become," his brother said, his voice steady yet filled with emotion. It was a beacon in the storm of emotions that raged within him. Touger nodded, tears glistening in his eyes, a silent acknowledgment of the unbreakable bond that united them in their loss and love.

His mother stepped closer, her hands warm as they clasped his. Her voice, a soothing balm for his wounded soul, held a quiet strength that only a mother could possess. "We miss him too, son. But he will always be with us in spirit, watching over us from above." Her words, imbued with love and resilience, wrapped around him like a comforting embrace.

In that moment of shared sorrow and remembrance, Touger felt a sense of peace begin to settle over him. The memories of his father, the laughter, the lessons, and the love all flooded back, not as a source of pain but as a testament to a life well lived. His father's legacy thrived in the hearts of those who cherished him.

The night deepened, the sky a canopy of twinkling stars, each one a reminder of the everlasting bond they shared. Together, they stood beneath the starlit sky, a family united by loss, bound by love, drawing strength from each other in their time of need. The darkness that threatened to consume him was now punctuated by moments of light, moments of love.

As the night waned and the first light of dawn painted the sky in hues of gold and pink, Touger knew he carried his father's memory with him—a guiding light in the darkness, a beacon of love that could never be extinguished. The dawn was more than just a new day; it was a symbol of hope and renewal.

With Father's Day approaching, a mixture of emotions swirled within him. He made a silent vow to cherish and love those who were still with him to honor his father's memory by showing appreciation and gratitude for the fathers who walked beside their children, both living and departed. It was a promise to himself and his father, a commitment to embrace life and the family he held dear.

On that day, as the world celebrated fatherhood in all its forms, Touger understood the preciousness of the bond between parent and child—a bond that transcended time and space, living on in the echoes of memory and whispers of love. It was a bond that, even in the absence of his father, felt unbreakable.

With a heart filled with gratitude and love, Touger embraced the day. He visited his father's favorite spot, a serene place where the river flowed gently and the birds sang a sweet melody. Here, he found solace, a connection to his father that transcended the physical. As he laid flowers by the riverbank, he whispered his thanks, knowing that his father watched over him, guiding him through the twists and turns of life.

The spirit of his father lived on, not just in the memories but in the legacy of love and remembrance Touger carried within him. It was a flame that would burn bright for all eternity, a testament to the enduring power of love and family. And as the sun set, casting a golden glow over the horizon, Touger felt at peace, knowing that his father's light would always guide him home.

THE FLUSHED AND THIRSTY

Mr. Neng Lee had always found solace in the mountains of Laos. The dense forests, the clear streams, and the vibrant life around him were all he had ever known. But in 1976, his life took an unexpected turn. As conflict-ravaged his homeland, Neng made the heart-wrenching decision to leave everything behind and seek a new life in America with his wife, Mai, and their two children, Khou and Pa.

Their journey began in a refugee camp in Thailand. After months of waiting, the day finally came when they were to board a flight to the United States. They had never been on a plane, nor had they ever seen a city as bustling as Bangkok. As they arrived at the international airport, the vastness of it all overwhelmed them. The noise, the lights, and the throngs of people were unlike anything they had ever experienced.

Amidst the chaos, Khou and Pa tugged at their father's sleeves, their eyes wide with curiosity and thirst. Spotting a water fountain, Mr. Neng led his family towards it, noticing how people bent down to drink from it. He watched closely, observing the water flow out when they approached.

"Look, Papa! Water!" Khou exclaimed, his face lighting up.

Confidently, Neng stepped forward, bending down to drink, but no water came out. Confused, he tried again, and again, but still, no water. His children looked up at him, their faces flushed and thirsty.

"Why no water, Papa?" Pa asked, her voice tinged with disappointment.

Neng stepped back, his heart sinking with each failed attempt. Embarrassment washed over him as he gestured to his children, "Maybe the fountain does not like us."

Mai, sensing his frustration, placed a comforting hand on his shoulder and shook her head. "It's okay, Neng. We will find another way."

But Neng was not one to give up easily. Determined to quench his children's thirst, he continued to observe. He watched how others used the fountain, trying to decipher the secret. It seemed so simple, yet he was met with failure each time. Frustration grew, and he felt the weight of his inadequacy in this modern world.

Finally, a kind passerby noticed his struggle. With a gentle smile, the woman approached him. She pointed to the base of the fountain, then gestured with her foot to the lever. "You need to press the lever with your foot," she said slowly, using simple English and clear gestures.

Neng looked down and saw the lever for the first time. Feeling a mix of relief and embarrassment, he pressed the lever with his foot. Water gushed out, much to the delight of Khou and Pa.

"Thank you," Neng said, his voice filled with gratitude. He quickly filled their cups and handed them to his children.

"Papa, you did it!" Khou cheered, taking a big gulp of water.

Mai smiled warmly at Neng. "We're learning, step by step," she said, gesturing reassuringly.

This small victory was a stark reminder of the challenges that lay ahead. The simple act of getting water had become a monumental task, a symbol of the vast chasm between his old life and the new one he was about to embrace. For Mr. Neng and his family, every day in this new world would be filled with such struggles as they navigated their way through an unfamiliar society, learning and adapting, one small step at a time.

When they finally arrived in Chicago, their sponsoring church welcomed them with open arms. But their new home presented a myriad of challenges. The Lee family did not speak any English, relying on gestures and sign language to communicate. The stove was a baffling contraption, and they didn't know how to operate the washing machine or the refrigerator. Simple tasks that were second nature to others became insurmountable obstacles for them.

One evening, Mrs. Peterson, a kind-hearted member of the church, came by to help. She pointed to the stove and mimed turning the knobs. "This is your stove," she said, showing them how to turn the knobs. "You need to light it like this." She demonstrated how to cook on it, her movements smooth and practiced. Neng and Mai watched intently, trying to absorb every detail.

"This," Mrs. Peterson said, pointing to the washing machine, "is how you use the washing machine." She mimed putting clothes in, adding soap, and turning the dial.

Neng and Mai exchanged glances, nodding gratefully. "Thank you," Neng said, his voice sincere though heavily accented.

Despite their best efforts, the transition was overwhelming. They missed the familiarity of their old life, the simplicity of the mountains, and the comfort of their community. But they pressed on, motivated by the hope of a better future for their children.

Then, tragedy struck. One cold night in their small apartment, Neng went to bed and never woke up. Mai found him the next morning, his face peaceful but lifeless. The community was shocked and heartbroken. Neng's death was the beginning of a disturbing trend among the Hmong refugees, perplexing authorities, and the medical community. Many Hmong men were dying in their sleep, a phenomenon that would later be termed Sudden Unexplained Nocturnal Death Syndrome (SUNDS). At the time, no clear explanation could be found, adding to the fear and uncertainty that gripped the Hmong community.

In a sterile conference room, the police, investigators, and medical doctors gathered to discuss the mysterious deaths. Detective Harris leaned forward; his brow furrowed. "Another Hmong man passed away in his sleep last night. That makes it five this month."

Dr. Roberts, a seasoned medical examiner, shook his head in frustration. "We've performed autopsies on all of them, and there's no clear cause of death. It's like they just... stopped living."

Dr. Nguyen, an epidemiologist specializing in immigrant health, interjected. "This pattern isn't new. It's been happening since the Hmong started arriving. We're calling it Sudden Unexplained Nocturnal Death Syndrome, or SUNDS, but we don't have any solid answers yet."

Officer Martinez, who had been working closely with the Hmong community, added, "The families are terrified. They believe it's some sort of curse or spirit. We need to give them answers, something to ease their fears."

Dr. Roberts sighed. "We've run every test we can think of. There are no signs of foul play, no drugs or toxins. It's like their hearts just... give out."

Detective Harris frowned. "Could it be stress? They've been through so much. War, displacement, adapting to a new country..."

Dr. Nguyen nodded. "That's a possibility. The trauma they've experienced, the drastic lifestyle changes, and the stress of adjusting to a new environment could be factors. But without more research, we can't be sure."

Dr. Bruce Thowpaou Bliatout, a Hmong and an expert on Hmong culture and health, had been following the situation closely. He decided to conduct a comprehensive study to understand the cultural and psychological aspects of these deaths. In 1982, he published a groundbreaking paper titled "Hmong Sudden Unexpected Nocturnal Death Syndrome: A Cultural Study."

Mrs. Peterson and Mr. Johnson stood by Mai and her children, providing support and comfort. Mrs. Peterson hugged Mai tightly, gesturing to her heart. "We're here for you, Mai. You're not alone."

The loss of Neng was a devastating blow, but Mai knew she had to be strong for Khou and Pa. With the help of their new friends, they continued to navigate their new world, each day a testament to their resilience and determination. They faced many more challenges, but with each one, they grew stronger, and their bond as a family deepened.

In those moments of triumph, no matter how small, they found the courage to continue their journey, holding on to the hope of a better future in a land they had yet to understand fully.

THE ILLUSION OF GRANDEUR

Harry Moua had always believed that life was his for the taking. Born into a world where money equated to power and success, he reveled in his accomplishments. Every deal he closed, every opulent party he threw, and every accolade he received bolstered his belief that he was invincible. He walked with the air of a man who owned the world, his pride and arrogance evident in every step.

One evening, at the height of his success, Harry hosted a grand gala at his mansion. The who's who of society attended, their laughter and chatter filling the lavishly decorated halls. Harry stood at the center, a glass of the finest champagne in hand, basking in the glow of admiration.

"Harry, you truly outdo yourself every time," said Jacob, an old friend and business associate. "This party is spectacular."

Harry smirked, "Only the best for my guests, Jacob. After all, what good is success if you can't enjoy it?"

Yet, amid the opulence, Harry's closest friend, Lily, noticed a flicker of emptiness in his eyes. She had known Harry long enough to see through his façade. Later that night, as the party wound down, she approached him.

"Harry, can we talk?" she asked softly, leading him to a quiet corner.

"Sure, Lily. What's on your mind?" Harry replied, his tone dismissive.

"Have you ever thought about what really matters in life? Beyond the money and the parties?" she pressed.

Harry laughed, "You're being dramatic, Lily. Life is about enjoying the fruits of our labor. Look around you; this is what matters."

Lily sighed, sensing the futility of her words. "I hope one day you'll see it differently."

Months passed, and Harry's empire continued to grow. But one morning, he woke up with an unusual heaviness in his chest. Brushing it off as exhaustion, he pushed through his day, unwilling to let anything slow him down. However, the discomfort persisted, and soon, he found himself confined to a hospital bed, doctors hovering over him with concerned expressions.

"Mr. Moua, your condition is serious," Dr. Evans explained. "You need to take this time to rest and recover."

Harry scoffed, "Rest? I have too much to do. Just fix me up so I can get back to work."

But the days turned into weeks, and Harry's condition worsened. He was forced to confront a harsh reality: his money and success couldn't save him from his failing health. As he lay in bed, he watched his life from a distance, unable to participate in the world he once dominated.

With each passing day, Harry grew more reflective. The constant stream of visitors began to dwindle, and soon, only a few loyal friends and family remained by his side. One evening, Lily visited, her eyes filled with a mix of sadness and determination.

"Harry, do you remember our conversation at your gala?" she asked gently.

Harry nodded, his voice weak. "Yes, I do. I was such a fool."

Lily smiled softly. "It's not too late to change, Harry. Life has a funny way of teaching us what's truly important."

Tears welled up in Harry's eyes. "I had everything, Lily. But now, I see that it was all meaningless. The money, the fame—it doesn't matter. What matters is the love and kindness we show to others."

Lily squeezed his hand. "I'm glad you've realized that, Harry. It's never too late to make amends and find peace."

As Harry's health continued to decline, he made an effort to reconnect with those he had wronged. He reached out to old friends, mended broken relationships, and sought forgiveness from those he had hurt in his relentless pursuit of success. His transformation was evident, and though his body grew weaker, his spirit shone brighter.

One afternoon, Harry's nurse, Maria, sat by his bed, offering him comfort. "You've come a long way, Mr. Moua. Your story is an inspiration."

Harry smiled faintly. "Thank you, Maria. I've learned that life is about more than what we can gain. It's about what we can give."

In his final days, Harry found solace in the love and support of those around him. He had lost his wealth and status, but he had gained something far more valuable: the understanding that true success lies in the connections we make and the love we share.

As Harry took his last breath, he felt a sense of peace wash over him. Life, with all its twists and turns, had taught him a profound lesson. He had laughed at its irony and cried at its cruelty, but in the end, he had found meaning in its simplest truth: we are all actors in the grand play of life, but it is our kindness and compassion that define our legacy.

And so, Harry Moua's story came to a close, a testament to the transformative power of love and redemption. Life may be funny, but in the end, it's the moments of genuine connection that truly make us laugh.

CHAPTER TWENTY-SIX
"I USED TO PLAY PIANO BY EAR, BUT NOW I USE MY HANDS."

WELL, I GUESS YOU FINALLY DECIDED TO GIVE YOUR FINGERS A BREAK AND LET YOUR HANDS DO ALL THE WORK.

THE EGG OF WISDOM

Mark had always been a man driven by ambition, but his track record was marred with failures. He had been scammed, lost money gambling, and watched his second business crumble. After numerous failed attempts, he was determined to find a foolproof way to success—one that involved no risk.

Hearing tales of a wise monk living in the mountains, Mark set out on a journey, hoping to gain the wisdom that would finally steer him away from failure. The monk was reputed for his deep understanding of success and failure, and Mark believed that this was his last hope.

After days of arduous travel, Mark finally reached the temple nestled high in the mountains. He stood before the imposing structure, his heart filled with anticipation. He was ready to learn something valuable—something that would ensure he would never taste failure again.

As he entered the serene courtyard, he saw the monk seated under a large banyan tree, radiating calmness and wisdom. Mark approached him with reverence and urgency.

"Master," Mark began, his voice trembling slightly, "I have come to seek your guidance. I have failed in so many things. I want to know how I can avoid any risks in life. I want to ensure that the next time I do something, it will be without any risk."

The monk looked at Mark with kind, piercing eyes and said, "I will help you, Mark, but first, answer me this: What is in the back of my hands?"

Mark, puzzled, asked, "I don't know. What is it that is in the back of your hands, Master?"

"An egg," replied the monk. "Now, tell me, is it broken or not?"

Mark was taken aback by the question. He pondered for a moment and then replied, "How would I know if it's a broken egg or not?"

The monk's gaze remained steady. "Well, that's the risk you have to take. Please answer: Is it a broken egg or not?"

Mark felt a wave of frustration. He thought to himself, if I say it's not broken, he might crush it. But if I say it's broken, it might not be. Torn by indecision, he finally said, "I don't know."

The monk smiled gently. "That's exactly right. Now, go home, Mark. The lesson is over. Don't take any chances, and you will get nothing in return."

Mark stood there, shocked. The monk's words began to sink in. The realization hit him with the force of a revelation. By refusing to take any risk, he was essentially ensuring that he would gain nothing.

Mark bowed deeply, gratitude and newfound understanding filling his heart. "Thank you, Master. I understand now."

The monk nodded, his eyes twinkling with wisdom. "Remember, Mark, life itself is a risk. To achieve anything meaningful, you must be willing to take chances, even if it means facing failure. It is through these experiences that we grow and ultimately succeed."

As Mark descended the mountain, he felt a renewed sense of purpose. He understood that taking risks was an essential part of the journey to success. Armed with this new perspective, he was ready to face the world again, knowing that even in failure, there was a lesson to be learned and a step toward eventual success.

LIFE IN AMERICA

Once upon a time, in a small town in the heart of the United States, the Moua family, refugees from Thailand, found themselves starting a new chapter of their lives. Mr. and Mrs. Moua, along with their three children, arrived in the land of opportunity with hopes and dreams of a better future, leaving behind the turmoil and hardships of their homeland.

Guiding them on this unfamiliar journey were their sponsors, Mr. and Mrs. John Thompson, a God-loving couple known for their kindness and generosity in the community. The Thompsons welcomed the Moua family with open arms, providing them with a place to stay, support, and guidance as they adjusted to their new life in America.

With gratitude in their hearts, the Moua couple set out to build a life for themselves in their new home. They found work, humble jobs that paid them $7 per hour, but they worked tirelessly and with determination to make ends meet and provide for their children.

As the years passed, the Moua family's dreams began to grow. They longed for a place to call their own, a home where they could create lasting memories and build a future for their children. However, the reality of their financial situation made this dream seem out of reach.

One day, with heavy hearts, Mr. and Mrs. Moua approached their sponsors, the Thompsons, with a request. They needed a loan of $5,000 to make a down payment on a house they had set their eyes on. Worried about being able to pay back the loan, the Moua family hesitantly made their plea to the Thompsons.

Mr. Moua: "Mr. and Mrs. Thompson, we have a humble request. We need a loan of $5,000 to make a down payment on a house for our family. We understand if it's too much to ask..."

Mrs. Thompson: "Oh, dear, you don't need to worry. We will help you. You have been working so hard all these years, and it's time for you to have a place to call your own."

To their surprise, three months later, the Thompsons paid a visit to the Moua family at their new home.

Mr. Thompson: "Hello, Moua family. We have something for you."

Mrs. Moua: "What is it, Mr. Thompson?"

Mr. Thompson: "It's a paper stating that the loan you took has been paid in full. Consider it a gift from us to you."

Overwhelmed with gratitude and disbelief, the Moua family couldn't believe the generosity and kindness shown to them by their sponsors.

Mrs. Moua: "We don't know how to thank you enough. You have truly been angels to us."

Through the love and support of the Thompsons, the Moua family not only found a home but also found a sense of belonging and hope in their new country. Their journey in America had been challenging, but with the compassion and selfless acts of their sponsors, the refugees had not just survived but thrived, proving that love and kindness knew no boundaries.

THROUGH THE FIRE

The warm glow of the fireplace illuminated the cozy living room as Grandma Mai settled into her favorite rocking chair. Her grandson, little Tommy, snuggled up next to her, his eyes wide with anticipation.

"Tell me a story, Grandma," Tommy asked, his voice full of curiosity.

Grandma Mai smiled, her eyes twinkling with a mixture of joy and nostalgia. "Alright, Tommy. I'll tell you the story of a brave little boy who faced many challenges but never gave up."

"In a small village in Laos, during a time of great war, a baby boy was born. His mother brought him into the world, but passed away soon after. His father, a soldier, had gone to fight and never returned. The baby was alone, but a kind neighbor took him in and named him Somchai, which means 'worthy man.'

"Somchai's village was destroyed, and Elder Kham carried him through the dangerous roads, away from the bombs and chaos.

"Somchai and Elder Kham found refuge in a camp in Thailand. Life there was hard. The boy often went without food and was very sick. But one day, a kind woman from a Catholic Charity, Sister Margaret, visited the camp. She saw Somchai's suffering and decided to help.

"'We can take him to America,' Sister Margaret told Elder Kham. 'He will have a chance at a better life there.' And so, they did."

"When Somchai arrived in America, everything was different. He went to live with a loving family, the Millers, who treated him like their own. But school was tough. He didn't speak the language well, and some kids were mean to him.

"One day, after being bullied, he came home in tears. Mrs. Miller hugged him tightly and said, 'You're special, Somchai. One day, they'll see that.' Those words gave him strength, and he worked very hard in school, becoming one of the best students."

"Years went by, and this boy grew up. He became a Doctor of Naturopathic Medicine because he wanted to help others like he had been helped. He opened a clinic and later started a company making natural health products. People respected him, and his business thrived.

"At the opening of his clinic, he told everyone, 'This clinic is a testament to the power of perseverance and faith. Together, we can build a healthier, happier future.'"

"But success brought challenges. Someone falsely accused him of fraud, and he was sent to prison. Somchai lost everything—his business, his home, and his reputation.

"In prison, he met a wise man named Frank. One night, Frank saw Somchai's sadness and said, 'When you've hit rock bottom, there's only one way to go—up. And faith, my friend, is the ladder.' Those words helped Somchai find hope again."

"After six and a half years, Somchai was released from prison. He had nothing, but he hadn't lost his spirit. He started offering free health consultations at a community center. Slowly, people began to trust him again.

"One day, a former patient approached him. 'Dr. Somchai, you saved my life once. I believe in you. Let's start a new clinic together.' With that support, Somchai began rebuilding his life."

"Somchai's new clinic became very successful. He shared his story with the community, saying, 'We don't live life by what we know or see, but by faith and hope in God, our source of power to overcome anything in this world.'"

Grandma Mai looked down at Tommy, her eyes filled with love. "And that, my dear, is the story of a little boy who never gave up, no matter how hard things got."

Tommy's eyes were wide with wonder. "Grandma, who is this little boy?"

Grandma Mai's smile grew even warmer. She gently took Tommy's hand. "That little boy was your father, Tommy. He is

Somchai, the brave man who grew up to be strong, kind, and resilient."

Tommy's mouth opened in surprise. "Really, Grandma?"

"Yes, my dear," she said, hugging him tightly. "Your father's journey shows us that with faith and hope, we can overcome anything. God is the source of his faith and hope."

In that moment, Tommy felt a newfound sense of pride and admiration for his father, knowing that he came from a lineage of strength and resilience.

Later that evening, when his father returned from work, Tommy ran to him and said, "Dad, I love you. I want to be just like you—strong, brave, and with faith in God."

LOVE IS FOR LOSERS

Lance was sipping his coffee at the corner table of the cozy cafe when he noticed Andy sitting at a nearby table, looking forlorn and lost in his thoughts. The cafe, a charming place with exposed brick walls and soft jazz playing in the background, was Lance's favorite spot to relax. Today, however, his attention was drawn to the stranger whose shoulders seemed to carry an invisible burden.

Lance, a friendly and outgoing man with a knack for sensing when others needed a lift, felt a pang of empathy for the man. He set down his coffee cup, smoothed his plaid shirt, and decided to approach him.

With a warm smile, Lance walked over to Andy's table and asked, "Mind if I join you? You seem a bit down, and I thought some company might help."

Andy looked up, startled by the kind gesture. His eyes, a deep blue clouded with sorrow, met Lance's for a moment before he nodded silently, welcoming Lance to take a seat across from him. The two men exchanged introductions, and soon, a conversation started to flow between them.

Noticing the melancholy expression on Andy's face, Lance gently asked, "What's troubling you? You look like you have the weight of the world on your shoulders."

Andy hesitated for a moment before replying, "It's a love issue. But you wouldn't understand."

Lance chuckled softly and said, "Try me. I may surprise you."

Andy sighed and began to open up, "Love is for losers. And I guess I'm a loser in that department."

Intrigued by Andy's cryptic statement, Lance leaned in and asked, "What do you mean by that?"

Andy gave a wry smile and explained, "Well, if you play tennis, you would understand. But sometimes, no matter how hard you try, you end up losing."

Lance couldn't help but laugh at Andy's analogy. "So, you lost a tennis match in love, huh?" he teased.

Andy chuckled softly, the heaviness in his heart momentarily lifted by Lance's lighthearted response. "Yeah, something like that. In tennis, when you haven't scored any points in a game, it's called 'love.' It means you're at zero. I was in the middle of the most important match of my life, and I couldn't get past love. My mind was elsewhere, thinking about my dad."

Lance's expression softened. "I'm sorry to hear that, Andy. Was he sick?"

Andy nodded, his eyes misting over. "Yeah, he was. I thought I could handle it, but during the match, I kept thinking about all the times he watched me play and how proud he was. I just couldn't focus."

Lance leaned back, absorbing Andy's story. "It's tough when life throws such curveballs. But you know, love for your dad isn't something that makes you a loser. It's what makes you human."

Andy looked thoughtful. "I guess. But it's hard not to feel like I let him down."

Lance nodded. "I get it. When we care deeply about someone, it can be overwhelming. But your dad wouldn't want you to beat yourself up over this. He'd want you to remember the good times and keep playing with the same passion."

Andy smiled faintly. "Maybe you're right. I just wish I could have won that match for him."

As the two continued to chat, sharing stories and experiences, a sense of camaraderie blossomed between them, bridging the gap of their initial strangeness. Lance shared his own tales of personal struggles and moments where love had both lifted him and weighed him down, making Andy realize he wasn't alone in his pain.

By the time they finished their coffee, Andy found himself feeling a bit lighter, grateful for the unexpected encounter with a kind stranger named Lance, who had helped him see his troubles from a different perspective. As they bid farewell and went their separate ways, Andy couldn't help but smile, knowing that sometimes, a chance meeting at a cafe could turn a gloomy day into a brighter one.

Just as Andy stepped out of the cafe, he turned back to see Lance still seated at the table, now absorbed in a book. For a moment, Andy considered inviting him to a tennis match, not as opponents, but as friends. Deciding against it, he took a deep breath and walked into the crisp afternoon, a newfound hope warming his heart.

THE FALL

Johnathan was a middle-aged man whose life was the very picture of success. Each morning, he would stand in front of his floor-to-ceiling window, surveying the city below with a sense of ownership. His posture radiated confidence and command.

He had clawed his way to the top, becoming the CEO of his own company. His leadership style was ruthless, and he showed no mercy even to the most loyal and hardworking of his employees. One fateful day in the boardroom, he announced the mass firing of several staff members. Among them was Mark, a dedicated employee who had served the company for over twenty years.

"You're all fired. Pack your things and leave," Johnathan declared coldly.

Mark stood up, his face a mixture of shock and despair. "But sir, I've given everything to this place," he pleaded.

Johnathan's eyes were steely and unfeeling. "No exceptions," he snapped, motioning for security to escort them out.

At the stock exchange, Johnathan relished his power. He watched the ticker with a grin, reveling in the numbers climbing ever higher. "Look at that! We're unstoppable," he boasted to a colleague, basking in his perceived invincibility.

But pride comes before a fall. One afternoon in his office, Johnathan's secretary, Lucy, handed him a piece of paper. As he read it, his face drained of color. The stock had plummeted, hitting rock bottom. Panic set in, and his world began to crumble.

The shareholders were livid. In a tense boardroom meeting, their leader, Mr. Thompson, pointed an accusatory finger at Johnathan. "Your mismanagement has cost us everything. We vote to remove you as CEO," he declared.

Johnathan protested, "You can't do this to me!" But security guards swiftly escorted him out of his own company, his defiance futile.

Stripped of his power and wealth, Johnathan wandered aimlessly through the crowded and dilapidated streets of downtown. His once-pristine tailored suit was now worn and dirty, a stark contrast to his former self. He found refuge in an abandoned building, huddling in a corner, shivering from the cold and consumed by hunger.

"How did it come to this?" he muttered to himself, reflecting on his downfall.

Days turned into weeks, and Johnathan found himself sitting on a street corner, holding a tattered cardboard sign that read, "Anything Helps." He had become invisible to the world he once ruled.

One day, a sleek black car pulled up in front of him, and a well-dressed man stepped out. It was Michael, a successful businessman. He looked at Johnathan with a mix of recognition and pity.

"Johnathan, is that you?" Michael asked, his voice laced with surprise.

Johnathan squinted at him, struggling to place the familiar face. "Do I... do I know you?" he stammered.

Michael smiled gently. "Oh, we've crossed paths before. Remember when you were on top of the world, and I was just one of the little people?"

Recognition dawned on Johnathan. "You... you bought my shares?" he whispered, his voice filled with regret.

Michael nodded, reaching into his pocket and pulling out a wad of cash. "Here, take this. It's not much, but it might help you get back on your feet," he said, offering the money.

Johnathan hesitated for a moment before accepting it, tears welling up in his eyes. "Thank you, Michael. I... I never realized the consequences of my actions until now."

Michael looked at him with sympathy. "Remember, Johnathan, wealth and power are fleeting. Be careful who you step on while climbing up because someday you may meet them on your way down."

As Michael got back into his car and drove away, Johnathan sat there, holding the money and contemplating his past. A newfound understanding of his actions and their consequences began to take root in his heart.

"I'll make things right," he whispered to himself, determined to rebuild his life with a new perspective.

CHAPTER TWENTY-SEVEN
"I'M NOT A COMPLETE IDIOT, JUST SOME PARTS ARE MISSING."

WELL, MAYBE YOU JUST NEED
A LITTLE 'ASSEMBLY'
TO BECOME A GENIUS.

A PILOT FOR ONE DAY

Sam: "Jimmy, you won't believe the story I read on Facebook last night. It was a dull evening, and I was just lounging in my creaky old rocking chair on the balcony, sipping on some hot coffee. I logged into Facebook, you know, just to kill time, and there I was, scrolling through the usual updates and cat videos."

Jimmy: "Yeah, those cat videos can get old fast."

Sam: "Exactly! Just as I was about to give up, I stumbled upon this post that caught my eye. It was about a guy named Tommy. Now, Tommy wasn't your average guy—he worked as a janitor at the airport, doing all the usual janitorial stuff."

Jimmy: "A janitor at the airport? That's a tough job."

Sam: "Yeah, and you'd think his day couldn't get any more interesting, right? But then, fate—or maybe just plain luck—led him to the cockpit of an airplane."

Jimmy: "Wait, how did he end up there?"

Sam: "I wish I knew! Anyway, there he was, and what does he find? The captain's flight manual, lying right there on the seat. And get this—it was titled 'HOW TO FLY AN AIRPLANE.'"

Jimmy: "Oh boy, this sounds like trouble."

Sam: "Big trouble! But Tommy, being the curious type, starts flipping through the manual."

Jimmy: "I can imagine where this is going."

Sam: "Step 1 says to push the blue button to start the engine. And guess what? Tommy pushes it, and voila—the engine comes to life!"

Jimmy: "No way!"

Sam: "I kid you not. Then, Step 2 says to push the yellow button to taxi the plane to the runway. Tommy, feeling adventurous, goes ahead and pushes that yellow button. Lo and behold, the plane started moving!"

Jimmy: "This is getting crazier by the minute."

Sam: "Just wait. Step 3 instructs him to push the green button to fly. And without a second thought, Tommy pushes it. Next thing you know, he's soaring into the sky, leaving the ground behind!"

Jimmy: "Unbelievable! But what about landing?"

Sam: "Ah, that's where it gets tricky. As Tommy's enjoying the unexpected flight, he suddenly realizes he has no clue how to land this thing. He frantically flips through the manual and finds, 'To land the plane, purchase manual volume number two.'"

Jimmy: "You've got to be kidding me! What did he do?"

Sam: "Well, the post didn't say, but just imagining the situation had me cracking up. But you know, it got me thinking about how important it is to be prepared and have the right guidance. Even in life, we need that."

Jimmy: "Absolutely. It's like jumping into something without knowing how to get out of it."

Sam: "Exactly! And it reminded me of the importance of having faith and wisdom to navigate through life's challenges. Just like Tommy needed that manual, we need God's guidance to steer us through life's ups and downs."

Jimmy: "Well said, Sam. These stories, as funny as they are, really do have some deep lessons."

Sam: "They sure do. As I closed my laptop and looked up at the stars, I couldn't help but feel thankful for the reminder. Never live life without having God in your life. Just like Tommy needed the complete pilot's manual, we need God's guidance to navigate through the turbulent skies of life."

Jimmy: "That's a great takeaway, Sam. Thanks for sharing that story."

Sam: "Anytime, Jimmy. Anytime."

THE MYSTERIOUS HOUSEKEEPER

Jennifer, a young single mother at the age of 35, took a deep breath and began to recount her astonishing tale to Bethany, her closest friend. With two young children depending on her, the strange occurrences in her life had added an extra layer of stress to her already demanding days.

"It all started a few months ago," Jennifer began, sipping her coffee nervously. "I would come home from work, and my house would be spotless. The vacuuming was done, the dishes were washed... It was the strangest thing."

Bethany's eyes widened in surprise. "Wow, that is strange. Did you think it was a neighbor or a friend helping out?"

"At first, I thought so," Jennifer replied. "But as time went on, no one came forward. It started to worry me. I mean, who was coming into my house when I wasn't there?"

Bethany leaned in, intrigued. "What did you do next?"

"I called the police," Jennifer continued. "They set up surveillance cameras in my house, hoping to catch whoever was behind it. But when they reviewed the footage, it turned out to be me all along. I was the one cleaning the house without even realizing it."

Bethany's brows furrowed in confusion. "Wait, you were the one doing all the cleaning? How is that possible?"

"It was a shock to me, too," Jennifer admitted. "The police explained that I was suffering from a dissociative disorder, causing me to perform tasks without being aware of it. It was like I was living a double life without knowing it."

Bethany gasped, her hand flying to her mouth. "That must have been so disorienting for you. How did you handle it?"

"It was a challenging time, for sure," Jennifer said somberly. "I sought help from a therapist and started treatment to manage my condition. It was a difficult journey, but I'm grateful for the support I received from my family and friends."

As Bethany processed the shocking revelation, she reached out and gave Jennifer a comforting hug. "I'm glad you're getting the help you need. You're so strong for sharing this with me."

Jennifer smiled gratefully. "Thank you, Bethany. It's been a tough road, but I'm taking it one step at a time. I've learned a lot about myself through this experience."

The two friends sat in silence, the weight of Jennifer's story hanging in the air. It was a tale of self-discovery, resilience, and the enduring power of friendship in the face of life's unexpected twists and turns.

At Mercy Mental Hospital, Dr. Ramon Diaz, a renowned psychiatrist, paused his dictation, reflecting on the extraordinary case of Jennifer. His diagnosis had uncovered not just the dissociative disorder that caused her to unknowingly perform household tasks but also the deeper emotional turmoil that stemmed from her loss. Jennifer had confided in Bethany, finding solace in her friend's comforting presence, only to realize later that Bethany was a figment of her mind—a manifestation of her late mother, who had passed away months before Jennifer's breakdown.

Dr. Diaz concluded in his note that Jennifer's mind had created Bethany to cope with her grief and loneliness. The discovery that she was both the mysterious housekeeper and that her comforting friend was a projection of her deceased mother was a testament to the mind's incredible if sometimes bewildering, capacity to heal and protect itself. He concluded his note by emphasizing the importance of continued therapy and support for Jennifer as she navigated her path to recovery.

HOME INVASION

In the quiet town of Sandspring, Bill and Martha enjoyed their retirement years who were known for their kindness and community service. One of Bill's favorite pastimes was his morning walks by the lake, savoring the peaceful sunrise.

One morning, upon returning home, Bill was startled to find a strange car parked in his driveway. His confusion turned to shock as he encountered unfamiliar faces in his home - an old woman, a young lady, and a young man, all of whom seemed strangely familiar yet foreign.

Bill's heart pounded with disbelief as he searched for Martha and their grandchildren, but he couldn't place the faces he saw before him. Determined to protect his home, he called the police.

Minutes later, police officers arrived at the scene. Officer Smith, the senior officer, approached Bill, who was visibly distressed.

Officer Smith: "Good morning, sir. I'm Officer Smith. Can you tell me what's going on?"

Bill: "Officer, these people are in my house, and I don't know who they are. They said they live here, but this is my home. My wife and grandkids are gone. I don't know what's happening."

Officer Smith: "Alright, Bill, we're here to help. Let's take a step back and sort this out. Ma'am, can you explain why you're here?"

Old Woman: "Officer, I am Martha. Bill, I'm your wife. This is our home. The young lady is our daughter, and the young man is our grandson."

Bill: "What? No, you can't be Martha. Martha is younger... This doesn't make any sense."

Officer Smith: "Okay, Bill, let's check your ID and any documents you might have. Ma'am, do you have any documents to support your claim?"

Martha: "Yes, officer. Here's our marriage certificate and some family photos."

As Officer Smith and his partner reviewed the documents and photos, it became evident that the old woman was indeed Martha, and the young lady and young man were their daughter and grandson.

Officer Smith: "Bill, these documents and photos show that these people are your family. Do you remember anything about them now?"

Bill: "I... I don't know. It all seems so confusing. I remember Martha differently."

Officer Smith: "We need to get to the bottom of this. Would you be alright if we called someone from your family or a close friend to help sort this out?"

Martha: "Please call Dr. Thao. He's been helping Bill with his condition."

The officers contacted Dr. Charles Thao, who soon arrived at the scene.

Dr. Thao: "Good morning, Officer Smith. I'm Dr. Thao. Bill, how are you feeling?"

Bill: "Dr. Thao, I don't understand any of this. They say they're my family, but I don't remember them like this. Martha looks different, and the kids... I don't know."

Dr. Thao: "Bill, remember we've talked about your Alzheimer's diagnosis. Sometimes, your memories might not align with reality. It seems that might be happening now."

Officer Smith: "Dr. Thao, can you shed some light on Bill's condition for us?"

Dr. Thao: "Bill has Alzheimer's disease. It can cause confusion and memory loss, making it difficult for him to recognize even close family members at times."

Officer Smith: "That makes sense. Bill, it seems your memory is playing tricks on you. Let's make sure you're safe and have the support you need."

Bill: "I just want to understand what's real. I don't want to forget my family."

Dr. Thao: "I understand, Bill. We'll work together to support you. Let's head to the hospital for a check-up, and we'll figure out the next steps."

As the officers ensured the situation was under control, Bill was taken to St. Mary Hospital, where Dr. Thao and his team provided the necessary care and reassurance. The community of Sandspring rallied around Bill and Martha, determined to face the challenges of Alzheimer's with compassion and support.

As the sun set over Sandspring, a new chapter began for Bill, Martha, and their community, united in their resolve to face the challenges of Alzheimer's with courage, resilience, and unwavering support.

THE LEGACY OF FAITH

As friends and family gathered in a serene park for a solemn occasion, Ryan stood before them, preparing to deliver a eulogy for his dear friend, Alex. The setting sun cast a golden glow over the scene, lending a sense of peace to the somber moment. The gentle rustling of leaves and the distant chirping of birds provided a poignant backdrop.

"Today, we gather to honor the life of Alex, a man whose journey left an indelible mark on all who knew him," Ryan began, his voice steady but filled with emotion. "I stand here not only to bid farewell to a cherished friend but also to share a story of transformation and the enduring power of faith."

He paused, scanning the familiar faces, some tear-streaked, others solemn, all sharing in the grief of their collective loss. "Thirty years ago, Alex and I engaged in many spirited debates about the existence of God. Alex, once a staunch atheist, challenged my beliefs with fervor and conviction. His skepticism often pushed me to question my own faith, leading me down a path of uncertainty and doubt."

A soft murmur rippled through the crowd. Ryan's wife, Emily, squeezed their daughter Cindy's hand, her eyes glistening with tears. Cindy, now a teenager, had grown up hearing stories about Uncle Alex and his lively debates with her father.

Ryan continued, "It was through Alex's unwavering dedication to his beliefs that I found my way back to faith. In the midst of our debates, I witnessed a profound transformation within him. Over time, Alex's perspective shifted, and he embraced Christianity with a fervor that inspired me."

A memory surfaced in Ryan's mind, one he hadn't shared with many. "I remember one night, after another heated discussion, Alex called me. His voice was different, softer. 'Ryan,' he said, 'I've been thinking a lot about what you've said, and... I think I'm starting to understand.' It was the beginning of his journey, a moment I'll never forget."

As the sun dipped below the horizon, casting a warm glow over the gathered mourners, Ryan's voice wavered with emotion. "Alex never ceased to talk about God - about the beauty of faith, the comfort it brought him, and the hope it instilled in his heart. His newfound conviction was a testament to the power of belief and the capacity for change that resides within each of us."

He looked over at Alex's parents, their faces etched with grief and pride. "In honoring Alex's memory today, let us remember not only the man he was but also the legacy of faith and transformation he leaves behind. May his journey serve as a guiding light for us all, illuminating the path to a deeper understanding of ourselves and the world around us."

With a final nod of reverence, Ryan stepped back, allowing the gentle embrace of twilight to envelop the gathering. As he did, Emily stepped forward, placing a comforting hand on his shoulder. "You spoke beautifully," she whispered, her voice breaking.

Cindy approached, hugging her father tightly. "I wish I could've known him better," she said softly.

Ryan kissed the top of her head. "He lives on in all of us, Cindy. In the stories we share, in the faith we hold, and in the love we give."

As the family and friends lingered, sharing stories and memories of Alex, a sense of peace settled over the park. The night was filled with quiet conversations, laughter through tears, and the comforting knowledge that Alex's legacy would endure, not just in faith but in the hearts of those who loved him.

DISTURBED DREAMS

In the dead of night, the quiet suburban street was suddenly pierced by the screeching sound of tires and the slamming of car doors. Federal agents, clad in dark uniforms and armed to the teeth, descended upon a house like a swarm of vengeful shadows. They moved swiftly and with purpose, their mission clear in their minds as they approached the target.

Inside the house, a man lay peacefully asleep in bed, his wife by his side, their dreams undisturbed by the chaos that was about to unfold. Suddenly, the bedroom door burst open with a loud crash, and the agents stormed in, their flashlights cutting through the darkness like knives.

"Get on the floor! Hands behind your back!" one of the agents barked as they yanked the man out of his bed with brutal force. His wife screamed in terror, her eyes wide with shock as she watched her husband being manhandled by the intruders.

"No, please! You have the wrong person! Please listen to me!" the man pleaded, his voice filled with desperation as he tried to reason with the agents.

"Shut up! You're coming with us!" another agent snarled, tightening his grip on the man's arm as they forced him to the ground.

The man's wife sobbed uncontrollably, her pleas for mercy being disregarded as the agents continued their assault. Witnesses peering through their windows said the agents were brutal, their actions fueled by a blind determination to capture their target at all costs.

With a knee pressed hard against his neck, cutting off his breath, the man gasped for air and struggled to speak. "I'm not who you think I am! Please, you're making a mistake!" he gasped, his words choked with fear and frustration.

As the man was dragged outside to the waiting car, the mayor of the city emerged from his house across the street, a look of shock and disbelief on his face as he witnessed the scene unfolding before him.

"I'm the mayor! You have the wrong man!" the mayor shouted, his voice echoing through the night. "Please, listen to me! This is a mistake!"

But the agents paid no heed to his pleas, their focus unwavering as they continued to haul the man away, their actions relentless and unforgiving.

After a few minutes, as the car sped away into the night, leaving behind a shattered family and a house in disarray, the agents finally realized their grave mistake.

"The suspect is across the street," one agent muttered, his voice filled with shame and regret. The truth hit them like a ton of bricks, a realization that would haunt them for days to come.

During the subsequent investigation by the FBI, witnesses came forward to testify about the brutal actions of the agents that night. Their accounts painted a disturbing picture of excessive force and disregard for the rights of the innocent.

After a thorough investigation, it was deemed an honest mistake, a case of mistaken identity that had led to a grave injustice. The mayor was released, his reputation tarnished, but his innocence proven.

Yet, as the dust settled and the truth came to light, one question remained unanswered. Why had the federal agents acted with such brutality and negligence, ignoring the pleas of the innocent and causing untold suffering in their wake?

In the end, none of the agents paid a price for their errors; their actions justified.

CHAPTER TWENTY-EIGHT

"I'M NOT ARGUING WITH YOU, I'M JUST EXPLAININ' WHY I AM RIGHT."

OH, I SEE, SO YOU'RE NOT ARGUING, YOU'RE JUST GENEROUSLY SHARING THE REASONS WHY YOU'RE ALWAYS RIGHT?

THE UNBROKEN PROMISE

Once upon a time, in a small town named Silver Stream, between rolling hills and lush forests, there lived a boy named Linus. He was a spirited and headstrong young man who often clashed with his father, a stern but loving man named Thomas.

As Linus approached his 18th birthday, he was filled with excitement at the promise his father had made to buy him a car as a gift. He had been dreaming of the freedom and independence that a car would bring him. However, on the day of his birthday, instead of a shiny new car sitting in the driveway, his father presented him with a worn Bible.

Linus was overcome with a mix of anger and embarrassment in front of his friends who had gathered for his birthday celebration. Feeling betrayed and hurt, he stormed out of the house, vowing never to return.

For 45 long years, Linus wandered the world, never staying in one place for too long. He carried with him the bitterness and resentment he felt towards his father, never once looking back.

When news reached him that his father, Thomas, had passed away, Linus found himself at a crossroads. Despite the years of estrangement, a sense of longing and regret stirred within him. With a heavy heart, he returned to his childhood home for his father's funeral.

Standing before the gathered mourners, Linus felt the weight of his choices bearing down on him. As he began to speak, his voice trembled with emotion. Tears welled up in his eyes as he recounted the story of his youth and the pain of feeling abandoned by his father.

But as he spoke, memories flooded back to him. Memories of a father who had always been there for him in his own quiet and steadfast way. Memories of a promise made and kept, hidden within the pages of a Bible.

After the funeral, alone in his old bedroom, Linus found the Bible tucked away under his pillow, just as he had left it all those years ago. With trembling hands, he turned the pages and discovered an envelope hidden inside.

Inside the envelope was a yellowed piece of paper—a check for the car his father had promised him all those years ago. In that moment, as the weight of his father's love and sacrifice washed over him, Linus realized the depth of his father's devotion.

Years later, as Linus lay in a hospital bed, surrounded by his family, his grandson Peter approached him, curiosity gleaming in his eyes.

"Grandpa," Peter began, his voice soft and curious, "Why did you leave and never come back? What was it that made you stay away for so long?"

Linus looked at Peter, his eyes filled with a mixture of sorrow and regret. Taking a deep breath, he began to recount the story of his past, the misunderstandings, and the pain that had driven him away.

As the conversation unfolded, Peter listened intently, his young heart open to the wisdom and experience of his grandfather. Together, they delved into the complexities of family, forgiveness, and the enduring power of love.

And as the sun set on Linus's final day, a sense of peace settled over him, knowing that he had found understanding and closure in the bond he shared with his grandson, a bond that transcended time and distance, carrying the legacy of their family forward into the future.

WILDERNESS AWAKENING

In the serene setting of the Appalachian mountains, a group of college students embarked on a camping adventure filled with anticipation and excitement. Eager to immerse themselves in the beauty of the outdoors, they set up camp in a lush forest clearing, ready to enjoy a weekend of relaxation and fun.

As the sun dipped below the horizon, the group gathered around a crackling campfire, roasting marshmallows and sharing stories late into the night. The peaceful ambiance of the woods enveloped them, offering a sense of tranquility and escape from the hustle and bustle of everyday life.

In the early hours of the morning, as the first light of dawn began to filter through the trees, Bethany stirred from her slumber and stepped outside the tent to take in the breathtaking sunrise. However, her moment of solitude was abruptly shattered when she heard a commotion coming from the camp's kitchen area.

Bethany: "What's going on over there?"

Rushing over to investigate, Bethany's eyes widened in shock as she saw Matt on his knees, inexplicably licking the kitchen floor with a look of dazed confusion on his face.

Bethany: "Oh my God, Matt! What are you doing?"

Alarmed, she called out for help, and soon, the rest of the group came running to see what was happening.

Steve: "What's happening? Is Matt okay?"

Bethany: "He's licking the floor! We need to stop him!"

Steve, one of the students, attempted to intervene and stop Matt's bizarre behavior, but the drug-induced delirium seemed to have a firm grip on him. With combined effort, the group managed to restrain Matt and prevent him from causing further harm to himself.

Steve: "Matt, snap out of it! What did you take?"

Realizing that Matt needed urgent medical attention, the group quickly decided to transport him to the nearest town, located 25 miles away, where a small country clinic was situated. The journey was tense and fraught with worry as they raced against time to get Matt the help he needed.

Bethany: "Hang in there, Matt. We're getting you help."

Upon arrival at the clinic, the medical staff quickly assessed Matt's condition and ran a series of tests. The results revealed that Matt had ingested K2, a potent and dangerous synthetic drug known to cause severe hallucinations, delusions, and impaired brain function.

Doctor: "He's lucky you brought him in when you did. K2 can be very dangerous."

For the next two days, Matt remained under the care of the medical team at the clinic, where he was closely monitored and treated for the effects of the drug. Slowly but surely, with the support of his friends and the medical professionals, Matt began to regain his bearings and return to a state of clarity.

As Matt was eventually discharged from the clinic, the group reflected on the harrowing experience and the importance of staying vigilant and looking out for one another, especially in unfamiliar environments. Despite the unexpected turn of events, the camping trip served as a poignant reminder of the fragility of life and the bonds of friendship that can help navigate even the most challenging of circumstances.

GRANDMA MISADVENTURE

On a sunny afternoon in a quiet neighborhood, a series of events unfolded that would leave everyone in stitches and make Grandma a local legend. It all began when the neighbor, Mrs. Jenkins, thought she heard some commotion coming from her backyard. Concerned, she peeked over the fence only to see a peculiar sight - Grandma, an energetic woman in her 70s, perched precariously on a tall oak tree.

Alarmed, Mrs. Jenkins dialed 911, and in no time, the police and fire department arrived on the scene. As they approached the tree, they found Grandma sitting calmly on a sturdy branch, seemingly oblivious to the chaos she had caused.

"Ma'am, why are you up there?" asked the police officer, to which Grandma just chuckled and shrugged, not understanding a word of English. Perplexed, the firefighters decided to seek help from the local social service agency for an interpreter.

Enter Mr. Leng, a kind Hmong man who arrived promptly to assist with the translation. With a warm smile, he asked Grandma in her native language, "Puj, Yog lecaag koj tsua dlaum ntoo rua sau kod nua?". In English, "Grandma, why did you climb the tree?"

With a twinkle in her eye, Grandma replied, "Tub yog puas taab ib tug mivnyuas dlev miv miv caum kuv. Kuv ntshai es kuv txhale dlaum ntoo naj. Taamsim nuav kuv nqeg tsi tau lawm. Paab kuv os."

A ripple of laughter broke out among the onlookers as Mr. Leng translated her words, "I climbed the tree because a little dog chased me. Now I can't come down."

Despite the absurdity of the situation, everyone couldn't help but chuckle at Grandma's explanation. The interpreter assured her, "Don't worry, we'll help you down. A firefighter will bring a ladder to get you safely back on the ground."

As the firefighter carefully ascended the ladder to reach Grandma, the local media had already caught wind of the bizarre incident. Reporters swarmed the scene, capturing the moment on camera and broadcasting it on the evening news.

That night, Grandma's unintentional tree-climbing escapade became the talk of the town. Her fearless encounter with a tiny dog had turned her into a local celebrity, with everyone sharing a good laugh at the hilarious turn of events.

From that day on, Grandma's tree-climbing misadventure was retold with amusement and fondness, ensuring her a place in the hearts of the townsfolk as the fearless lady who conquered a tree to escape a playful pup.

GRANDMA GO TO CHURCH

In the heart of a bitterly cold winter in Wheaton, Illinois, an extraordinary incident unfolded at the local church, leaving the congregation in awe and wonder. It was a Sunday that would be forever etched in the memories of those who bore witness to the remarkable events that transpired.

Just two months prior to that fateful day, Grandma, a recent immigrant from Laos, found herself in a land vastly different from her sun-kissed homeland. Unfamiliar with the harsh winter climate and the need for proper attire, she had bravely ventured out barefoot to attend church, her determination carrying her through the snow-covered path.

As the church service ended, a concerned church member rushed outside and discovered Grandma standing barefoot in the snow, seemingly unaffected by the freezing temperatures that surrounded her.

"Grandma, what are you doing out here without any shoes on? You'll catch a cold!" the church member exclaimed, rushing to her side.

With a serene smile, Grandma replied, "Back in Laos, we didn't have shoes. I'm used to it."

The church member, astonished, quickly called for an Emergency Medical Technician (EMT) to assess Grandma's condition. The EMT knelt down beside her, examining her feet with a mix of curiosity and disbelief.

"Ma'am, are you feeling any pain or numbness in your feet?" the EMT asked, gently touching Grandma's bare skin.

Grandma shook her head. "No, I'm feeling fine. I've walked like this all my life."

The EMTs, perplexed by Grandma's resilience, muttered to themselves, "I've never seen anything like this before."

The pastor alerted to the situation, hurried over to Grandma, his expression a mix of concern and admiration.

"Grandma, why did you walk here without shoes in this cold weather?" the pastor inquired, his voice filled with genuine curiosity.

With a twinkle in her eye, Grandma replied, "I had to come to church. It's important to me. The cold doesn't bother me much."

As word of Grandma's barefooted journey spread through the church, a sense of reverence and wonder enveloped the congregation. How could this newcomer endure such conditions with such grace and fortitude?

In a world where material possessions often held great importance, Grandma's simple existence served as a powerful reminder of the strength and resilience of the human spirit. She was a living testament to faith, perseverance, and the enduring power of the human heart.

And so, on that cold winter day in Wheaton, Illinois, Grandma's barefooted miracle became a tale that would be shared for generations, inspiring all who heard it with its message of courage, resilience, and unwavering faith.

THE WEDDING

In the small, tight-knit town of Riverdale, everyone knew everyone. The residents shopped at the same grocery store, attended the same church, and cheered for their local team at the same baseball game every Friday night. Among them was Willy, who had been the nerdy, awkward kid in junior high school. But time had transformed him into a strikingly handsome young man, capturing the attention of many of the town's young women.

Willy, however, had eyes only for one person: Mary Beth, the most beautiful girl in Riverdale. She had won the town's teen pageant and had been crowned queen of the July 4th parade. Her smile could light up the entire town, and her grace was unmatched.

Finally, Willy was getting married to Mary Beth, a dream come true. He was sending out wedding invitations to everyone in Riverdale. In his mind, his wedding would be a grand affair, one that would make those who had bullied him in his youth green with envy. He envisioned Mary Beth walking down the aisle toward him, her eyes shining with love and joy. They would be happy forever, sharing a life filled with love and laughter.

But this was all just a fantasy.

Willy sat at a corner booth, staring at a piece of paper. It was a mock-up of his wedding invitation. His best friend, Tommy, slid into the seat across from him, noticing the faraway look in Willy's eyes.

"Hey, Willy. What's that you've got there?" Tommy asked.

Willy quickly folded the paper and shoved it into his pocket, forcing a smile. "Oh, nothing. Just some doodles."

Tommy raised an eyebrow, sensing there was more to it. "Come on, man. I know that look. What's going on?"

Willy sighed, his shoulders slumping. "It's... it's an invitation. To my wedding."

Tommy's eyes widened in surprise. "Wedding? Since when are you getting married? And to whom?"

Willy hesitated the weight of his secret crush heavy on his heart. "I can't tell you."

Tommy leaned back, crossing his arms. "Oh, I know. Mary Beth? The same Mary Beth we went to school with? The one who's dating Johnny?"

Willy nodded, his gaze dropping to the table. "I know it's crazy, but I can't help it. I've loved her since high school. I just... I just want to believe that one day she'll see me the way I see her."

Tommy softened, understanding the depth of Willy's feelings. "Look, Willy. I know you've got a big heart, and Mary Beth is amazing. But you can't live in a fantasy. You deserve someone who loves you back, man. Someone who sees how incredible you are."

Willy sighed, his dreams of a perfect wedding fading into the harsh light of reality. "I know you're right, Tommy. It's just hard to let go."

Tommy reached across the table, placing a hand on Willy's shoulder. "You'll find someone, Willy. Someone who'll make you forget all about Mary Beth. Just give it time."

Willy nodded, forcing a smile. Deep down, he knew Tommy was right. But for now, he needed to let his dream linger a little longer if only to ease the ache in his heart.

As the weeks went by, Willy tried to move on. He attended the town events, always with a smile, always hoping. But Mary Beth remained a distant star, beautiful and out of reach. And though his wedding invitations remained hidden in his desk drawer, they served as a reminder of the love he held in his heart, a love that might never be returned.

In reality, Mary Beth was happily dating Johnny, and Willy was just another face in the crowd. His grand wedding, the envious stares from his former bullies, and the life he dreamed of with Mary Beth were nothing more than a figment of his imagination. But in the quiet moments when he was alone, Willy allowed himself to dream, if only to feel a little closer to the happiness he longed for.

CHAPTER TWENTY-NINE

SOMEONE POSTED, "IT'S SO NICE TO WAKE UP IN THE MORNING KNOWING THAT GOD HAS GIVEN YOU ANOTHER DAY TO LIVE. TAKE A MINUTE TO THANK GOD."

BUT REMEMBER, IT'S ALSO NICE TO WAKE UP IN THE LATE AFTERNOON. TAKE 30 MINUTES TO PRAY FOR OVERCOMING LAZINESS—YOU'RE GOING TO NEED IT!

THE INVISIBLE

Paul Wang had always been a man of contradictions. Once a faithful servant in his local church, he became known for his fiery sermons and relentless charity work. But beneath his charismatic exterior lay a man grappling with his own demons. His marriage crumbled under the weight of his infidelities, and his finances were drained by reckless gambling. Paul's fall from grace was swift and public, leaving him alienated from the very community he once served.

One rainy evening, as Paul stumbled through the desolate streets, he found himself standing before the church he once called home. The grandeur of the building seemed to mock his downfall. The doors, once wide open to him, now felt like they were sealed shut. He could still hear the whispers of the congregation, their judgmental stares burning holes into his back.

Paul found solace among society's outcasts. The homeless, the addicts, the felons—these were now his companions. Each night, he huddled under a bridge with them, sharing stories of their past lives. They called themselves "the invisible ones," shunned by society and forgotten by the church.

One night, as they gathered around a small fire, Paul spoke about his experiences. "The church... they only want the good ones," he said bitterly. "They say they preach love and acceptance, but they turn away those who need it the most. People like us."

His words struck a chord with the group. They nodded in agreement, their eyes reflecting years of pain and rejection. Paul realized that they were not just invisible to society—they were invisible to God's house as well.

It was in this darkness that Paul met David. David was an older man with kind eyes and a gentle demeanor who volunteered at a local shelter. He had a way of seeing past the grime and the sorrow directly into the heart of a person. One day, he approached Paul with a warm smile.

"Mind if I sit?" David asked, gesturing to the spot beside Paul.

"Suit yourself," Paul replied gruffly, not bothering to look up.

David sat down and handed Paul a warm cup of coffee. "I've heard your story, Paul. It's a tough one."

Paul scoffed. "Heard it from who? The good folks in the church?"

David chuckled softly. "No, from the people here. You've become a sort of legend among them. A man of faith who lost his way."

Paul remained silent, staring into the fire.

"Do you believe in second chances, Paul?" David asked, his voice filled with genuine curiosity.

Paul looked up, meeting David's gaze for the first time. "I used to."

David nodded. "You know, Jesus didn't come for the righteous but for the sinners. He didn't come to call the good ones, but the bad ones. People like us. In the word of the Apostle Paul, 'Christ Jesus came into the world to save sinners'—and I am the worst of them all." (1 Timothy 1:15).

Over the next few weeks, David continued to visit Paul and the others, bringing food, clothing, and, most importantly, hope. He never preached or judged, but his actions spoke volumes. Slowly, Paul began to see a glimmer of light in his dark world.

One night, David invited Paul to a small, humble gathering in a rundown building on the outskirts of town. "It's a church," David explained. "But not like the ones you've known. It's a place for the broken, the lost, and the outcasts."

Paul hesitated but decided to go. Inside, he saw people from all walks of life—including addicts, felons, divorcees, and the homeless. They were singing, praying, and sharing their stories. For the first time in years, Paul felt a sense of belonging.

Paul's journey of redemption was not an easy one. He struggled with his past, battled his addictions, and faced his inner demons. But with David's guidance and the support of his newfound community, he slowly rebuilt his life.

He started sharing his testimony, speaking about his fall and how he found redemption through Christ's love. His message was simple yet powerful: "God doesn't turn away the broken; He embraces them. The church may forget the invisible, but God never does."

Paul's transformation became a beacon of hope for many. He reached out to those shunned by society, offering them the love and acceptance he had once craved. Through his actions, he reminded the church of its true mission—to love and serve all, especially the fallen.

Paul stood before a packed congregation in a modest church, his voice strong and clear. "I was lost, but now I'm found. I was shunned, but now I'm embraced. This is the message of Christ's love and redemption. It's not just for the good ones, but for the broken, the outcasts, and the invisible."

The congregation listened in rapt attention, many moved to tears. Paul's story was a challenge to the church, a call to remember its true purpose. As he finished, he looked out at the sea of faces and saw a reflection of his journey—a journey from darkness to light, from sin to redemption, from invisibility to being seen by God.

And in that moment, Paul knew that he was no longer a mess. He was a messenger of God's transformative love, a living testament to the power of redemption.

Paul concluded his speech with a powerful reminder, his voice filled with conviction and love. "The power and love of God is to transform and redeem the lost, the unwanted, and the invisible. In some cases, the ones that the church rejected or shunned away. Jesus loves them and brings them back to the Kingdom. Remember this, for it is not just our duty but our privilege to be the hands and feet of Christ to the fallen. For in God's eyes, no one is beyond redemption. Jesus Christ offers a second chance to the fallen, broken, and invisible. Through the confession of sins, repentance, and being born again in baptism, the Holy Spirit empowers the broken to live for Christ rather than for themselves.

THE OLD MAN: SAMUEL

Brandon had an eye on the bank in the small town of Marysville. He watched the bank customers going in and out every day. He tracked their routines, noting who seemed weak but had money in the bank. One day, he spotted an old man, Samuel, coming to the bank to make deposits and withdrawals. Brandon watched him and tracked his routine for a month. To him, Samuel seemed like a good target to rob. He was old, appeared weak, and seemed easy prey.

Every Friday at 4:00 PM, Samuel would come to make deposits and sometimes withdrawals. He owned a small bookstore in town. Brandon decided this was his opportunity. He waited until Samuel made a withdrawal from the bank. As Samuel walked to the elevator, Brandon followed. Once inside the elevator, Brandon turned to Samuel and demanded, "Give me the money, or I'll hurt you bad."

The old man, in his seventies, looked up at Brandon, his eyes wide with fear. "Please," he begged, his voice trembling, "I don't want any trouble. Just take it."

Suddenly, everything went black for Brandon.

He woke up in the hospital, disoriented and in excruciating pain. His body felt like it had been hit by a truck. He tried to move but found himself handcuffed to the bed. Panic set in. What happened? How did he end up here? He could barely remember anything after entering the elevator with Samuel.

The duty nurse entered the room, and he asked, "Why am I handcuffed? What happened to me?"

The nurse, looking somewhat disdainful, replied, "You were involved in an incident. The police will explain."

A police officer, standing guard, walked in. "You're under arrest. Once you're discharged, you'll be going to jail."

Brandon, confused and in pain, asked, "Why? What happened?"

The officer handed him a news article. "Because you tried to rob an old man at a bank. Read this, and you'll know why."

Brandon read the article with growing horror. The headline read: "Local Bookstore Owner and Martial Arts Master Foils Robbery Attempt." The article detailed how Samuel, a master martial arts teacher, had defended himself against an attempted robbery. Despite his age, he had incapacitated his attacker with precision and skill, leaving Brandon severely injured.

Brandon dropped the article, his hands shaking. "I...I didn't know," he muttered, eyes wide with disbelief.

"Well, now you do," the officer replied sternly. "Maybe next time, you'll think twice before picking on someone just because they seem weak."

As Brandon lay there, he realized too late that appearances could be deceiving and that Samuel was anything but weak. The lesson, learned in pain and regret, would stay with him for the rest of his life.

THE JAZZ LEGENDS

Ladies and gentlemen, family and friends, Thank you for gathering here today to honor and remember the incredible life of my grandfather, Johnathon Thornton. My name is Gabriel Thornton, and it is my privilege to share with you the story of a man whose legacy is woven with threads of humility, kindness, and unwavering generosity.

In the bustling metropolis of New Orleans, my grandfather, Johnathon Thornton, graced the jazz clubs with a presence that enchanted audiences far and wide. Yet, behind the dazzling facade of musical stardom lay a side of him that few had the privilege to witness—a side brimming with humility and kindness that transcended the boundaries of performance.

One stormy evening, Grandpa found himself outside a chic jazz club, awaiting entry to a celebration for the release of his latest album. Despite his renown, he stood incognito amidst the rain-soaked crowd, his unassuming aura blending seamlessly with the city's nocturnal symphony.

Inside the club, the owner was taken aback upon discovering that Johnathon had been waiting outside. "I had no idea that Johnathon was out there in the rain, patiently biding his time. Not a word escaped his lips," the club owner marveled, astonished by my grandfather's understated demeanor.

"He's a man of the people, you know," a discreet waiter murmured to a colleague, marveling at Johnathon's down-to-earth persona.

"He's known to share moments with the less fortunate on the streets, offering them a glimmer of hope," whispered a bartender, recounting tales of Johnathon's clandestine acts of benevolence that often went unnoticed by the public eye.

At the age of 56, my grandfather's life was a tapestry woven with threads of extraordinary generosity and empathy. He could often be found relishing a simple po' boy sandwich in the park, conversing effortlessly with passersby, his celebrity status a mere footnote in those candid interactions.

Following the release of an iconic "Jazz Legends" album, Johnathon astounded the recording crew by presenting each member with a custom-made saxophone as a token of his gratitude for their unwavering dedication and skill.

In another remarkable gesture, he selflessly relinquished a substantial portion of his "Jazz Legends" earnings to ensure that the sound engineers and backup musicians were duly acknowledged for their pivotal contributions to the album's success.

For his role in "The Blues of the Bayou," Johnathon willingly trimmed his own compensation to accommodate the inclusion of the venerable B.B. King, driven by his profound respect for King's craft and artistry.

LOL AND SORROW

Amidst a series of personal tribulations—the loss of a cherished friend, the tragic passing of his girlfriend's child, and his sister's brave battle with leukemia—Johnathon's resilience and compassion radiated like a beacon in the darkness. Despite the upheavals that assailed his life, he stood unwavering, a pillar of solace and support for those in need.

He bestowed a generous $5 million donation upon the clinic that treated his sister, standing steadfast by her side during her arduous leukemia battle and placing her well-being above all else. He suspended his career to be her rock, showering her with unwavering love and care in her hour of need.

In homage to his sister and all warriors against leukemia, Johnathon established a Leukemia Foundation, earmarking a portion of his musical earnings to bolster research efforts and provide aid to those fighting the disease.

Through his deeds and enduring humility, my grandfather, Johnathon Thornton, the enigmatic jazz musician, embodied the essence of altruism and benevolence. His life served as a poignant testament that genuine greatness transcends the glitz and glamour, manifesting in the compassion and kindness we extend to others.

As we remember Johnathon Thornton today, let us not only celebrate his accomplishments in the world of jazz but also strive to emulate the profound kindness and humility he exemplified in his everyday life. One time, a reporter asked about his faith, and he replied, "The poorest person is not the one without money. It is the one without God." He was a jazz legend, but more importantly, a man of faith, which he would want us to remember about him. Thank you.

THE FORBIDDEN LAND

In the forbidden Muslim country, a group of daring missionaries led by Pastor David embarked on a dangerous mission to distribute Bibles to the underground Christian community, risking their lives in the face of strict laws that prohibited the practice of Christianity.

As they journeyed through the treacherous terrain, evading government patrols and facing imminent danger at every turn, the missionaries found themselves in a hidden cave deep in the rugged mountains, seeking refuge from the relentless pursuit of the authorities.

Their hearts heavy with the weight of the dangers that surrounded them, the missionaries huddled together in the shadows, knowing that discovery could mean certain capture and imprisonment. Sarah whispered anxiously, "What if they find us here? We won't stand a chance against the authorities."

Michael, his eyes scanning the darkness for signs of danger, replied grimly, "We must stay vigilant and ready to defend ourselves. Our mission is to bring hope and faith to those in need, no matter the risks we face."

Just then, the sound of approaching footsteps echoed through the cavern, signaling the arrival of the village police. The missionaries held their breath, their hearts pounding with fear as the officers drew nearer, their lanterns casting eerie shadows on the rocky walls.

With quick thinking and silent prayers on their lips, the missionaries concealed themselves in the shadows as the police entered the cave, their weapons drawn and their eyes sharp with suspicion. Pastor David, his heart pounding in his chest, prayed for divine intervention as the officers passed within arm's reach of their hiding place.

Despite their best efforts to remain hidden, a misplaced step caused a small rock to tumble, alerting the officers. The sound, though minor, was enough to draw their attention. One of the officers, keen-eyed and wary, noticed the disturbance and signaled the others. The missionaries' hearts sank as they realized their concealment had failed.

The officers, now on high alert, moved methodically through the cave, uncovering the missionaries' hiding spot. Pastor David and his companions were forced out into the harsh light of the lanterns, their faces reflecting both fear and resolve.

Subjected to harsh interrogations, threats, and demands to renounce their faith in Christ, Pastor David and his companions endured days of relentless questioning. The authorities, hoping to break their spirits, applied increasing pressure, but the missionaries refused to deny their faith, even in the face of grave danger.

When the officers demanded that Pastor David spit on the Bible as a final act of defiance, he looked them straight in the eye and declared, "I will not deny my Lord and Savior, no matter the consequences. Our faith is stronger than any earthly trial you may subject us to."

Impressed by the missionaries' unwavering commitment to their beliefs, the officers revealed their true identities as members of a secret Christian society within the law enforcement. They explained that they had orchestrated the elaborate test to ensure the missionaries' sincerity and authenticity in their faith.

Filled with gratitude and relief, the missionaries were released from captivity and escorted to a safe location by the officers, who had risked their own safety to protect them. In a secluded sanctuary hidden from prying eyes, the missionaries gathered for a worship service unlike any they had experienced before.

As they raised their voices in songs of praise and prayers of thanksgiving, Pastor David offered heartfelt gratitude for the trials they had endured and the miraculous deliverance they had received. United in their shared journey of faith and perseverance, the missionaries knew that no obstacle or threat could extinguish the light of God's love that burned brightly within their hearts.

THE SAHARA DESERT

The story of Dylan and Michael's expedition in the Sahara Desert captures a gripping tale of perseverance and discovery. Their journey is marked by the harsh realities of the desert, the strain on their friendship, and the ultimate reward of finding the legendary moving stone. This account, shared by Dylan with the rescued investigators at the hospital after their treatment for dehydration, serves as a testament to their resilience and the power of hope in the face of seemingly insurmountable challenges. Here is a refined version of your story:

The sun hung high in the sky, a relentless orb of fire determined to sap every last bit of energy from the two friends trudging through the endless dunes of the Sahara Desert. Dylan and Michael had set out on an expedition to investigate a legendary tale about a moving stone—a stone that supposedly wandered the desert at night and rested by day. The allure of uncovering such a mysterious phenomenon had driven them deep into the heart of West Africa's vast desert.

But now, a week into their journey, the situation was dire. Their satellite GPS and compass had malfunctioned, leaving them disoriented. They had been walking for hours, their bodies weakened by thirst and exhaustion. The scorching heat seemed to press down on them, a physical weight that made every step a monumental effort.

Michael stumbled, his legs trembling with fatigue. Dylan, a few feet ahead, turned and called out, his voice hoarse. "Come on, Michael! You can't stop now. We have to keep moving!"

Michael's vision blurred, the landscape wavering like a mirage. He reached into his backpack and pulled out a small bottle of water. Without a word, he unscrewed the cap and poured the precious liquid over his head, the cool droplets momentarily reviving him.

Dylan's eyes widened in disbelief. "Michael, you had water all this time, and you didn't bother to mention it. I could have died of thirst?"

Michael shrugged, wiping the water from his face. "Well, you didn't ask."

Dylan shook his head in frustration, his voice rising. "People need some common sense these days, some consideration too, you know."

Michael offered the bottle to Dylan, his expression apologetic. "Oh, do you want some?"

Dylan snatched the bottle and took a small sip, savoring the brief relief. "We need to find our way out of here, Michael. We can't afford to waste any more time."

The two friends resumed their trek, their steps heavy and arduous. The desert stretched out endlessly before them, a vast expanse of golden sand and oppressive heat. Hours passed, and the sun began its slow descent toward the horizon, casting long shadows across the dunes.

As night fell, the temperature dropped, bringing a welcome respite from the day's scorching heat. The moon rose, casting an eerie glow over the desert. Dylan and Michael made camp under the stars, their bodies too exhausted to continue.

"Do you think we'll ever find that moving stone?" Michael asked, his voice barely above a whisper.

Dylan stared up at the sky, the stars twinkling like distant beacons of hope. "I don't know, Michael. But we have to believe that we will. It's the only thing keeping us going."

The night passed slowly, each hour marked by the sounds of the desert—distant animal calls, the whisper of the wind across the sand. As dawn approached, Dylan awoke to find Michael staring intently at something in the distance.

"What is it, Michael?" Dylan asked, rising to his feet.

Michael pointed, his eyes wide with wonder. "Look."

Dylan followed his gaze and saw it—a large stone unlike any they had seen before. It stood in the middle of the desert, casting a long shadow in the early morning light. As they watched, the stone seemed to shift slightly as if it were alive.

"Could it be?" Dylan whispered, his heart pounding.

Michael nodded. "The moving stone. We found it."

With renewed determination, they approached the stone, their exhaustion momentarily forgotten. The stone was smooth and cool to the touch, its surface marked with strange, intricate patterns.

As they stood there, marveling at their discovery, the sun began to rise, casting its golden light over the desert. Dylan and Michael knew that they still had a long journey ahead of them, but for the first time in days, they felt a glimmer of hope.

"Let's get some rest," Dylan said, his voice filled with new resolve. "And then we'll figure out how to get back."

Michael smiled, the fatigue in his eyes replaced by a spark of excitement. "Agreed. We might be lost, but we're not beaten."

And so, the two friends lay down beside the moving stone, the desert wind gently blowing over them. They had come seeking a legend, and in the process, they had found something even more valuable—a renewed sense of purpose and the unbreakable bond of friendship.

CHAPTER THIRTY

"SOMEONE ONCE SAID,
"YOU MUST SEE YOURSELF AS A KING
BEFORE OTHERS CAN BELIEVE IN YOU."

WELL, I SEE MYSELF AS A KING NOW.
SO, OBEY ME AND BELIEVE IN ME!"

THE RUNAWAY TRAIN

The train roared down the tracks at an impossible speed, a silver streak under a moonlit sky. The passengers clung to their seats, a mix of panic and disbelief plastered on their faces. No one could reach the engineer. No one knew how to stop it. It felt like a nightmare, but the cold metal under their fingertips and the screech of wheels on rails told them otherwise.

In the third carriage, a woman clutched her young daughter's hand. "Stay calm, sweetie. It's just a dream," she whispered, though she wasn't sure she believed it herself. Across the aisle, Mr. Mason, a retired teacher with a shock of white hair, tried to use his phone for the umpteenth time. "No signal," he muttered, shaking his head. He looked at the young man next to him, a tech-savvy college student named Jacob. "Any luck on your end?"

Jacob frowned at his screen. "Nothing. It's like we're cut off from the world." He glanced around nervously. "What the hell is going on?"

A few rows back, an elderly woman named Mrs. Johnson began to pray aloud, her rosary beads clicking softly. "Lord, protect us in this hour of need," she murmured, her eyes closed tightly.

Suddenly, a high-pitched beeping sound echoed through the carriage. Heads turned, searching for the source, but it seemed to come from everywhere and nowhere at once. Mr. Mason's eyes widened. "Do you hear that?"

"Yes," Jacob replied, standing up to look around. "But where is it coming from?"

A young mother in the front of the carriage shook her head. "I don't hear anything," she said, her voice trembling.

"Me neither," added an older man with a cane. "Maybe it's just in our heads."

The beeping grew louder, more insistent. Panic spread like wildfire. Some passengers covered their ears, while others frantically searched for the source.

"Everyone, stay calm!" Mr. Mason shouted, trying to restore order. "Panicking won't help us."

But just as suddenly as it began, the beeping stopped. Silence fell over the carriage, thick and oppressive. Mr. Mason slumped back in his seat, his heart pounding.

Before anyone could react, the train lurched violently. Screams filled the air as the world outside the windows blurred into a whirl of lights and shadows. The screeching of metal on metal was deafening.

Mr. Mason closed his eyes, his last conscious thought a prayer for survival.

Mr. Mason awoke to the harsh, sterile light of a hospital room. His body ached, and his head throbbed. Blinking against the brightness, he tried to sit up, only to be gently pushed back by a nurse.

"Easy there, Mr. Mason," she said softly. "You've been through quite an ordeal."

"Where am I?" he croaked, his throat dry.

"You're in the hospital," she replied. "The train you were on... it derailed."

Memories flooded back, and Mr. Mason's eyes widened in horror. "The passengers...?"

The nurse's expression turned somber. "Some didn't make it. Others are still fighting for their lives."

Mr. Mason closed his eyes, grief, and relief washing over him in equal measure. "What happened? Why couldn't we stop the train?"

"We're still investigating," she said. "But right now, you need to rest. You've been through a lot."

As she left the room, Mr. Mason stared at the ceiling, the memories of the nightmare train ride playing over and over in his mind. The beeping sound, the helplessness, the crash—everything felt surreal, like a terrible dream. But the pain in his body and the loss in his heart reminded him that it was all too real.

THE PERFECT CHURCH

For nearly twenty years, Lucas wandered from church to church, seeking the perfect spiritual home. Each one fell short of his expectations. Some were too traditional, others too modern. Some focused too much on charity, while others seemed obsessed with wealth and prosperity. None struck the balance he yearned for, and his frustration grew with each passing year. For many years, he did not attend church. He attended a home church with his kids and wife and no other members and did not affiliate with any denomination.

One Sunday morning, feeling particularly despondent, Lucas wandered into a small chapel on the outskirts of town. The sign read, "Church of the Heavenly Gate," and the building's simplicity appealed to him. He decided to attend the service, thinking it would be just another disappointment.

Inside, he met Pastor Ethan, a charismatic and gentle man with a profound presence. Ethan's sermons were unlike any Lucas had ever heard. They were filled with wisdom, compassion, and a deep sense of connection to God. Ethan spoke of a direct relationship with the Father, one that transcended the rituals and formalities that had always alienated Lucas from other churches. For the first time in two decades, Lucas felt he had found a place that resonated with his soul.

Ethan seemed almost savior-like to Lucas. He had an aura of serenity and understanding that captivated everyone who attended his services. Lucas began to attend the Church of the Heavenly Gate regularly, feeling a sense of belonging and peace he had never experienced before. He became close to Ethan, often staying after services to discuss theology and spirituality.

However, as time went on, Lucas noticed something unsettling. Ethan's teachings began to diverge from traditional Christian doctrine. He spoke of exclusive revelations and divine messages that only he received. The church members were increasingly encouraged to sever ties with those outside the church to devote all their time and resources to Ethan's vision. Doubt crept into Lucas's mind, but he pushed it away, not wanting to lose the community he had finally found.

One evening, Lucas decided to investigate further. He researched the church's history and Ethan's background. What he discovered alarmed him. The Church of the Heavenly Gate was listed among several watch groups as a potential cult. Ethan's supposed direct relationship with God was a common tactic used by cult leaders to control their followers. Lucas realized with horror that he had been drawn into something dangerous.

Determined to save himself and others, Lucas confronted Ethan, but the pastor dismissed his concerns, accusing him of a lack of faith. Lucas knew he had to leave, but it was heart-wrenching. He had to abandon the community he had grown to love and the peace he thought he had found.

As he walked away from the Church of the Heavenly Gate, Lucas reflected on his long search for the perfect church. He realized that his ideal did not exist. Churches are made up of flawed people, just like himself, and expecting perfection was unrealistic. He learned that true faith was about finding a community where he could grow, support others, and be supported in return, imperfections and all.

Lucas decided that if he wanted a perfect church, he would have to create it himself—starting with himself and his own home. He began hosting small gatherings, not with the intention of starting a new church but to share his journey and experiences with others who might be seeking the same sense of belonging and spiritual fulfillment.

One evening, Lucas invited some friends over who were also church shopping, struggling to find a place that felt right to them. Over coffee and snacks, he shared his story, from his years of searching to his disillusionment with the Church of the Heavenly Gate.

"Friends," Lucas began, "I spent twenty years looking for the perfect church. I thought I had found it with Ethan and the Church of the Heavenly Gate, but I was wrong. It was a cult, not a true community of faith. What I've learned is that if you're looking for the perfect church, it's impossible unless you start one on your own at home but without any members or joining a cult. Churches are made up of imperfect people, and that's what makes them real."

His friends listened intently, nodding in agreement. Sarah, who had been to nearly as many churches as Lucas, spoke up. "I've felt that way too. Every church has something that doesn't quite fit, but maybe that's the point."

"Exactly," Lucas replied. "It's about finding a community where you can grow, support others, and be supported in return, despite the imperfections. We need to stop expecting perfection and start looking for a place where we can be ourselves, flaws and all."

As the evening went on, the friends shared their own experiences and concerns. They realized that their quest for the perfect church had led them to miss out on the beauty of community and shared faith. Lucas's story had opened their eyes to a new way of thinking.

In the end, they decided to continue meeting at Lucas's home, not to start a new church but to support each other in their spiritual journeys. They learned that true fulfillment came from accepting imperfection and finding a community where they could grow and thrive despite it.

The lesson: The only perfect church is the one you start or a cult you join. The church of Jesus Christ is made up of sinners and people with flaws.

REGRET BY MISUNDERSTANDING

Once upon a time, in the quaint town of Yellow Creek, there lived two lovers named Claire and Jack. They were deeply in love and spent their days exploring the town, sharing dreams, and planning their future together. One sunny afternoon, as they sat by the river, Jack received an urgent message on his phone but couldn't read it at that moment.

Unbeknownst to Jack, the message was from Claire's best friend, Lily, who had written to inform him that Claire had been involved in a car accident and was in critical condition at the hospital. However, due to poor cell reception in the area, the message appeared incomplete, and Jack only caught a glimpse of the words "Claire" and "accident." Distraught and fearing the worst, Jack misunderstood the message to mean that Claire had passed away.

Heartbroken and unable to bear the thought of living without Claire, Jack decided to leave Yellow Creek and start afresh in a distant city, hoping to numb the pain of his loss. Meanwhile, back in Yellow Creek, Claire woke up in the hospital, confused and disoriented but relieved to find herself alive. She had suffered minor injuries in the accident and was on the path to recovery.

Days turned into weeks, weeks turned into months, and both Jack and Claire tried to move on with their lives, carrying the weight of the misunderstanding that had torn them apart. Jack found solace in his work and new surroundings, but his heart still ached for the love he had lost. Claire, on the other hand, focused on her rehabilitation and healing, but a part of her remained incomplete without Jack by her side.

Years passed, and both Jack and Claire eventually built new lives and families of their own. Jack married a kind-hearted woman named Emily, and they had two children, while Claire found love again with a gentleman named Thomas, and they, too, started a family. Despite their new lives, the memory of their lost love lingered in the corners of their hearts.

One fateful day, Jack's job brought him back to Yellow Creek for a business meeting. While walking through the familiar streets, he passed by the hospital where Claire had been treated after the accident. A rush of memories flooded back, and he couldn't shake the feeling of longing that gripped his heart.

Curiosity got the better of him, and Jack decided to visit the hospital, hoping to find closure and perhaps a glimpse of the past he had left behind. As he entered the hospital, he saw a familiar face in the distance—it was Claire, standing by the reception desk, looking as beautiful as ever.

Their eyes met, and in that moment, the world stood still. Words failed them as years of unspoken emotions and misunderstandings hung heavy in the air. Finally, with tears in her eyes, Claire whispered, "I thought you were gone forever."

Jack, with a lump in his throat, replied, "And I thought I had lost you forever. But here we are, after all this time."

Despite the deep connection that still existed between them, they both knew their lives had taken different paths. They talked for hours, sharing their journeys, their families, and the life they had each built. The bittersweet reality of their situation weighed heavily on them, knowing they could never return to what once was.

As they parted ways, Jack and Claire realized they would always carry the regret of their misunderstanding, a poignant reminder of what might have been. They returned to their respective families, cherishing the love they had now while keeping the memories of their past tucked away in their hearts.

And so, in the town of Yellow Creek, Jack and Claire's love story remained a tale of what could have been, a testament to the impact of fate and the unyielding passage of time. Though they never got back together, they found solace in the lives they had created, forever bonded by the memories of their shared past.

ONLY IN AMERICA, AGAIN!

Gavin slumped against the cold, unforgiving walls of the jail cell, the metallic clang of the door echoing in his ears. He closed his eyes, replaying the events that led him here. The argument, the confrontation, the betrayal—each moment seared into his memory.

It was a humid summer evening. Gavin walked into the living room, his shirt sticking to his back, and saw Amelia on the phone, her voice low and secretive. Suspicion had been gnawing at him for weeks, and tonight, he couldn't hold it in any longer.

"Who are you talking to, Amelia?" Gavin demanded, his voice tense.

"It's none of your business, Gavin. Just leave me alone," Amelia replied, irritation clear in her tone.

"None of my business? I'm your husband! I have every right to know who you're sneaking around with," Gavin's anger flared.

"You're being ridiculous! You're always looking for a fight," Amelia yelled back.

The argument intensified, voices rising, each word sharper than the last. Amelia's phone was still connected, and her lover, Brandon, was listening from another state.

"Amelia, just hang up! I'll call the police. You don't have to deal with this," Brandon's anxious voice came through the phone.

"No, Brandon, don't! It's not that serious," Amelia replied, her voice pleading.

"So, it's Brandon, huh? How long has this been going on?" Gavin's voice was accusatory.

"That's it, Gavin! I'm done with this!" Amelia tried to push past Gavin, but he grabbed her arm, his frustration boiling over. She struggled to free herself, their movements becoming a violent dance of accusation and betrayal.

In the heat of the moment, Amelia managed to break free and ran to the other side of the room, clutching her arm where Gavin had held her.

"I'm calling 911. Stay safe, Amelia," Brandon's frantic voice came through the phone.

Brandon dialed 911, his voice urgent as he explained the situation. The police were dispatched immediately.

The police arrived with sirens blaring and lights flashing, casting eerie shadows on the walls. They burst into the house, separating Gavin and Amelia.

"Gavin Johnson, step away from her and put your hands behind your back," an officer sternly commanded.

"This is my house! What the hell is going on?" Gavin protested, confused and resisting.

The officers wrestled Gavin to the ground, his forehead scraping against the rough pavement. Blood dripped from his wound as they dragged him to the police cruiser, his mind reeling from the betrayal and confusion.

Amelia stood to the side, her face a mixture of anger and guilt. She watched as Gavin was taken away, knowing that Brandon's call had sealed her husband's fate, at least for now.

Gavin spent two agonizing weeks in the county jail, waiting for a hearing that never came. Eventually, the case was dismissed due to lack of evidence, but the damage was done. His marriage was over, and Amelia had moved in with Brandon.

It all started fifteen years prior. Gavin had always believed he had found his perfect match in Amelia. They had met during their college years and quickly fell in love. Just two years shy of graduating, Gavin and Amelia married in the quaint town of Riverdale. Their love was a beacon of joy, and fifteen years and four children later, Amelia was still as radiant as ever.

Amelia had recently landed a prestigious job as a nursing station administrator at a renowned hospital. Her coworkers adored her, and some secretly admired her beauty and competence. Despite company policies prohibiting personal relationships, temptation entered Amelia's life when Brandon, a charismatic computer contractor, came to fix her office computer.

"You know, Amelia, if computers could talk, yours would be singing your praises all day," Brandon said with a smile.

"Oh, Brandon, you're such a charmer," Amelia laughed.

"It's hard not to be when I'm around someone as captivating as you," Brandon leaned in.

Their flirtations grew bolder with each passing day until one day, they crossed a line that couldn't be uncrossed. Amelia and Brandon became lovers, their affair hidden from the world but not from Gavin's growing suspicions.

"Amelia, who were you on the phone with? You've been acting strange lately," Gavin's frustration was evident.

"It's none of your business, Gavin. You're being paranoid," Amelia defended.

"Paranoid? Or maybe I'm just seeing things clearly for once!" Gavin's anger rose.

The argument escalated, voices rising and emotions boiling over. In another state, Brandon listened helplessly to the confrontation over the phone.

"Amelia, hang up! I'll call the police. Just get out of there!" Brandon's voice was panicked.

Moments later, the police arrived at Gavin's home.

"Only in America," Gavin muttered to himself, "where the boyfriend of your wife can call the police to arrest you, and it's somehow considered righteous."

Years later, Gavin shared this painful chapter of his life with his new wife, Evelyn. As they sat by the fireplace, he held her hand and said, "I wanted you to know everything about my past, Evelyn. My failed marriage, my mistakes, and my regrets. But I promise you, I'll never let history repeat itself. I love you, and I'll always be honest with you." Evelyn squeezed his hand, understanding the depth of his confession and the promise of a new beginning.

REFLECTIONS ON ROUTE 66

Driving along the iconic Route 66, Evan Yang embarked on a journey to visit his grandmother in Springfield, Missouri, unaware of the unexpected turn of events that awaited him on the open road.

As Evan changed lanes abruptly, narrowly avoiding a collision with another passing vehicle, tensions flared between the two motorists. The other driver responded with a rude gesture and a barrage of curses, triggering Evan's impulsive temper. Despite claiming to be a Christian, Evan succumbed to anger and retaliated in kind, tailgating the other driver in a bid to assert dominance on the highway.

Fifteen minutes later, Evan pulled into a gas station to refuel, only to realize that his wallet was missing, lost at a previous stop miles behind him. Panic set in as Evan frantically searched his car, his mind racing about how to remedy the situation.

A stranger, who had been observing the scene unfold, approached Evan with an unexpected offer of assistance. He volunteered to cover the cost of Evan's gas and even handed him $100 as a gesture of goodwill. Evan was taken aback by the stranger's kindness, especially in light of their earlier confrontation on the road.

In a moment of reflection, Evan approached the stranger, his heart heavy with regret for his earlier outburst. He questioned the stranger's motives, puzzled by the discrepancy between their current interaction and their hostile exchange on the highway.

With a compassionate gaze, the stranger gently revealed a startling truth to Evan. "It was not me who flipped you off," he explained calmly. "It was your own reflection, a projection of your inner turmoil and tendency to blame others for your own actions."

Shocked and humbled by this revelation, Evan's facade of anger crumbled, replaced by a profound sense of self-awareness. The stranger's words pierced through Evan's defenses, forcing him to confront the truth of his behavior and the impact of his unchecked emotions.

In that moment of clarity, Evan saw himself for who he truly was—a man plagued by unresolved anger and a reluctance to accept responsibility for his actions. With a newfound sense of humility and gratitude, Evan apologized to the stranger, acknowledging his own faults and vowing to embark on a journey of self-improvement and growth.

Driving away from the gas station, the sun setting in the distance, Evan carried with him a renewed sense of purpose and a commitment to face his inner demons head-on. As the miles flew by on Route 66, Evan's heart felt lighter, his spirit cleansed by the unexpected lesson he had learned from a stranger on the open road.

CHAPTER THIRTY-ONE

THE AGE-OLD QUESTION, "HAVE YOU RECEIVED JESUS CHRIST AS YOUR LORD AND SAVIOR?"

WELL, I HAVE. NOW, WHAT IS THE NEW-AGE QUESTION?

THE DEALMAKER

Once upon a time, in the bustling city of Minneapolis, there was a young Hmong man named Lue who had recently arrived in America in search of a better future. Lue was hardworking, determined, and eager to make a life for himself in his new homeland.

After settling in and finding a job at a local factory, Lue decided that it was time to buy a car to make his daily commute easier and more convenient. He had saved up enough money from his job and was excited to finally own his own vehicle.

Lue went to a nearby car dealership, where he was greeted by a friendly salesman named Mike. Lue looked around at the various cars on the lot, trying to decide which one would be the best fit for him. After much deliberation, he finally found a car that he liked and was ready to make the purchase.

The negotiation process began, with Lue and Mike going back and forth on the price of the car. Lue was determined to get a good deal and wanted to make sure he was not overpaying. After a long period of haggling, Mike finally said, "It's a deal, Lue!"

Lue's face scrunched up in confusion. "No deal, no deal," he protested, shaking his head.

Mike was perplexed. "But Lue, we agreed on the price. It's a good deal for this car."

Lue shook his head again. "No deal, no more dealing," he insisted.

Mike realized that there was a misunderstanding. Lue, still learning English as a second language, had misinterpreted the word "deal." In his mind, he thought "deal" meant more negotiations and haggling, not an agreement on the price.

Smiling, Mike explained to Lue the meaning of the word "deal" in this context. Understanding dawned on Lue's face, and he chuckled at his mistake. "Oh, I see! Deal means agreement. Yes, it's a deal then!"

With a handshake and a smile, the deal was finally sealed. Lue drove off the lot in his new car, grateful for the lesson learned and excited for the adventures that awaited him in his new life in America. And from that day on, Lue never forgot the meaning of the word "deal."

ADOPTION

In a bustling city, where skyscrapers towered over the streets, and the noise of traffic filled the air, there was a man named Danny. Once a local hero whose act of bravery had made national news, Danny now found himself living on the streets, forgotten by most but still remembered by a few.

One chilly evening, as Danny lay huddled under a thin blanket in a quiet alley, a young woman named Sarah stumbled upon him. She paused, her eyes widening in recognition as she heard his name whispered by a passerby.

"Danny?" Sarah called softly, unsure if her memory served her right.

Danny stirred from his sleep and looked up, his eyes meeting Sarah's in surprise. "Do I know you, miss?"

Sarah took a step closer, her heart racing with a mix of emotions. "You saved me when I was a little girl from a burning house. You were my hero."

A flicker of recognition crossed Danny's weathered face, and a warm smile spread across his lips. "Sarah? Is that you? My, how you've grown!"

Tears welled up in Sarah's eyes as she embraced Danny, overwhelmed by the flood of memories and emotions from that fateful day. As they sat together on the cold pavement, they shared stories and caught up on the years that had passed.

Through their conversation, Sarah learned that Danny had fallen on hard times after his heroic deed, finding himself without a home or purpose. And Danny discovered that Sarah had been abandoned by her father, leaving her and her mother to fend for themselves, which later her mother passed sway to, leaving her alone.

A spark of an idea ignited in Sarah's mind as she looked at Danny with newfound determination. "Danny, would you consider coming home with me? I want to adopt you as my father to repay the debt of gratitude I owe you."

Danny's eyes widened in disbelief, touched by Sarah's offer. "But I have nothing to offer you, my dear. I'm just a homeless man."

Sarah shook her head, her eyes shining with sincerity. "You have something far more valuable to offer – your heart, your wisdom, and your kindness. You may not have wealth, but you have something even greater – the spirit of a true hero."

And so, in an unconventional twist of fate, Sarah brought Danny into her home, where he became not just a father figure but a beloved member of their family. Together, they found solace and happiness in each other's company, healing old wounds and forging new bonds.

As days turned into years, the once-homeless hero found a new purpose in life, guiding and nurturing Sarah with the love and care of a devoted father. And Sarah, in turn, flourished under Danny's gentle guidance, grateful for the second chance at family that fate had brought her way.

And so, in a city of towering skyscrapers and bustling streets, an unlikely family found their own little piece of paradise, where a hero's redemption led to a happily ever after.

NOBODY TO SOMEBODY

The skies over Laos were a fiery orange as warplanes roared overhead, their bombs exploding in the distance. Amid the chaos and destruction, in a small ramshackle hut, a baby boy was born. His cries mingled with the sounds of war, a poignant reminder of the fragility of life. His parents, desperate and impoverished, named him Nobody. The name was a reflection of their belief that in the vastness of the world and the brutality of their circumstances, they were insignificant.

Nobody's childhood was a grim tale of survival. His days were spent scavenging for food and avoiding the dangers of the war. The nights were the hardest, filled with the sound of distant explosions and the fear of the unknown. Despite the darkness surrounding him, a spark of resilience burned within Nobody. He clung to the stories his mother whispered to him, tales of a better life and the hope that one day they would find peace.

When the conflict reached their doorstep, Nobody's family fled to Thailand, joining the throngs of refugees seeking safety. The journey was perilous. They trudged through dense jungles, crossed treacherous rivers, and narrowly escaped enemy patrols. Each step was a testament to their determination to survive.

The refugee camp in Thailand was a stark contrast to the life they had known. Crowded tents, scarce resources, and the constant uncertainty of the future marked their new reality. But it was here, in the midst of hardship, that Nobody encountered the transformative power of faith.

One evening, as the sun set over the camp, a group of missionaries arrived. Among them was Miss Doris Whitelock, a kind-hearted woman with a gentle smile. She gathered the children and began to share stories from the Bible. Young Nobody was captivated by the tales of Moses parting the Red Sea and David defeating Goliath.

"Remember, child," Miss Whitelock said, looking directly at Nobody with compassionate eyes, "God has a plan for you. No matter how difficult life seems, He is always with you."

These words planted a seed of hope in Nobody's heart, a hope that would sustain him through the darkest of times.

Through the efforts of charitable organizations, Nobody and his family were granted asylum in the United States. The journey to America was filled with a mix of fear and excitement. They arrived in a bustling city, the skyscrapers towering above them like giants.

Settling into a modest apartment in a rough neighborhood, Nobody faced new challenges. The language barrier, cultural differences, and the harsh realities of urban life were daunting. But he was determined to succeed. With relentless effort, he learned English, excelled in school, and worked multiple jobs to support his family.

Years of perseverance paid off when Nobody founded a technology company. His innovative ideas and tireless work ethic transformed it into a multimillion-dollar enterprise. He married his high school sweetheart, Mai, and together they built a life of luxury and comfort. Their mansion was a testament to his hard work, filled with the finest furnishings and the latest gadgets.

However, with success came scrutiny. Rivals envied his achievements, and whispers of suspicion began to circulate. Nobody's world, which seemed invincible, was about to crumble.

One crisp autumn morning, as Nobody arrived at his sleek, glass-walled office, federal agents stormed the building. Accusations of tax evasion, fraud, and corruption echoed through the hallways. His employees watched in shock as he was led away in handcuffs, his once-proud name now associated with disgrace.

The trial was a media spectacle. Every detail of his downfall was splashed across headlines. His assets were seized, his company dismantled, and his reputation shattered. In the cold, sterile confines of a prison cell, Nobody felt utterly broken. The walls seemed to close in on him, the silence a constant reminder of his fall from grace.

"God, why have you forsaken me?" he cried out in the darkness, his voice breaking with despair. The once unshakable faith seemed distant and unreachable.

Months turned into years, and prison became a place of reflection and spiritual renewal for Nobody. The prison chapel, a small sanctuary within the harsh environment, became his refuge. He spent countless hours reading the Bible, praying, and finding solace in the teachings he had once heard as a child.

One Sunday, during a particularly moving service, the prison chaplain spoke words that resonated deeply with Nobody. The chaplain, a former convict himself, had a way of reaching the hearts of the broken.

"God doesn't measure your worth by your achievements or failures," the chaplain said, his voice echoing in the small chapel. "In His eyes, you are always somebody, valuable and loved."

These words ignited a new flame within Nobody. He realized that his identity was not defined by his wealth or status but by his faith and resilience.

Upon his release, Nobody faced the daunting task of rebuilding his life. With no money, no home, and a tarnished reputation, he turned to his faith. He volunteered at a local church, offering his skills to help others who were struggling. He found joy in serving meals at the soup kitchen, tutoring children, and mentoring ex-convicts.

Gradually, through hard work and dedication, he began to rebuild his life. He reconnected with his family, mended broken relationships, and found a humble job that allowed him to support his loved ones. Though he no longer had the wealth and status he once enjoyed, Nobody's faith remained unshaken. He understood that true riches lay in the love of God and the strength it gave him to endure.

Years later, Nobody stood before a congregation, sharing his story. The church was filled with people from all walks of life, each facing their own battles. His voice was steady, his eyes filled with conviction.

"I lost everything," he said, his voice carrying a quiet strength, "but I found the greatest treasure of all—God's love. No matter how low you fall, remember that you are never alone. God is with you, and through Him, you can rise again."

The audience listened in rapt silence, moved by his journey from despair to hope. Nobody had become a testament to the enduring power of faith, a living reminder that in the eyes of God, everyone is somebody.

The congregation erupted in applause, tears streaming down many faces. In that moment, Nobody realized that his journey had come full circle. He had been stripped down to nothing, but through the love and power of God, he had been rebuilt into a new man—a man of faith, resilience, and unwavering hope.

Like Nobody, if you are enduring losses, devastation, or tragedy, and it seems like life is unjust, you are not alone. Many others are facing similar, or even greater, hardships. The encouraging news is that we do not live by sight or rely solely on what we perceive or understand but by faith and hope. This faith is not based on empty promises or wishful thinking; rather, God is the foundation or evidence of our faith. If you don't know who He is, I invite you to explore and investigate. He will reveal Himself to you. In Him, you are a precious somebody.

THY NEIGHBOR

In a small town, Springfield, nestled between rolling hills and lush greenery, there lived a man named Charles who found himself entangled in a web of unfortunate circumstances that landed him behind cold iron bars for six and a half agonizing years. Charles, once a free spirit, now found himself confined within the bleak walls of a prison, his spirit weighed down by the heaviness of his solitude.

As days turned into weeks and weeks melted into years, Charles felt the cruel sting of isolation seeping into his very being. The world outside, his friends and families, seemed to have totally forgotten him, and the once vibrant colors of life had faded into shades of gray within the confines of his cell.

One afternoon, as Charles sat on the edge of his bunk, staring blankly at the cracked ceiling, he heard the guard call out, "Charles, you've got mail."

With a mixture of surprise and curiosity, Charles walked to the front of his cell and took the envelope from the guard. Inside, he found a letter and a money order for $300. The letter read:

"Dear Charles,

We haven't met formally, but I heard about your situation and felt compelled to help. I hope this money can make your time a little easier.

Stay strong,

Daniel Diaz"

Charles felt a lump in his throat. He hadn't expected anyone to care, let alone a stranger. Over the next few months, more letters and money orders arrived like clockwork. One letter, however, stood out. It was from Elizabeth, Daniel's wife.

"Dear Charles,

My husband, Daniel, has been sending you money regularly. I want you to know that we both believe in you and your ability to overcome this challenging time. Remember, no matter how dark it gets, there is always a light at the end of the tunnel.

With prayers and best wishes,

Elizabeth Diaz"

One day, Charles received a visit request. It was Daniel. They sat across from each other in the lobby together.

"Why are you doing this for me?" Charles asked, his voice thick with emotion.

Daniel smiled warmly. "It's because it's what Jesus would do."

Tears welled up in Charles' eyes. "You've given me more than just money, Daniel. You've given me hope."

Months turned into years, and the support from Daniel and Elizabeth never wavered. Every three months, without fail, a sum of $300 to $500 found its way into Charles' commissary account, a lifeline that helped him endure the harsh realities of prison life.

For Charles, the impact of Daniel and Elizabeth's benevolence was profound. Amidst a sea of indifference and abandonment, their unwavering support shone like a beacon of hope in the darkness. Through their actions, Charles learned the true meaning of being a good neighbor, a friend, and a brother in Christ.

Reflecting on his journey, Charles couldn't help but draw parallels to a story told long ago by a man named Jesus. The tale of the Good Samaritan, a parable that transcended time and space, resonated deeply within Charles' heart. Just as the Samaritan had shown compassion to a stranger in need, Daniel and Elizabeth had become his Samaritans in the midst of his trials.

In the annals of history, the legacy of Daniel and Elizabeth Diaz would forever be etched as a testament to the transformative power of kindness and compassion. Through their simple yet profound acts of generosity, they had not only provided for Charles' physical needs but had also nourished his spirit, reminding him that even in the darkest of hours, there are rays of light that can pierce through the shadows and illuminate the path to redemption.

Someone once said, "When someone doesn't have much, but they give it anyway, that's love." We can conclude this story by saying that this is exactly who Daniel and Elizabeth are. They are the embodiment of this statement. In this book, the author is grateful and dedicated to them.

PLAYING CATCH UP

I returned to my favorite café, The Travellers House Coffee and Tea, in Springfield, Missouri, a cozy spot tucked away in a quiet corner of town. The place is an oasis of tranquility with its soft lighting, warm wooden interiors, and the comforting aroma of freshly brewed coffee wafting through the air. Settling into my usual seat by the window, my thoughts began to drift toward my next book. The bustling life outside the window served as a perfect backdrop for my creative musings.

Moments later, Daniel walked in. A tall, lanky man with a friendly demeanor that lit up any room. His face brightened when he spotted me. "Hey, Charles! How's it going?" he greeted, making his way to the table with a noticeable spring in his step.

"Hey, Daniel," I replied, my smile warm and welcoming. "Good to see you. How are things?"

"Not bad, not bad. Keeping busy as usual. How about you? How's *LOL AND SORROW* doing?" Daniel asked as he settled into the chair across from me, the chair that had almost become his unofficial spot in the café.

"It's doing really well," I said, my eyes twinkling with satisfaction. "The response has been great. Readers seem to really connect with it. It's been quite a journey."

"That's fantastic! I knew it would resonate," Daniel said with genuine enthusiasm. "What's next for you?"

"Actually, I've already started on another book venture," I revealed a hint of excitement in my voice. "It's coming soon. It's a story I think my readers won't want to miss. It's a bit different, but I think it has a lot of heart."

"By the way, Daniel," I continued, leaning forward slightly, "have you had a chance to read *LOL AND SORROW* yet?"

"Yes, I did," Daniel replied enthusiastically. "It was amazing. The way you weave humor and sorrow together is truly something. I laughed, I cried. I can't wait for your next book."

"I'm glad to hear that," I said, my smile widening. "I'm really excited about this new project. It's been consuming my thoughts in a good way."

As we sipped our coffee, our conversation flowed easily. We talked about everything from the intricacies of character development to the subtle art of plot twists. The café buzzed around us with the soft hum of other patrons and the occasional clinking of cups and saucers, but in our little corner, it felt like we were in our own world, discussing dreams and stories.

"Do you remember when we used to sit here and talk about our wild ideas before any of this was real?" Daniel mused, his eyes reflecting a nostalgic glow.

"Of course," I responded. "Those were the days of dreams and endless possibilities. It's amazing how far we've come."

"Indeed. And to think it all started with a shared passion for storytelling," Daniel said, raising his cup in a mock toast.

We continued reminiscing about our journey, the challenges we faced, and the triumphs we celebrated. I shared snippets of my upcoming book, giving Daniel a sneak peek into the world I was creating. Daniel, in turn, offered insights and suggestions, his enthusiasm infectious.

As the afternoon sun began to cast a golden hue over the town, we finished our coffee and stood up to leave. The air outside was warm and inviting, filled with the promise of a beautiful evening.

"Well, Charles, as always, it was great catching up," Daniel said, clapping me on the back.

"Likewise, Daniel. Thanks for the great conversation. It's always inspiring," I replied, my spirits buoyed by our chat.

As we walked out into the sunshine, both of us felt uplifted, our hearts light with the joy of friendship and the promise of new adventures. For me, the conversation had reignited my passion, filling me with fresh ideas and a renewed sense of purpose for my next book. And for Daniel, it was a reminder of the power of dreams and the beauty of sharing them with friends.

LOL AND SORROW

With a final wave, we parted ways, each heading toward our own paths, but with the knowledge that our journeys would always be intertwined through the stories we shared and the memories we created together. Watching Daniel disappear around the corner, I turned and walked home, my mind buzzing with ideas, ready to pour my heart into my next literary endeavor.

Charles Cawv Thao

THANK YOU, DEAR READER, FOR EMBARKING ON THIS JOURNEY WITH ME.

THE END

SEE YOU IN THE NEXT BOOK ADVENTURE!

Printed in the USA
CPSIA information can be obtained
at www.ICGtesting.com
CBHW051647021024
15220CB00006B/92